Power and Performance
Software Analysis and Optimization

Power and Performance
Software Analysis and Optimization

Jim Kukunas

AMSTERDAM • BOSTON • HEIDELBERG • LONDON
NEW YORK • OXFORD • PARIS • SAN DIEGO
SAN FRANCISCO • SINGAPORE • SYDNEY • TOKYO

Morgan Kaufmann is an imprint of Elsevier

Morgan Kaufmann is an imprint of Elsevier
225 Wyman Street, Waltham, MA 02451, USA

British Library Cataloguing in Publication Data
A catalogue record for this book is available from the British Library

Library of Congress Cataloging-in-Publication Data
A catalog record for this book is available from the Library of Congress

For information on all Morgan Kaufmann publications
visit our website at www.mkp.com

ISBN: 978-0-12-800726-6

This book is dedicated to God, my wife Riley, my mother and father, my brother Stephen, my friends, colleagues at Intel, and everyone who helped me with this book.

Contents

Introduction

As engineers, we are constantly striving to perfect our craft: aspiring to architect flawless systems, diligently pursuing bug-free deliverables, and zealously sharpening our skillset on the proverbial whetstone of experience. As a product of these joint experiences, the relatively young discipline of software engineering continues to rapidly mature in fields such as validation and verification, software prototyping, and process modeling. However, one important aspect of software engineering is often overlooked: software optimization, that is, the craft of tuning software to efficiently utilize resources in such a way as to impact the user's experience.

This definition yields three important insights. Firstly, because software optimization is the craft of tuning software, it is an ongoing data-driven process that requires constant feedback in the form of performance measurements and profiling. Secondly, all computing resources are limited and of varying scarcity, and thus their allocation must be carefully planned. Thirdly, optimizations must have an impact on the user experience. This impact can manifest itself in many different ways, such as improved battery life, the ability to handle increased datasets, or improved responsiveness.

Unfortunately, some developers look at performance analysis and optimization as arcane and unnecessary; a fossil of computing antiquity predating optimizing compilers and multi-core systems. So are these engineers correct in their assessment? Is performance a dated and irrelevant topic? The answer is a resounding, "No!" Before we dive into the methodologies and background for performance analysis, let's first discuss why performance analysis is crucial to modern software engineering.

PERFORMANCE APOLOGETIC

There are two primary reasons why software optimization is necessary. The first reason is that software that performs well is often power-efficient software. This obviously is important to developers whose deliverables run on mobile devices, such as laptops, tablets, and phones, but it also is important to engineers of desktop and server products, whose power issues manifest themselves differently, typically in the form of thermal issues and high operating costs. For instance, data centers often, as part of their arrangements with the utility company, have minimum and maximum daily power consumption limits. This, combined with the fact that few engineers have the luxury of knowing or controlling where their users will install their software, means that every software engineer should care about writing power-efficient software. The second reason is that performance, and the related costs, have a powerful effect on usage patterns.

PERFORMANCE IS POWER EFFICIENCY

It's natural to think about power efficiency and performance as diametrically opposed concepts. For example, consumers tend to understand that while our server-class Intel® Xeon® processor line provide stellar performance, they won't be as power-efficient in a tablet as our mobile Intel® Atom™ platform. Many users are familiar with the tunables, exposed by the drivers of hardware such as wireless and graphics cards, asking users to choose between power-efficient operation, maximum performant operation, or a balance between the two. However, when dealing with software, this distinction doesn't exist.

In the next few chapters, we'll dive deeper into the details of the power management features available in Intel® processors. For now, it is enough to understand that there are two general ways the CPU saves power dynamically at runtime. The first technique, known as frequency scaling, temporarily reduces the operating frequency and voltage of the processor. For example, a CPU might have a maximum operating frequency of 1.6 GHz, and the ability to scale the frequency as low as 600 MHz during light loads.

The second technique, known as deep sleep, is where the processor is halted, that is, the CPU stops executing instructions. The amount of power saved depends on how deep of a sleep the processor can enter, because in deeper sleep states various resources, such as the caches, can be powered off for additional savings. For instance, as the author sits here typing this chapter, the processor can enter a shallow sleep state in between keystrokes, waking up to process each keystroke interrupt, and can enter a deeper sleep state while the author is proofreading what he just typed.

In general, while frequency scaling can provide some power-savings, the largest savings come from the deep sleep states. Because of this, writing power-efficient software revolves around keeping the CPU asleep, and therefore not executing instructions, for as long as possible. Therefore if work needs to be done, it needs to be done as quickly as possible, so the CPU can return to its slumber. This concept is known as "race to idle." Harking back to the earlier definition of software optimization where it was asserted that tuning is a data-driven process requiring constant feedback, it is illuminating to note that while "race to idle" is a good rule of thumb for the majority of cases, there may be cases where it provides suboptimal power-savings. This is why measurement is so important.

Both of these power-saving techniques, frequency scaling and deep sleep, are handled transparently by the operating system, so user space applications don't need to explicitly worry about requesting them. Implicitly however, applications do need to be conscious of them, so they can align their behavior in such a way as to allow the operating system to fully utilize them. For instance, each deep sleep state has an entry and exit latency, with the deeper sleep states having higher latencies than the lighter sleep states. The operating system has to deduce how long the processor can afford to sleep before its next scheduled task, and then pick the deepest sleep state that meets that deadline.

From this it follows that the hardware can only be as power-efficient as its least efficient software component. The harsh reality is that a power-efficient hardware platform, and a finely optimized software stack are naught if the user downloads a poorly, or maliciously, written application that prevents the hardware from taking advantage of its power-saving features.

PERFORMANCE AND USAGE PATTERNS

The ultimate purpose of computing is to increase the productivity of its user, and thus users, consciously or unconsciously, evaluate software features on whether the benefits to their productivity outweigh the associated costs.

To illustrate this point, consider the task of searching for an email in a mail client. Often the user is presented with two methods to complete this task; either manually searching through a list sorted by some criteria, or utilizing a keyword search capable of querying metadata. So how does a user decide which method to use for a specific query? Avoiding a discussion of human-computer interaction (HCI) and cognitive psychology, the author submits that the user compares two perceptions.

The first perception is an estimate of the duration required for performing the manual search. For instance, perhaps the emails are sorted by the date received, and the user remembers that the email was received very recently, and thus perceives a short duration, since the email should be near the top of the list. Or instead, perhaps the user was asked to scrounge up a long forgotten email from months ago, and the user has no idea where in the list this email would appear, and thus perceives a long duration. The second perception is an estimate of the duration required for utilizing the search function. This second perception might consist of prior search performance and accuracy, as well as other considerations, such as the user-interface performance and design.

The user will compare these two perceptions and choose the one with the shorter perceived duration. Therefore, as the perceived duration for the keyword search increases, its perceived value to the user approaches zero. On the other hand, a streamlined and heavily optimized search might completely displace the manual search.

This concept scales from individual software features all the way up to entire computing devices. For instance, consider a user fleetingly interested in researching a piece of trivia. If the user's computer is powered off and takes ten minutes to boot, the user will probably not bother utilizing it for such a small benefit. On the other hand, if the user's computer boots in 5 s, the user will be more likely to use it.

It is important to note that these decisions are based on the user's perceptions. For instance, a mail client might have a heavily optimized search algorithm, but the user still might perceive the search as slow if the user-interface toolkit is slow to update with the query results.

A WORD ON PREMATURE OPTIMIZATION

So now that we've discussed why performance is important, let's address a common question about when performance analysis and optimization is appropriate. If a software engineer spends enough time writing software with others, the engineer will eventually hear, or perhaps remark to a colleague, the widely misused quote from Donald Knuth, "premature optimization is the root of all evil" (Knuth, 1974).

In order to understand this quote, it is necessary to first establish its context. The original source is a 1974 publication entitled "Structured Programming with Goto Statements" from the ACM's *Computing Surveys* journal. In one of the code examples, Knuth notes a performance optimization, of which he says, "In established engineering disciplines a 12% improvement, easily obtained, is never considered marginal ..." (Knuth, 1974). So clearly Knuth didn't mean, as some have misconstrued him to, that *all* optimizations are bad, only *premature* optimizations. This then raises the question of what constitutes a premature optimization. Knuth continues, "It is often a mistake to make a priori judgements about what parts of a program are really critical ..." (Knuth, 1974). In other words, a premature optimization is one made without first analyzing the program to determine what optimizations are impactful.

These words might ring truer today than they did back in 1974. Modern systems are significantly more complex, with advances in optimizing compilers, stacked caches, hardware prefetching, out-of-order execution, and countless other technological innovations widening the gap between the code we write, and how our code executes, and thus subsequently performs. As such, we as engineers must heed Knuth's warning and ensure that our optimizations target the critical code.

Since an optimization requires analysis, does that mean that all optimization should wait until the software is completely written? Obviously not, because by that time it will be too late to undo any inefficiencies designed into the core architecture.

In the early stages of architecture and design, performance considerations should revolve around the data structures utilized and the subsequent algorithms that accompany them. This is an area where Big-O analysis is important, and there should be a general understanding of what algorithms will be computationally challenging. For those not familiar with Big-O analysis, it is a method for categorizing, and comparing, algorithms based on the order of growth of their computational costs in relation to their best, average, and worst cases of input. Early performance measurements can also be obtained from models and prototypes.

As architecture manifests as code, frequent performance profiling should occur to verify that these models are accurate. Big-O analysis alone is not sufficient. Consider the canonical case of quicksort versus mergesort and heapsort. Although mergesort and heapsort are in the worst-case superlinear, they are often outperformed by quicksort, which is in the worst-case quadratic.

THE ROADMAP

So hopefully, you now have a basic understanding of why performance analysis and optimization is important, and when it is appropriate. The rest of this book focuses on the how and the where. The following content is divided into four parts. The first part provides the necessary background information to get you started, focusing on Intel® Architecture and the interactions between the hardware and the Linux software stack. The second part begins by covering performance analysis methodologies. Then it provides instructions on utilizing the most popular performance profiling tools, such as Intel® VTune™ Amplifier XE and perf. The third part outlines some of the various common performance problems, identified by the tools in Part 2, and then provides details on how to correct them. Since each performance situation is different, this part is far from comprehensive, but is designed to give the reader a good starting point.

Throughout this book, AT&T syntax is used for assembly instructions. Hexadecimal numbers are prefixed with $0x$, binary numbers are written with a subscript two, such as 0101_2, and all other numbers are in base ten.

REFERENCE

Knuth, D.E., 1974, dec. Structured programming with go to statements. ACM Comput. Surv. 6 (4), 261–301. doi:10.1145/356635.356640. http://doi.acm.org/10.1145/356635.356640.

Background
Knowledge

Early Intel® Architecture

1

CHAPTER CONTENTS

The power button is pressed, causing the #RESET pin to be asserted, that is, the voltage is driven into the predefined threshold that represents the active state logic level. After a predefined number of clock cycles pass, the #RESET pin is then deasserted, invoking the hardware reset. The hardware reset is responsible for initializing the processor to a known state. This includes setting the registers, including the general purpose, control and status registers, to their documented initial values.

This first "breath" leaves the processor in an execution state significantly different from the one which most developers are familiar. The processor begins execution in 16-bit Real-Address mode. This journey between 16-bit Real-Address mode and 64-bit, or 32-bit, Protected Virtual-Address mode occurs every time the processor is powered on. In doing so, this process mirrors the historical evolution of the Intel® Architecture, from the 16-bit 8086 of 1978 to the 64-bit Intel® Core™ processor family of the twenty-first century. As the computer is booted, more than 40 years of advancements in processor technology unfold in the blink of an eye.

The author imagines that some readers are wondering what benefit could possibly come from the retention of all these relics of computing antiquity in modern processor design. Backwards compatibility, which by definition involves maintaining older designs, directly benefits the reader. As readers, hopefully, continue through this book, they will find references to many architectural features. Education on and usage of these features is an investment of the reader's time. By strictly maintaining backward compatibility, Intel ensures that the investments made by the reader today continue to pay dividends for the foreseeable future. Consider that original bytecode compiled in the late 1970s will still run unmodified on a modern Intel® processor fabricated in 2014.

Other detractors argue that Intel Architecture is inelegant. Since elegance is in the eyes of the beholder, this claim is hard to refute. The author is not a hardware engineer; however, as a software engineer, the author sees an interesting parallel between hardware and software in this claim. Many software projects are architected to be elegant solutions to a well-defined problem. This elegance erodes over time as new features, which were unimaginable during the design phase, are requested and bug fixes and workarounds are introduced. After enduring these unavoidable harsh realities of the software lifecycle, a software's worth comes not from elegance, but from whether that software still works, is still reliable, and can still be extended to meet future needs. The author submits that x86 still works, is still reliable, and can still be extended.

Covering every aspect of Intel Architecture would require an entire book, as opposed to a couple of chapters. The goal of the next three chapters is to introduce the fundamentals of the architecture, in order to provide just enough knowledge to enable the reader to understand the later content in this book, as well as begin to reason effectively about power consumption and performance.

Because Intel Architecture has been in a constant state of evolution for the last 40 years, and has been steadily increasing in complexity, the author has divided the introduction to Intel Architecture into three separate chronologically ordered chapters, sampling the general timeline of Intel products. Despite following the timeline, history is only being used as a convenient tool. Not all processors or architectural details will be covered in the sections that follow. Also, unless explicitly stated, not all technologies are discussed in the section corresponding to the processor that introduced them. Instead, each section will utilize the given processor as a vehicle for simplifying and explaining important concepts of the modern x86 architecture. This has the dual benefit of gradually introducing the concepts of the modern x86 architecture in a natural and logical progression, while also providing the context necessary to understand the reasoning behind the technical decisions made through the years.

This chapter examines some of the earliest members of the x86 family. The majority of these processors are 16-bit. The chapter ends with the first 32-bit x86 processor, and the first processor to run Linux, the Intel® 80386.

1.1 INTEL® 8086

The 8086, introduced in 1978 and shown in Figure 1.1, was not the first processor developed by Intel, however it was the first processor to implement what would be known as the x86 architecture. In fact, the two digits in the name x86 correspond to the fact that the first x86 processor designations all ended with 86, such as 8086, 80186, 80286, 80386, and so on. This trend was continued by Intel until the Pentium® processor family. Despite being introduced in 1978, the 8086 was continually produced throughout the 1980s and 1990s. Famously, NASA had been using the 8086 in their shuttles until 2011.

In stark contrast to the thousands of pages in the modern Intel® *Software Developer Manual* (SDM), the 8086 user manual, including a full reference on the system behavior, programming tools, hardware pinout, instructions and opcodes, and so on, fits within about two hundred pages. This simplified nature makes the 8086 an excellent introduction to the fundamental concepts of the x86 architecture. The rest of this book will build further on the concepts introduced here.

In the architecture of the 8086, there are three fundamental design principles (Intel Corporation, 1979). The first principle is the usage of specialized components to isolate and distribute functionality. In other words, rather than one large monolithic system architecture, building an 8086 system provided flexibility in the peripherals selected. This allowed system builders to customize the system to best accommodate the needs of the given situation. The second principle is the inherent support for

FIGURE 1.1

Intel® 8086 (Lanzet, 2009).

parallelism within the architecture. At the time of the 8086, this parallelism came in the form of combining multiple processors and coprocessors together, in order to perform multiple tasks in parallel. The third principle was the hierarchical bus organization, designed to support both complex and simple data flows.

To illustrate these principles, consider that along with the 8086, there were two other Intel processors available, the 8088 and 8089. The 8088 was an identical processor to the 8086, except that the external data bus was 8 bits, instead of 16 bits. The 8088 was chosen by IBM® for the heart of the "IBM compatible PC." The 8089 was a separate coprocessor, with it's own instruction set and assembler, designed for offloading data transfers, such as Direct Memory Access (DMA) requests. Interestingly, the 8089 was not chosen by IBM® for the "IBM compatible PC," and therefore was never widely adopted.

One or more of each of these chips could be mixed and matched, along with a selection of peripherals, to provide systems highly tailored for software requirements. For example, consider the system diagram in Figure 1.2. This diagram, taken from the *8086 User Manual*, demonstrates a multiprocessor configuration consisting of one primary 8086 processor, along with three 8088 processors, driving three graphics peripherals, and five 8089 processors, with three accelerating I/O to the graphics peripherals and two accelerating access to a database.

This modularity can be seen throughout the design of the 8086. For example, the internal architecture of the 8086 is cleanly divided into two categories: the execution unit (EU), and the bus interface unit (BIU). The EU contains all of the resources

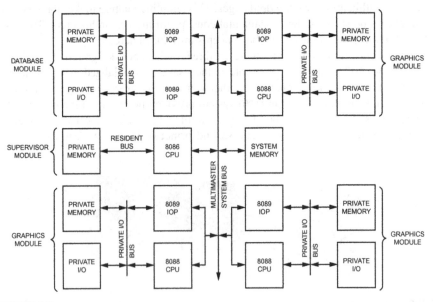

FIGURE 1.2

Example Multiprocessor Intel® 8086 system diagram (Intel Corporation, 1979).

for maintaining and manipulating the internal processor state, including the CPU registers and arithmetic/logic unit (ALU). The EU, however, is unable to access the system's memory, which requires usage of the system bus. The BIU is solely responsible for interfacing with the system bus. This separation allows for the two units to operate in parallel, with the BIU fetching data over the bus *while* the EU is executing instructions.

To accommodate this asynchronous nature, the two units interface with an instruction queue, therefore allowing the BIU to prefetch instructions before they are required. When the BIU detects that there is an available slot in the queue, it begins to fetch an instruction to fill that slot. When the EU detects that there is a valid entry in the queue, it removes that entry and begins executing it. If the EU requires the evaluation of a memory operand, it passes the effective address to the BIU, which suspends instruction prefetching and retrieves the desired system information.

Beginning to understand the x86 architecture starts with the realization that a processor is simply a state machine with states, described by the contents of memory and the registers, and inputs that transition between different states, the instruction set.

1.1.1 SYSTEM STATE

For the general case, there are three members of the 8086 storage hierarchy: the processor's registers, the system's external memory, that is, RAM, and persistent storage, that is, the disk drive. The *registers* provide fast volatile storage located very close to the processor on the die. Since this memory is very fast, it is also very expensive, and therefore very scarce. On the other hand, the volatile external memory is significantly cheaper than the registers, and therefore more prevalent than the registers, but is also orders of magnitude slower. Similarly, the persistent storage is significantly cheaper than the external memory, and therefore is available in greater quantities, but is also orders of magnitude slower than external memory. To quantify the inverse relationship between storage density and speed, consider that the 8086 might be paired with a 10 MB hard drive, was capable of addressing 1 MB of external RAM, and had seven 16-bit registers.

Address space

The 8086 is comprised of two different address spaces, the memory address space, capable of addressing 1 MB, and the I/O address space, capable of addressing 64 KB.

External peripherals can either be mapped into the I/O address space or memory-mapped. Device registers in the I/O address space are manipulated with the IN and OUT instructions, while memory-mapped device registers can be manipulated with general purpose instructions, just like external memory.

In order to address 1 MB of memory with a 16-bit processor, which would normally be limited to 2^{16} bytes of memory, the 8086 utilizes a technique referred to as *segmentation*. Segmentation divides the memory space into four 64 KB segments. The definition of the segments is completely up to the programmer to control. There are no restrictions on their configuration. For instance, nothing prevents segments from overlapping.

A segmented address, referred to as a logical address, is comprised of two components, a segment selector and an offset. The segment selector takes the form of a segment register. The offset is a 16-bit pointer, which represents the displacement of the address from the segment's base address. Since the 16-bit offset is unsigned, an overflow or underflow results in a wrap around effect within the segment. Therefore, the offset can be considered modulo the segment.

For the 8086, there are four segments: (0) the code segment, described by the CS segment selection register, (1) the stack segment, described by the SS segment register, (2) the data segment, described by the DS segment register, and (3) the extra data segment, described by the ES segment register. Some instructions imply the usage of a specific segment. For instance, instructions that manipulate the stack imply the stack segment and instruction fetches imply the code segment. In other cases, the segment register will need to be explicitly provided, or the default segment register will need to be overridden.

The EU only handles logical addresses, with address translation from logical to physical being handled by the BIU. In order to translate a logical address into a 20-bit physical address, the segment register is logically shifted left by 4 bits, which is equivalent to multiplying by 16, and then added to the offset.

1.1.2 REGISTERS

Aside from the four segment registers introduced in the previous section, the 8086 has seven general purpose registers, and two status registers.

The general purpose registers are divided into two categories. Four registers, AX, BX, CX, and DX, are classified as data registers. These data registers are accessible as either the full 16-bit register, represented with the X suffix, the low byte of the full 16-bit register, designated with an L suffix, or the high byte of the 16-bit register, delineated with an H suffix. For instance, AX would access the full 16-bit register, whereas AL and AH would access the register's low and high bytes, respectively.

The second classification of registers are the pointer/index registers. This includes the following four registers: SP, BP, SI, and DI, The SP register, the stack pointer, is reserved for usage as a pointer to the top of the stack. The SI and DI registers are typically used implicitly as the source and destination pointers, respectively. Unlike the data registers, the pointer/index registers are only accessible as full 16-bit registers.

As this categorization may indicate, the general purpose registers come with some guidance for their intended usage. This guidance is reflected in the instruction forms with implicit operands. Instructions with implicit operands, that is, operands which are assumed to be a certain register and therefore don't require that operand to be encoded, allow for shorter encodings for common usages. For convenience, instructions with implicit forms typically also have explicit forms, which require more bytes to encode. The recommended uses for the registers are as follows:

AX Accumulator
BX Data (relative to DS)
CX Loop counter
DX Data
SI Source pointer (relative to DS)
DI Destination pointer (relative to ES)
SP Stack pointer (relative to SS)
BP Base pointer of stack frame (relative to SS)

Aside from allowing for shorter instruction encodings, this guidance is also an aid to the programmer who, once familiar with the various register meanings, will be able to deduce the meaning of assembly, assuming it conforms to the guidelines, much faster. This parallels, to some degree, how variable names help the programmer reason about their contents. It's important to note that these are just suggestions, not rules.

Additionally, there are two status registers, the instruction pointer and the flags register.

The instruction pointer, IP, is also often referred to as the program counter. This register contains the memory address of the next instruction to be executed. Until 64-bit mode was introduced, the instruction pointer was not directly accessible to the programmer, that is, it wasn't possible to access it like the other general purpose registers. Despite this, the instruction pointer was indirectly accessible. Whereas the instruction pointer couldn't be modified through a MOV instruction, it could be modified by any instruction that alters the program flow, such as the CALL or JMP instructions.

Reading the contents of the instruction pointer was also possible by taking advantage of how x86 handles function calls. Transfer from one function to another occurs through the CALL and RET instructions. The CALL instruction preserves the current value of the instruction pointer, pushing it onto the stack in order to support nested function calls, and then loads the instruction pointer with the new address, provided as an operand to the instruction. This value on the stack is referred to as the *return address*. Whenever the function has finished executing, the RET instruction pops the return address off of the stack and restores it into the instruction pointer, thus transferring control back to the function that initiated the function call. Leveraging this, the programmer can create a special thunk function that would simply copy the return value off of the stack, load it into one of the registers, and then return. For example, when compiling Position-Independent-Code (PIC), which is discussed in Chapter 12, the compiler will automatically add functions that use this technique to obtain the instruction pointer. These functions are usually called __x86.get _pc_thunk.bx(), __x86.get_pc_thunk.cx(), __x86.get_pc_thunk.dx(), and so on, depending on which register the instruction pointer is loaded.

The second status register, the EFLAGS register, is comprised of 1-bit status and control flags. These bits are set by various instructions, typically arithmetic or logic instructions, to signal certain conditions. These condition flags can then be checked in order to make decisions. For a list of the flags modified by each instruction, see the Intel SDM. The 8086 defined the following status and control bits in EFLAGS:

Zero Flag (ZF) Set if the result of the instruction is zero.

Sign Flag (SF) Set if the result of the instruction is negative.

Overflow Flag (OF) Set if the result of the instruction overflowed.

Parity Flag (PF) Set if the result has an even number of bits set.

Carry Flag (CF) Used for storing the carry bit in instructions that perform arithmetic with carry (for implementing extended precision).

Adjust Flag (AF) Similar to the Carry Flag. In the parlance of the 8086 documentation, this was referred to as the Auxiliary Carry Flag.

Direction Flag (DF) For instructions that either autoincrement or autodecrement a pointer, this flag chooses which to perform. If set, autodecrement, otherwise autoincrement.

Interrupt Enable Flag (IF) Determines whether maskable interrupts are enabled.

Trap Flag (TF) If set CPU operates in single-step debugging mode.

1.1.3 INSTRUCTIONS

Continuing the scenario described in the introductory section, once the #RESET pin is asserted and deasserted, the processor initializes the program registers to their predefined values. This includes the predefined value of the instruction pointer, providing the BIU the first location to fetch and decode for the execution unit.

This first location is always the last 16 bytes in the physical address space. For a 16-bit processor with 20-bit physical addresses, this is $0xFFFF0$. This provides just enough room for a JMP to the BIOS's real initialization code.

To understand the reasoning behind this, consider that the very first instructions executed, which are responsible for initializing the system and preparing a standardized execution environment before booting the operating system, belong to the BIOS. The BIOS is mapped into the physical address space, but it doesn't reside in physical memory. Instead, the BIOS is stored in a ROM chip, located on the motherboard, connected with a Low Pin Count (LPC) Bus. This ROM is memory mapped at the very top of the physical address space, such that the last byte of the ROM is at the very top. Therefore, differently sized ROMs have different starting addresses within memory. For example, a 1-KB ROM would start at $0xFFFFF - 0x400 + 1 = 0xFFC00$, where as 4-KB ROM would start at $0xFFFFF - 0x1000 + 1 = 0xFF000$. These first instructions executed, the last bytes of the BIOS ROM, are the only address guaranteed to contain valid BIOS code, and since it belongs to the BIOS, it is guaranteed to know where in physical memory the rest of the initialization code resides.

From this point on, the processor continues its loop of fetching new instructions, decoding those instructions, and then executing those instructions. Each *instruction* defines an operation that transitions the state machine from one state to another.

Each individual instruction is comprised of one or more forms, that is, various encodings handling different operand types. An *operand* is simply a parameter for the instruction, defining what aspect of the state should be acted upon. Examples

Table 1.1 Forms for the ADD Instruction on the Intel® 8086

Operand Form	Example	Note
register, register	add %ax, %dx	dx = ax + dx
register, memory	add %ax, (%dx)	*(short *)dx = *(short *)dx + ax;
memory, register	add (%dx), %ax	ax = ax + *(short *)dx;
immediate, register	add $10, %ax	ax = ax + 10;
immediate, memory	add $10, (%bx)	*(short *)bx = *(short *)bx + 10;
immediate	add $10	ax = ax + 10;

of operands include a specific register, memory address, or an immediate, that is, a constant value at the time of assembly. As mentioned earlier, operands can be either explicit or implicit.

To illustrate this, consider the ADD instruction, which at the time of the 8086, had six unique forms. These forms are listed in Table 1.1. Notice how the first five forms are explicit, whereas the last form has an implicit operand, AX.

The 8086 had an instruction set comprising of about one hundred unique instructions, not accounting for different forms. These instructions can be divided into five logical groupings. For a full reference of the available instructions, along with their meanings and operands, see the Intel SDM.

Data movement

The first group contains instructions that move data from one operand to another. This includes instructions like MOV, which can move data from one operand to another, PUSH and POP, which pushes an operand onto the stack or pops the top of the stack into the operand, and XCHG, which atomically swaps the contents of two operands.

Integer arithmetic

The second group contains instructions that perform integer arithmetic. This includes instructions that perform the standard familiar arithmetic operations, such as ADD, SUB, MUL, and DIV.

Additionally, x86 supports instructions for performing these operations "with carry" or "with borrow." This is used for implementing these operations over an arbitrarily large number of bytes. In the case of a carry, the bit in EFLAGS is preserved for the next instruction to interpret. For example, each ADC, add with carry, instruction uses this bit to determine whether the result should be incremented by one, in order to borrow the bit carried from the previous ADC operation.

Typically each of these instructions sets the relevant status bits in the EFLAGS register. This often obviates the need to issue an explicit comparison instruction for some checks, like checks for zero, or less than zero. Instead, the flag can simply be reused from the arithmetic operation.

As mentioned earlier, the AX register is designated the accumulator register, so most arithmetic instructions have implicit forms that perform operations on, and store the result in AX.

Boolean logic

The third group contains instructions that perform boolean logic. This includes instructions like AND, which only sets bits in the result that are set in both operands, OR, which only sets bits in the result that are set in at least one of the operands, and XOR, which only sets bits in the result that are set in one operand and not the other.

Similar to the arithmetic group, these instructions also favor AX for their results. Additionally, they set the same bits in EFLAGS, sans the carry bits.

Flow control

The fourth group contains instructions that modify the program flow. Unlike a high level language, there are no if statements or for loop constructs. Instead, arithmetic and logical instructions set bits in the EFLAGS register, which can then be acted upon by control flow instructions. For example, consider the following two equivalent code snippets:

```
1   if (x > 255) {
2           x = 255;
3   }
```

LISTING 1.1

C version.

```
1   cmp     $255, %ax
2   jle     .Lskip_saturation
3   mov     $255, %ax
4   .Lskip_saturation:
```

LISTING 1.2

x86.

In the assembly version, the CMP instruction checks the contents of the register operand, AX, against an immediate, that is, a constant at assemble time, and sets the status flags in the EFLAGS register accordingly. While the JMP instruction unconditionally performs the jump, there are also conditional jump instructions. These instructions take the form of Jcc, where *cc* is a condition code. A condition code represents a predefined set of one or more conditions based on the status of EFLAGS. For example, the JNZ instruction only performs the jump if the Zero Flag (ZF) is not set. In the listing above, the JLE instruction only jumps to .Lskip_saturation when *AX* is less than or equal to 255, thereby skipping the saturation that occurs on line 3.

String

The fifth group contains instructions designed to operate on strings. This includes instructions for loading, LODS, storing, STOS, searching, SCAS, and comparing, CMPS, strings.

The string instructions are designed to heavily utilize implicit operands. The current character, either being loaded from, stored to, or scanned for, is held in AX. The source and destination pointers to strings are stored in DS:SI and ES:DI, respectively. The length of the strings are typically held in CX.

For example, the LODS instruction loads the byte at DS:SI into the AX register and then decrements or increments, depending on the status of the direction flag in EFLAGS,

Table 1.2 Meanings of the REP Prefix
(Intel Corporation, 2013)

Prefix	Meaning
REP	Repeat until CX = 0
REPE/REPZ	Repeat until EFLAGS.ZF != 0
REPNE/REPNZ	Repeat until EFLAGS.ZF == 0

SI. Conversely, the STOS instruction stores the byte in AX into the memory location ES:DI, and then updates the pointer accordingly.

The SCAS instruction compares the value of AX to the byte located at the memory location pointed to by ES:DI, updates the EFLAGS register accordingly, and then autoincrements or autodecrements DI. The CMPS instruction, designed for fast string comparison, compares the bytes located at ES:DI and DS:SI, updates the EFLAGS register, and then autoincrements or autodecrements both DI and SI.

While these string instructions perform one stage of their respective operations, they can be extended to perform the full operation by combining them with the REP prefix. This prefix repeats the instruction until the given condition is satisfied. This condition is specified through the suffix of the REP prefix. Table 1.2 lists the available REP prefixes and their subsequent meanings.

1.1.4 MACHINE CODE FORMAT
One of the more complex aspects of x86 is the encoding of instructions into machine codes, that is, the binary format expected by the processor for instructions. Typically, developers write assembly using the instruction mnemonics, and let the assembler select the proper instruction format; however, that isn't always feasible. An engineer might want to bypass the assembler and manually encode the desired instructions, in order to utilize a newer instruction on an older assembler, which doesn't support that instruction, or to precisely control the encoding utilized, in order to control code size.

8086 instructions, and their operands, are encoded into a variable length, ranging from 1 to 6 bytes. To accommodate this, the decoding unit parses the earlier bits in order to determine what bits to expect in the future, and how to interpret them. Utilizing a variable length encoding format trades an increase in decoder complexity for improved code density. This is because very common instructions can be given short sequences, while less common and more complex instructions can be given longer sequences.

The first byte of the machine code represents the instruction's *opcode*. An opcode is simply a fixed number corresponding to a specific form of an instruction. Different forms of an instruction, such as one form that operates on a register operand and one form that operates on an immediate operand, may have different opcodes. This opcode forms the initial decoding state that determines the decoder's next actions. The opcode for a given instruction format can be found in Volume 2, the Instruction Set Reference, of the Intel SDM.

Some very common instructions, such as the stack manipulating PUSH and POP instructions in their register form, or instructions that utilize implicit registers, can be encoded with only 1 byte. For instance, consider the PUSH instruction, that places the value located in the register operand on the top of the stack, which has an opcode of 01010_2. Note that this opcode is only 5 bits. The remaining three least significant bits are the encoding of the register operand. In the modern instruction reference, this instruction format, "PUSH r16," is expressed as "0x50 + rw" (Intel Corporation, 2013). The rw entry refers to a register code specifically designated for single byte opcodes. Table 1.3 provides a list of these codes. For example, using this table and the reference above, the binary encoding for PUSH AX is 0x50, for PUSH BP is 0x55, and for PUSH DI is 0x57. As an aside, in later processor generations the 32- and 64-bit versions of the PUSH instruction, with a register operand, are also encoded as 1 byte.

If the format is longer than 1 byte, the second byte, referred to as the Mod R/M byte, describes the operands. This byte is comprised of three different fields, MOD, bits 7 and 6, REG, bits 5 through 3, and R/M, bits 2 through 0.

The MOD field encodes whether one of the operands is a memory address, and if so, the size of the memory offset the decoder should expect. This memory offset, if present, immediately follows the Mod R/M byte. Table 1.4 lists the meanings of the MOD field.

The REG field encodes one of the register operands, or, in the case where there are no register operands, is combined with the opcode for a special instruction-specific meaning. Table 1.5 lists the various register encodings. Notice how the high and low byte accesses to the data group registers are encoded, with the byte access to the pointer/index classification of registers actually accessing the high byte of the data group registers.

In the case where MOD = 3, that is, where there are no memory operands, the R/M field encodes the second register operand, using the encodings from Table 1.5.

Table 1.3 Register Codes for Single Byte Opcodes "+rw" (Intel Corporation, 2013)

rw	Register
0	AX
1	CX
2	DX
3	BX
4	SP
5	BP
6	SI
7	DI

Table 1.4 Values for the MOD Field in the Mod R/M Byte (Intel Corporation, 2013)

Value	Memory Operand	Offset Size
00	Yes	0
01	Yes	1 Byte
10	Yes	2 Bytes
11	No	0

Table 1.5 Register Encodings in Mod R/M Byte (Intel Corporation, 2013)

Value	Register (16/8)
000	AX/AL
001	CX/CL
010	DX/DL
011	BX/BL
100	SP/AH
101	BP/CH
110	SI/DH
111	DI/BH

Otherwise, the R/M field specifies how the memory operand's address should be calculated.

The 8086, and its other 16-bit successors, had some limitations on which registers and forms could be used for addressing. These restrictions were removed once the architecture expanded to 32-bits, so it doesn't make too much sense to document them here.

For an example of the REG field extending the opcode, consider the CMP instruction in the form that compares an 16-bit immediate against a 16-bit register. In the SDM, this form, "CMP r16,imm16," is described as "81 /7 iw" (Intel Corporation, 2013), which means an opcode byte of $0x81$, then a Mod R/M byte with MOD $= 11_2$, REG $= 7 = 111_2$, and the R/M field containing the 16-bit register to test. The iw entry specifies that a 16-bit immediate value will follow the Mod R/M byte, providing the immediate to test the register against. Therefore, "CMP DX, 0xABCD," will be encoded as: $0x81$, $0xFA$, $0xCD$, $0xAB$. Notice that $0xABCD$ is stored byte-reversed because x86 is little-endian.

Consider another example, this time performing a CMP of a 16-bit immediate against a memory operand. For this example, the memory operand is encoded as an offset from the base pointer, $BP + 8$. The CMP encoding format is the same as before, the difference will be in the Mod R/M byte. The MOD field will be 01_2, although 10_2 could be used as well but would waste an extra byte. Similar to the last example, the REG field will be 7, 111_2. Finally, the R/M field will be 110_2. This leaves us with the first byte, the opcode $0x81$, and the second byte, the Mod R/M byte $0x7E$. Thus, "CMP 0xABCD, [BP + 8]," will be encoded as $0x81$, $0x7E$, $0x08$, $0xCD$, $0xAB$.

1.2 INTEL® 8087

Unlike the 8086, the 8087, shown in Figure 1.3, wasn't a standalone processor, but a coprocessor, similar to the 8089. But unlike the 8089, which accelerated I/O operations, the 8087 was developed to accelerate mathematical operations. Notice that in the instructions described in the previous section, all mathematical operations operate only on integers. As a result, all computations involving real numbers needed to be manually implemented in software. Unfortunately, this resulted in a suboptimal situation where the quality, accuracy, and functionality of available software math libraries varied greatly, thus impeding the ability of software to aid in tasks involving real numbers.

To remedy this situation, the 8087 was designed to consolidate as much of the common and error-prone computations into hardware as possible, freeing software engineers to focus on their application's calculations, rather than on implementing low level math routines. These features include floating point operations, numeric conversions, and common functions, such as the trigonometric and square root functions.

1.2.1 IEEE 754 FLOATING POINT

Intel recognized, as they were beginning development of the 8087, that a standardized floating point format, to be used from then on for all future architecture generations, was required. By standardizing the format, developers would be able to perform numerical analysis of their algorithms once, rather than repeatedly for each hardware generation. Also, once adoption of the new standard had taken hold, developers would be freed from writing custom code for each vendor's floating point solution, thus increasing software portability.

FIGURE 1.3

Intel® 8087 (Israel, 2009).

In order to accomplish this, Intel worked closely with the IEEE committee responsible for developing a standardized format for binary floating point arithmetic, the IEEE 754 standard. This standard, along with the international IEC 559:1989 standard, which is identical in content, defines the floating point format and arithmetic behavior, as well as the minimum precision and environment required for a compliant implementation. The original IEEE 754 format was finalized in 1985 and remained unchanged for twenty-three years, until the standard was extended in 2008. The 2008 revision to the standard retained most of the 1985 standard, and thus its content, along with the design of the 8087, still govern the format and behavior of floating point computations today, as of 2014. It is still important to note that, despite the fact that the standard did much to improve the situation of floating point portability and consistency, *the standard does not guarantee that different systems will produce identical results*.

Because the full 754 standard wasn't finalized until 1985, and the 8087 was released in 1980, the 8087 doesn't technically implement the full standard. Despite this, the 8087 implemented the current draft at the time of its release and both the hardware and Intel played an important role in the development of the standard. Notably, Dr. William Kahan, who was on the IEEE committee and is an expert in numerical analysis, was contracted by Intel to help design the 8087. The author recommends the reader visit Dr. Kahan's faculty website at Berkeley, located at http://www.eecs.berkeley.edu/~wkahan/, and read some of his publications on the rationale and history behind the standard, and on accuracy and error analysis in floating point computations.

Unlike an unsigned or signed 16-bit integer, which only allows for the representation of whole numbers between $[0, 2^{16} - 1]$ or $[-2^{15}, 2^{15} - 1]$ respectively, floating point allows for the representation of real numbers, as well as very large and small numbers beyond the integer limits. As the name implies, floating point utilizes scientific notation, which decomposes a number into a signed significand and a signed exponent. For example, the number 0.0005 would be represented as 5.0×10^{-4}.

However, using scientific notation introduces a problem, which is that the same number can be represented in multiple ways. For example, 5000.0×10^0, 500.0×10^1, and 5.0×10^3 are all the same number. Obviously, this could be problematic when comparing two floating point numbers. In order to remedy this, floating point requires that the scientific notation format is *normalized*. A number in normalized scientific notation has only a single nonzero digit before the decimal point. So in the previous example, 5.0×10^3 would be the normalized format.

Up to this point, all of the previous examples of scientific notation have been in base 10, hence the $\times 10^x$ component, however, all floating point numbers assume a base of 2. In order to encode a fraction in the significand in binary, each bit, n, represents $\frac{1}{2^n}$. Because of the normalized binary format, it's unnecessary to physically represent the leading bit of the significand. Therefore, this bit is implied and an extra bit of precision is gained. The exception to this case, 0, is handled with a reserved exponent of 0.

Formats, precision, and environment

The IEEE 754 standard defines four floating point types: basic single, basic double, extended single, and extended double. Compliance to the standard requires providing at least one basic type. The single type, corresponding to the `float` C type, is 32 bits, reserving 24 bits, 23 physical bits plus the implied leading bit, for the significand and 8 bits for the exponent. The double type, corresponding to the `double` C type, is 64 bits, providing 53 bits, 52 physical bits plus the implied leading bit, for the significand and 11 bits for the exponent. The MSb of each format is the sign bit for the significand.

For the extended types, the standard provides only the minimum length requirements. The single extended type is required to be at least 43 bits, with at least 32 bits for the significand and at least 11 bits for the exponent. The double extended type, corresponding to the `long double` C type, is required to be at least 79 bits, with at least 64 bits for the significand and 15 bits for the exponent. The bit encoding for the extended types is defined to be implementation-dependent.

One of the goals of the IEEE 754 format was to enable fast floating point sorting that could be performed by the regular integer ALU. One challenge to achieving this goal was how to handle the exponent component, since with a two's complement encoding extra logic would be needed to compare numbers based on their exponent's sign. In order to remedy this, a bias was introduced to the exponent component. A *bias* is simply an offset, added to the exponent, that ensures that the smallest possible value is expressed as all zeros, while the largest possible exponent is expressed as all ones. Because the bias is directly related to the number of elements that can be encoded, and therefore the number of bits in the representation, the bias varies with regards to the type. The standard defines the bias of a single basic type to be 127 and the bias of a double basic type to be 1023. Typically, the notation used for differentiating between biased and unbiased exponents is e and E, respectively.

The largest and smallest exponents, all ones and all zeros, are reserved for encoding special numbers. The largest exponent, $e = 255$ for floats and $e = 2047$ for doubles, is reserved for the encoding of infinity, both positive and negative according to the sign bit, and NaN, that is, Not A Number. Infinity is represented by a zero significand while NaN is represented by a nonzero significand. Infinity is designed to represent an edge of representable values, but is designed to compare properly with other numbers. NaNs are the result of an invalid operation and are designed to allow for errors to slowly propagate, which may be acceptable in some situations, as opposed to early termination of the computation with an exception. To accommodate both use cases, there are two types of NaNs, signaling and quiet, with the difference being that signaling NaNs generate an exception.

The smallest exponent, $e = 0$, is reserved for representing values for which the implicit leading bit in the significand does not apply. The obvious case for this is zero, which is represented by a zero exponent and a zero significand. As mentioned previously, floating point numbers are normalized; however, a special case exists for numbers too small for the standard format. These types of numbers are known as *denormals*, and are represented with $e = 0$, and the significand set to the relevant fraction.

In order to promote consistency in computations, the IEEE 754 standard also specifies four user-selectable rounding modes:

Round to Nearest The default rounding mode. As the name suggests, rounds to the closest representable number in the destination's format.

Round to Zero Always round toward zero.

Round to Negative Infinity Always round down toward negative infinity.

Round to Positive Infinity Always round up toward positive infinity.

In the case of certain conditions, floating point exceptions can be signaled either through the setting of a status flag or with the generation of a signal that invokes a trap handler. There are five defined exceptions:

Invalid Operation Raised when the requested computation cannot be performed. If no trap handler is specified, the result is a NaN.

Division by Zero If no trap handler is specified, the result is infinity.

Overflow If no trap handler is specified, the result is rounded based on the current rounding mode.

Underflow Same behavior as overflow

Inexact Raised when the rounding of a result is unable to be precisely represented or results in an overflow.

C99 support

Extensive support for the functionality described in this section is available in the C programming language, as of the C99 language revision. For a full reference, see *Annex F* of the C99 specification, along with section 5.2.4.2.2, which describes the characteristics of the format, and section 7.6, which describes access to the floating point environment. Another useful reference is the contents and man pages for the `fenv.h`, `float.h`, and `math.h` header files.

1.2.2 x87 FLOATING POINT

Unlike the 8086, the 8087 exposes its registers as a stack, instead of flat registers. Each of these eight registers is 80 bits in length, and thus each value is internally stored and computed in a double extended format. Values from memory, or the 8086's registers, are converted from integers, floats, and doubles into this 80-bit format when they are pushed onto the stack. Computations are then performed either with values from the stack or from memory locations. Unlike a traditional stack, each register is also directly addressable as a register relative to the top of the stack. The top of the stack is designated as the ST or $ST(0)$ register. Subsequent registers are designated with an index offset from the top of stack, such as $ST(1)$, $ST(2)$, and so on.

Usage of a stack makes the FPU operate much like a Reverse Polish Notation calculator. For example, in order to add two numbers, they could both be pushed onto the stack before executing an `FADD` instruction. This instruction will pop both numbers off of the stack, perform the addition operation and push the result onto the stack.

A stack was chosen for the registers as it is intuitive for mathematical operations, like RPN, and accommodates one operand instructions. Using the FXCH instruction, two stack registers can be swapped, and thus the stack registers could be utilized in a fashion that simulates flat registers (Kahan, 1990).

Aside from the stack registers, the 8087 also had a 16-bit status register, a 16-bit tag register, and a 16-bit control register. The status register for the FPU is similar to the EFLAGS register for the CPU. The first 6 bits correspond to the five IEEE 754 exceptions that can be raised during a computation, plus an additional bit to indicate a denormalized operand. Additional entries include 3 bits dedicated to the index of the current register at the top of the stack, 4 bits for expressing condition codes, that is, codes similar to the flags in EFLAGS that are used for comparisons and branches, and a bit representing an interrupt request. The tag register, with 2 bits per stack register, stores the status of the stack register. Each register can be marked as either having a valid entry, an entry of zero, a special reserved number, or as being empty. The control register allows for the masking and unmasking of exception interrupts, as well as control of the rounding mode and precision mode.

Similar to the parallel architecture of the 8086, the 8087 is also divided into two components. The first component, the control unit (CU), is responsible for handling instructions and memory operands, and remains synchronized with the main processor, and thus mirrors the BIU of the 8086. The second component, the numeric execution unit (NEU), is responsible for performing actual computations, and thus mirrors the EU of the 8086. While the floating point unit (FPU), the 8087, was executing a floating point instruction, the CPU was free to execute general purpose instructions, thus providing parallelism to improve performance.

The 8087 and subsequent coprocessors remained separate chips until the 80486 processor, which integrated the FPU into the CPU. While later processor introduced features like MMX™ technology, SSE, and Intel® Advanced Vector Extensions (Intel® AVX), which are also capable of floating point operations, the x87 FPU is still heavily utilized in areas where additional precision is needed.

1.3 INTEL® 80286 AND 80287

After the 8086 and 80186, the 80286 was introduced in 1982. What makes the 80286 worthy of mention is that it was the first x86 processor designed for multitasking. Much of this multitasking support came through the addition of a memory protection scheme designed to isolate tasks from one another.

Up until this point, no memory protection existed for x86, meaning that every byte in the address space was treated equally, regardless of whether it belonged to the operating system or a user application. This meant that there was no mechanism to prevent a user application from tampering with the code and data of another application or of the operating system. Obviously, this was less than optimal for security, for application isolation, or for operating system constraints on application behavior. To remedy this, the 80286 included an on-chip Memory Management Unit (MMU), which was responsible for transparently translating between logical, that is, segmented addresses consisting of a segment selector and offset, and physical addresses, and for enforcing memory protection. Therefore, each process on the system could be isolated in a separate address space.

1.3.1 PROTECTED AND REAL MODE

Because this represented a paradigm shift in the processor's programming model, the two models were split into two separate processor modes. The legacy mode, which was utilized by the 8086 and 80186, was called Real-Address mode, or simply real mode. The new MMU mode with memory protections was called Protected Virtual-Address mode, or simply protected mode. To retain compatibility with legacy applications for the 8086 and 80186, the processor booted into real mode, ensuring that these applications would see the 80286 as simply a faster and better 8086. Applications that wished to take advantage of the features in the new model would boot into real mode and then switch into protected mode. This technique, making new software request new features, is a common trend in x86 for making disruptive changes to the architecture while retaining backwards compatibility.

Transitioning from real mode to protected mode is a fairly straightforward process. The first step is to create and load all of the protected mode memory structures, so that the protected environment operates correctly immediately after the switch. Secondly, the PE bit in the first control register, $CR0$, is set, which effectively enters protected mode. Finally, a jump instruction is performed to flush any processor caches. At this point, the processor is now executing in protected mode and any new functionality can be utilized. Once protected mode was entered, there was no method for returning to real mode, without resetting the processor.

The 80286 introduced the concept of a privilege level, ranging from level 0, which had the most privileges, to level 3, which had the least. These privilege levels were enforced by the MMU, which wouldn't permit a task operating at a lesser privilege level to access a memory region marked at a greater privilege level. Four levels were provided in order to provide fine level of control for operating systems that desired it. For example, an operating system's core functionality might run at privilege level 0, the kernel drivers at level 1, the user space drivers at level 2, and user applications at level 3. This privilege system is part of modern x86, although the Linux kernel only utilizes level 0, for kernel space, and level 1, for user space.

1.3.2 PROTECTED MODE SEGMENTATION

Support for these memory protected regions meant that the current segmentation memory model had to be extended. Originally, segments had been fixed in size; however, that made memory protection more cumbersome, since the fixed sizes were too large for fine grained task control. In order to solve this, segments in protected mode were now of variable size. All of these changes, combined with additional changes designed to allow for the implementation of advanced features, such as swapping, simply wouldn't work within the confines of the existing segment register format.

To accommodate this, the segment register format and behavior in protected mode is completely different from the segment register format and behavior in real mode.

Remember that originally the segment registers simply contained a base address that was shifted and added to the offset to produce a larger address size. In this new model, the segment registers needed more room for the accounting required to support these new features. Therefore, in protected mode only, segments now didn't reference the base address of the segment, but instead pointed to a descriptor entry in a table of segment descriptors. Each 8-byte entry in this table describes the 24-bit base address, 16-bit size, and 8 bits for the privilege and access information, which is used for marking segments as read only, executable, and so on. The remaining 16 bits store the segment selector, which when loaded into the 16-bit segment register effectively load the segment. To improve performance, by avoiding the need to touch memory each time a segment operation needs to be checked, the other 48 bits of the segment descriptor are cached in a hidden register when the segment selector is loaded.

In order to make segmentation usable for both the operating system and user applications while still enforcing memory protections, two segment descriptor tables exist. The global descriptor table (GDT) is a table of segment descriptors that the operating system, privilege level 0, controls, while the local descriptor table (LDT) is controlled by the user application. Two registers, the GDTR and LDTR, exist for storing the base address of these tables. The global and local descriptor registers are loaded and stored with the LGDT and SGDT, and LLDT and SLDT instructions, respectively. Each segment selector has a special bit indicating whether the descriptor is located in the local or global table.

Each segment descriptor also had a present bit, indicating whether the corresponding segment was currently loaded into memory. If the segment descriptor was loaded into a segment selector register and the present bit in the descriptor was not set, the user program would be paused and an exception would be raised, giving the operating system a chance to load the relevant segment into memory from disk. Once the segment had been loaded, the user program would be resumed. All of this occurred transparently to the user program, and thus provided an early form of hardware supported virtual memory swapping. With swapping, more virtual memory could be allocated by the operating system than was physically available on the computer.

1.3.3 TASK CONTROL

Since the processor is only capable of running one application at a time, the job of a multitasking operating system is to provide the illusion that the processor can run multiple tasks at once. Whereas in a single-tasking operating system each job runs from start to completion before moving to next job, a multitasking operating system divides the processor time across each of the required jobs. This switching has to occur quickly and smoothly enough that it is transparent to the user applications, and appears that the processor is running all of the tasks concurrently.

The action of switching the processor from running one process to running a different process is referred to as a *context switch*. In order to perform a context switch, the operating system must keep track of the full execution state of the processor, including the contents of the registers and memory, for each executing task. On a context switch, the process which was running is paused and the contents of the execution state are saved into storage, while the execution state of the next process to run is loaded from storage into the processor.

The process of determining which process should be run and for how long is referred to as *process scheduling*. Process scheduling is a well researched problem in computer science that attempts to address many concerns, such as fairness in scheduling or balancing response time with throughput, for many different types of situations involving different numbers of processes with different performance requirements. As such, processor scheduling is a fairly large field, which won't be discussed in detail within this book. At the time of this writing, most of the processor scheduling research for Linux revolves around optimally scheduling tasks to complement current power-saving techniques. For a good introduction to the fundamental concepts and algorithms, the author recommends *Modern Operating Systems* by Andrew Tanenbaum.

The 80286 introduced a new feature that allowed for context switches to be handled automatically in hardware. This was facilitated through a special segment, a task state segment. Within the task state segment, all of the execution state for a process is preserved. By issuing a JMP, CALL instruction, or returning from an interrupt, where the destination is the processes' TSS descriptor, a context switch automatically occurs. The execution state of the currently executing process is automatically copied into the relevant section of the TSS. Once this is complete, the new execution environment, of the process being switched to, is automatically loaded into the processor, and execution of the new process can continue from where it had been previously paused.

Despite full support for context switches in hardware, Linux performs all of its context switches manually with software. This has been done for performance reasons, because the hardware context switch loads and validates all of the execution state, whereas Linux has historically performed some of the loads lazily and optimized some loads based on what actually needs to be restored.

1.4 INTEL® 80386 AND 80387

After the 80286, the 80386, shown in Figure 1.4, was introduced in 1985, and was continually produced by Intel, by popular demand, until September 2007. The 80386 was the first 32-bit processor in the x86 family, and also expanded many of the fundamental concepts introduced in the 80286. Perhaps even more importantly, since this book focuses on Linux, the 80386 was the first processor that ran Linux. In fact,

FIGURE 1.4

Intel® 80386 (Lanzet, 2008).

80386 support existed in the kernel until it was removed in 2012 (Molnar, 2012). To quote the original Usenet post from Linus Torvalds describing the Linux project:

> *"I'm doing a (free) operating system (just a hobby, won't be big and professional like gnu) for 386(486) AT clones. ...It uses every conceivable feature of the 386 I could find, as it was also a project to teach me about the 386. (Torvalds, 1991)"*

Whereas the 80286 introduced the real and protected processor modes, the 80386 introduced an additional mode. This mode, Virtual 8086 mode, was designed to address the fact that the 80286 did not allow returning to real mode from protected mode, and thus there was previously no way to run legacy and modern applications side by side. Virtual 8086 mode is a special mode designed to be entered from protected mode. This allows for the processor to execute 8086 programs, that is, programs written for real mode, from protected mode. Linux supports Virtual 8086 mode, with `CONFIG_VM86`, for certain drivers and legacy applications that need to access real mode.

1.4.1 **32-BIT MODE**

Having already been familiarized with the 16-bit ISA of the early x86 processors, the transition from 16 to 32 bits is straightforward. In 32-bit mode, both memory addresses and integers are extended from 16 to 32 bits, that is, `sizeof(int) = sizeof(void *) = 4` bytes. This increases the physical address space to 4-GB, 2^{32}.

The extended general purpose registers are prefixed with a letter *E*. For instance, the 16-bit *AX* register extends to the 32-bit *EAX* register. The previous register names operate on a subset of the corresponding extended registers. For instance, the *AX* register references the least significant word of *EAX*, and the *AH* and *AL* registers reference the two least significant bytes of *EAX*.

In Real-Address mode, everything continues operating exactly as it had before. All instructions in Real-Address mode default to their 16-bit versions. Within protected mode, a new bit was added to the segment descriptors, known as the *default bit*, or D-bit. When this bit is clear, instructions within the code segment default to 16-bit mode. When this bit is set, instructions within the code segment default to 32-bit mode.

While this bit controls the default size for a given segment, the mode of an individual instruction can override the default size with a special instruction prefix. This prefix, 0x66, is known as the *Operand-size override* prefix. By using this prefix, it is possible to execute 16-bit instructions in 32-bit Protected Virtual-Address mode, and to even execute 32-bit instructions in 16-bit Real-Address mode.

Aside from adding this new instruction prefix, the 80386 also extends the machine code format. These additions include support for 32-bit immediates, 32-bit displacements, and a new addressing format. As mentioned in Section 1.1.4, there were previously some restrictions on how memory operands could be addressed. These restrictions limited addressing to a base, contained within either the *SI*, *DI*, *BX*, or *BP* registers, and an optional displacement. Additionally, if the base was stored in *SI* or *DI*, an optional offset, also known as an *index*, could be encoded in *BX* or *BP*.

In 32-bit mode, the base and offset encodings in the Mod R/M byte are no longer limited to this subset of general purpose registers. Instead, any general purpose register can be used for either the base or index. In order to accommodate some of these encodings, a new optional byte, the *scale-index-base* (SIB) byte, may need to follow the MOD R/M byte.

The two most significant bits within the SIB byte encode the scaling factor. A value of zero encodes a scaling factor of one, a value of one encodes a scaling factor of two, a value of two encodes a scaling factor of four, and a value of three encodes a scaling factor of eight. The next 3 bits encode the register containing the index, which is scaled and then added to the base. The last 3 bits, the three least significant bits, encode the register containing the base. Both the index and base registers are encoded using the same values as in the Mod R/M byte for the 8086, as shown in Table 1.5.

In other words, 32-bit x86 memory operands are expressed as:

$$EA = \text{base} + (\text{index} \times \text{scale}) + \text{displacement}$$

The result of this calculation, which can be obtained with the *LEA* instruction, is referred to as the *effective address*. In AT&T assembly syntax, this is formatted as `displacement(base, index, scale)`. Because *LEA* can perform up to two additions and a multiplication, and doesn't modify any flags, it has historically been used as an optimization for general purpose integer arithmetic; however, on modern x86, this is no longer a fruitful optimization.

To illustrate this concept, consider how to load the ith element of an array of integers `foo[]`. Assume that the index, i, is stored in the *ECX* register, that the base address of `foo[]` is stored in the *EAX* register, and that the desired destination of the contents of `foo[i]` is the *EBX* register. Accessing `foo[i]` translates to the following pointer arithmetic:

$$foo[i] = *((uintptr\_t)foo + (i * sizeof(foo[0])))$$

Since each element of `foo[]` is an integer, `sizeof(foo[0])` $= 4$, the ith element could be loaded into *EBX* with:

```
mov (%eax, %ecx, 4), %ebx
```

The next element, $i + 1$, could be loaded either by incrementing *ECX* or by adding a displacement of four:

```
mov 4(%eax, %ecx, 4), %ebx
```

1.4.2 PAGING

Up to this point, memory address translations have occurred in one phase, logical, that is, a segmented address consisting of a segment selector and an offset, to a physical address. The 80286 extended segmentation in order to accommodate the needs of rapidly advancing operating system designs. The design of the 80386 recognized that segmentation alone was not enough to meet these needs, and therefore paging was introduced.

With paging, memory address translations occur in two separate phases. In the first phase, the logical address is converted to a linear address, through the translation method for segmentation. In the second phase, the linear address, produced in the first phase, is converted to a physical address, through the translation method for paging. Notice that paging doesn't replace segmentation, but instead was designed to complement it.

In a system that implements paging, the address space is divided into multiple pages. A *page* is simply a fixed-size chunk of memory, which may or may not be currently present in memory. The available physical memory of the system is divided into page frames. A *page frame* is a memory region capable of holding a page in memory. As required, various pages are swapped in and out of the physical page frames.

Mappings are created between the linear and physical address space through a hierarchical memory structure comprising of multiple tables, referred to as *page tables*. The page tables are divided into multiple levels, with each level representing pages of a different size. Each entry in the page tables can either map a page of the current size, or reference another table, which can then either map a page of a smaller size or reference another table, and so on.

In the classic x86 paging mode present in the 80386, the page tables are divided into two levels, the *page directory* and a set of *page tables*. Each entry in the first level, known as a *page directory entry* (PDE), can either map a 4-MB page or reference one of the second level page tables. Each entry in the page tables, known as a *page table entry* (PTE), maps a 4-KB page. The page directory table and each of the page tables are the size of a 4-KB page, meaning that each consists of 1024 entries of 4-B pointers. Therefore, only one page directory table is required to cover the whole 4-GB linear address space, since $1024 \times 4\text{-MB} = 4\text{-GB}$. The base physical address of this page directory table is stored in the *CR*3 register. Additionally, the 1024 entries in each page table cover the 4-MB region that would otherwise be mapped by the corresponding PDE, since $1024 \times 4096 = 4\text{-MB}$.

When a PDE or PTE maps a page, it points to the beginning of either a 4-MB or 4-KB page, so the entry pointer is guaranteed to be at least page aligned. The page directory and page tables are also required to be page aligned. As a result, the bottom 12 bits of the PDE and PTE are guaranteed to be zero, by definition. Rather than wasting these bits, they are used to encode the page's protection information, whether the page is currently present in memory, and whether the pointer maps a page or references another table. Within these 12 bits are four important bits: the present bit, the read/write bit, the supervisor/user bit, and the dirty bit. As mentioned previously, the present bit indicates whether the current page is present in memory. Attempting to access a page whose present bit is not set will generate a page fault, giving the operating system a chance to load the desired page into memory before continuing. The read/write bit controls whether the page is read-only, if the bit is clear, or if it is writable. The supervisor/user bit controls whether the page is owned by the operating system, if the bit is clear, or by a user task. Attempts to access a page belonging to the supervisor from a user application will result in a fault. Finally, the dirty bit indicates whether a page has been modified. If so, when the page is swapped out of memory, it will need to be written back to the disk. If not, it can be simply discarded, which is much less expensive.

A linear address, in this two-level system, is comprised of three components: a directory offset, a page offset, and then an address offset. Translation begins by reading the physical address of the page directory table from the *CR*3 register. The directory offset component of the linear address is added to this address in order to obtain the corresponding PDE. If the page size bit, bit seven, in the PDE is set, then the PDE maps a 4-MB page. In this situation, the PDE points to the physical base address of a 4-MB page and the rest of the linear address is treated as an offset from the beginning of that page. This base address and offset are added to produce the final physical address that completes the translation. If the page size bit in the PDE is not set, then the PDE references a page table. In this situation, the PDE points to the physical base address of the corresponding page table. The page offset component of the linear address is added to this address in order to obtain the corresponding PTE. The PTE points to the physical base address of a 4-KB page. Finally, the address offset component of the linear address is added to this base address to produce the final physical address that completes the translation.

At this point, the reader might be wondering about all of the memory accesses required to translate a linear address into a physical address. At the very least, the page directory will need to be accessed for every address translation. In the common case, both the page directory and a page table will need to be accessed. If this address translation, known as walking the page tables, occurred for every memory access, it would introduce a significant amount of overhead. To prevent this, a cache, known as the Translation Lookaside Buffer (TLB), was introduced. Once an address translation is completed, the result is stored in the TLB, including the page accounting bits. From that point forward, until that TLB entry is evicted or invalidated, all address translations involving the relevant page will be satisfied from the TLB, avoiding the page table walk. Leveraging locality of data, recent translations are added to the TLB while older translations, the least recently used, are evicted to make room for the new entries. Whenever the page table mappings are modified, the corresponding TLB entries must be explicitly invalidated to ensure that the new mappings are visible.

Unlike segmentation, which is always enabled, paging must be explicitly enabled by software. In order to activate paging, the PG bit is set in the *CR*0 control register, and the physical address of the top level page table, the page directory, is set in the *CR*3 control register.

The Linux kernel splits the linear address space for each process into two address ranges, one for the kernel, kernel space, and one for the user process, user space. For 32-bit Linux, this split is controlled through the CONFIG_VMSPLIT_* Kconfig options, which set CONFIG_PAGE_OFFSET to the beginning of kernel space. Therefore, any linear address above or equal to CONFIG_PAGE_OFFSET is a kernel address and any address below CONFIG_PAGE_OFFSET is a user space address. By default, the 4-GB linear address space is divided into a 1-GB kernel space range and a 3-GB user space range, that is, a page offset of 0*x*C0000000. In other words, regardless of how much physical memory is being used, an application can only map 3-GB worth of pages simultaneously.

While segmentation can't be disabled, it can be bypassed if it isn't desired. This is achieved by creating and loading flat memory segment descriptors, where each segment begins at the beginning of the address space and is the size of the full address space. This means that the logical to linear address translation is a one-to-one direct mapping, and therefore a nop. By default, Linux maintains two groups of segments, one that encompasses all of kernel space and one that encompasses all of user space.

REFERENCES

IEEE Standard for Binary Floating-Point Arithmetic, 1985. ANSI/IEEE Std 754-1985. doi: 10.1109/IEEESTD.1985.82928.

Intel Corporation, 1979, 10. The 8086 Family User's Manual, Computer Hardware Manual.

Intel Corporation, 1986. Intel 80386 Programmer's Reference Manual, Computer Hardware Manual.

Intel Corporation, 1987. Intel 80286 Programmer's Reference Manual Computer Hardware Manual.

Intel Corporation, 2013, 10. Intel 64 and IA-32 Architectures Software Developer's Manual Computer Hardware Manual.

ISO Joint Technical Committee JTC1, Subcommittee SC 22, Working Group 14, 2007, 10. ISO/IEC 9899:TC3 Draft C language Specification.

Israel, J., 2009, 02. Ic-photo-Intel–D8087-2-(8086-FPU). Used with permission. http://www.happytrees.org/main-images/chip-v2/ic-photo-Intel--D8087-2-(8086-FPU).png, PNG converted to greyscale and EPS.

Kahan, W., 1990, 11. On the advantages of the 8087's stack, Unpublished Course Notes.

Kahan, W., Palmer, J., 1979 oct. On a proposed floating-point standard. SIGNUM Newsl. 14 (si-2), 13–21. doi:10.1145/1057520.1057522. http://doi.acm.org/10.1145/1057520.1057522.

Lanzet, K., 2008, 6. KL Intel i386DX – CPU collection Konstantin Lanzet. Used with permission. http://commons.wikimedia.org/wiki/File:KL_Intel_i386DX.jpg#mediaviewer/File:KL_Intel_i386DX.jpg, JPEG convered to greyscale and EPS.

Lanzet, K., 2009, 4. KL Intel D8086 – CPU collection Konstantin Lanzet. Used with permission. http://upload.wikimedia.org/wikipedia/commons/e/e1/KL_Intel_D8086.jpg, JPEG convered to greyscale and EPS.

Molnar, I., 2012, 12. Nuke 386-dx/sx support, Git Pull Request, SHA1 in tree: 743aa456c1834f76982af44e8b71d1a0b2a82e21.

Palmer, J.F., 1980, The Intel 8087 numeric data processor. Proceedings of the May 19-22, 1980, National Computer Conference. AFIPS '80, Anaheim, California. ACM, New York, NY, pp. 887–893. http://doi.acm.org/10.1145/1500518.1500674.

Patterson, D.A., Hennessy, J.L., 2007. Computer Organization and Design: The Hardware/Software Interface, third ed. Morgan Kaufmann, Burlington, MA.

Torvalds, L., 1991, 08. What would you like to see most in minix? https://groups.google.com/forum/#!topic/comp.os.minix/dlNtH7RRrGA%5B1-25-false%5D, Usenet post.

Intel® Pentium® Processors 2

CHAPTER CONTENTS

In the previous chapter, the early history of the x86 architecture was introduced. While the early 16-bit processors introduced many of the fundamental principles of the x86 architecture, the Intel® 80386 truly embodies the aspects of what is considered by many developers to be the traditional x86 architecture. Aside from extending the architecture to 32 bits, the 80386 added many of the process isolation and memory protection features that are an integral part of modern operating systems.

The requirements placed on technology increase at a large order of growth, and therefore processor technology must continually improve to support these demands. In the time following the release of the 80386, most of these demands revolved around computational performance. The consumer market was surging with performance-intensive applications, such as 3D games and multimedia, while at the same time the rising availability of the Internet created a demand for infrastructure capable of supporting these new workloads.

This changing technological landscape significantly shaped the processor design of the time. The successor to the 80386, the Intel® 80486, focused on improving the performance of the functionality introduced with the 80386. For example, the floating point coprocessor was integrated directly into the processor, as opposed to requiring a separate chip. Additionally, a memory cache was added to the 80486, reducing the number of accesses to external memory. The Intel® Pentium® processor family redesigned how the execution pipeline of Intel® Architecture operated. This provided significant performance gains without requiring any direct intervention from the programmer.

The rest of this chapter investigates the important changes to Intel Architecture made during this era that affect performance, ranging from the Pentium® to Intel® Pentium® 4 processors.

2.1 INTEL® PENTIUM®

After the 80486, the first of the four, technically five, Intel Pentium processors, shown in Figure 2.1, was introduced in 1993. The name Pentium is derived from the Greek word πέντε (pente), which means five, since the Pentium is the fifth hardware revision, that is, the P5 microarchitecture. Despite this, the Pentium name was also used for later processors that were not based on the P5 microarchitecture.

Whereas the 80486 had a 8-KB cache for storing both code and data, the Pentium had a 16-KB cache, with 8-KB reserved for caching data and 8-KB reserved for caching instructions. Whereas the 80486 achieved instruction-level parallelism (ILP) through instruction pipelining, the Pentium processor was 2-wide superscalar, which significantly improved ILP. The Pentium also introduced MMX™ technology, the first set of Single Instruction Multiple Data (SIMD) extensions to the x86 instruction set.

FIGURE 2.1

Intel® Pentium® (Israel, 1996).

2.1.1 SUPERSCALAR

Prior to the 80486, the predecessor to the Pentium, each instruction was executed serially. In other words, each instruction began and finished execution before the execution of the next instruction could begin. This resulted in inefficient utilization of the processor's resources, as instruction execution did not require all of those resources simultaneously.

The 80486 introduced the concept of instruction pipelining. Instruction pipelining partitions the execution process into multiple independent steps capable of occurring in parallel. Instructions traverse these partitions one stage at a time. Once an instruction progresses to the next step, the next instruction can take its place in the pipeline, and so on. As a result, the pipeline can simultaneously execute multiple instructions. This leads to better utilization of the processor's resources, as each instruction only consumes a subset of the total resources. In other words, instruction pipelining provides a finer level of granularity for the allocation of processor resources.

The execution pipeline of the 80486 is partitioned into five stages, meaning that ideally five instructions are executing simultaneously. As the pipeline advances, effective utilization depends on each stage making forward progress to the next stage, with the oldest instruction exiting the pipeline and a new instruction entering the pipeline. A situation where forward progress cannot be made is referred to as a *hazard*. There are three types of pipeline hazards:

Structural Hazards Two instructions both require the same hardware resource.
Data Hazard Two instructions share a data dependency. For example, one instruction might depend on the result of another instruction.
Control Hazard Instructions within pipeline were speculatively executed but the branch was predicted incorrectly.

When a hazard occurs, the pipeline stalls in order to allow the hazard to pass. This stall is referred to as a *bubble* in the pipeline, since there is an empty gap introduced.

The Pentium processor increased the ILP of the 80486's instruction pipeline even further. Whereas the 80486 had one pipeline capable of executing five instructions simultaneously, the i586 architecture had two pipelines each capable of executing five instructions simultaneously. This is referred to as *multiple issue*, because multiple instructions are ideally entering and exiting the pipeline at each step. In order to accommodate this, the Pentium processor adds duplicate execution units to support the second pipeline.

The number of instructions the processor can issue each cycle is referred to as the processor's *width*, so the Pentium processor is described as 2-wide. It is important to understand that the two pipelines are not identical. As a result, there are restrictions on which instructions can be issued together. If any of these restrictions are violated, then only one instruction can be issued. This decision, whether to issue one or two instructions, is performed automatically in hardware during execution.

Therefore, the Pentium processor is classified as a *dynamic multiple issue* processor, that is, *superscalar*. This is opposed to a *static multiple issue* processor, where the programmer and compiler are responsible for scheduling instructions to obey the restrictions.

2.2 INTEL® PENTIUM® PRO

After the first Pentium, the Intel Pentium Pro, shown in Figure 2.2, was introduced in 1995. The Pentium Pro was the first processor to utilize the new P6 architecture, that is, the i686. The P6 architecture introduced a significant number of improvements to the first Pentium, and therefore remained a staple of the Pentium lineup, until the introduction of the NetBurst architecture with the Pentium 4.

Whereas the 80486 and first Pentium processor only contained one memory cache on-die, the Pentium Pro added a second, larger but slower, cache. This cache is known as the *second level cache* or L2 cache. Additionally, the introduction of the Physical Address Extensions (PAE) increased the amount of usable physical memory from 4-GB to 64-GB. The Pentium Pro also brought improvements to the execution pipeline, introducing out-of-order execution and *μops*, and by extending the processor's width to 3-wide superscalar.

2.2.1 PAE

The PAE increase the number of the processor's physical address pins, expanding the size of the physical address space. It is important to understand that this change only

FIGURE 2.2

Intel® Pentium® Pro (Israel, 1995).

extends the physical address space, not the linear or logical address spaces. With PAE enabled, pointers are still 32 bits in length and each process can still only map up to 4-GB worth of pages at the same time. The benefit is that the processor can address more memory, and therefore more pages can be kept resident in memory, rather than being swapped to and from slow storage, simultaneously.

Remember from Section 1.4.2 that traditional 32-bit paging utilizes one page directory table, with entries capable of either mapping a 4-MB page or referencing a page table, and a set of page tables, with entries mapping 4-KB pages. Both the page directory and page tables are 4-KB in size, with 1024 32-bit entries.

In order to accommodate the extended physical memory region when PAE is enabled, the entries in both types of tables are extended from 32 to 64 bits. Accounting for the reserved and configuration bits, these 64-bit entries are capable of handling a maximum of 52 physical address pins, that is, 4-PB; however, this is limited by the number of the processor's physical address pins. Starting with the Pentium Pro, the number of pins was increased from 32 to 36, increasing the physical address space to 64-GB, 2^{36}.

While the size of each entry doubled, the size of the different tables was not increased, so the number of entries in each table is reduced from 1024 to 512. As a result, a page table spans 2-MB of the linear address space, 4096×512, instead of 4-MB. Therefore, with PAE enabled a PDE maps a 2-MB page instead of a 4-MB page. Additionally, the linear address coverage of the page directory table shrinks from 4-GB to 1-GB, $(1024 \times 1024 \times 2) \times 512$, meaning that one page directory is no longer sufficient to cover the entire linear address space. Therefore, another level is added to the paging hierarchy, known as the *page directory pointer table* (PDPT). The PDPT has four 64-bit entries that each point to a page directory.

2.2.2 *μops*

Processor architectures are classified as either a Reduced Instruction Set Computer (RISC) or as a Complex Instruction Set Computer (CISC). The difference between the two classifications is that RISC architectures have a small number of simple general purpose instructions that each perform one single operation, essentially providing the basic building blocks for computations. CISC architectures, on the other hand, have a large number of more complex instructions, that are each capable of performing multiple internal operations.

For example, consider performing an arithmetic operation on a value in memory. For a RISC architecture, the corresponding arithmetic instruction would only be capable of operating on a register. As a result, before the operation could begin, a load instruction would be issued to fetch the value from memory and store it into a register. Once that is complete, the operation would be performed, with the result stored in a register. Finally, a store instruction would be issued to commit the result back to memory. On the other hand, the arithmetic operation's instruction for a CISC architecture would accept a memory operand. Assuming the memory operand is the instruction's destination operand, this form of the instruction would automatically fetch the value from memory, perform the operation, and then commit the result back to memory, all in one instruction.

As a result, CISC architectures are often able to perform an algorithm in less instructions than a RISC architecture, since one CISC instruction can perform the equivalent work of multiple RISC instructions. On the other hand, due to the simplified nature of their instructions, RISC architectures are often less complex, and therefore require less silicon. Additionally, due to the logical separation of different instructions for specific tasks, RISC architectures are capable of scheduling and executing instructions at a finer granularity than CISC architectures.

The x86 family of processors are classified as CISC, since x86 instructions are capable of performing multiple internal operations. Starting with the Pentium Pro, Intel Architecture is actually a hybrid approach between the two. The instruction set is not modified, so x86 instructions are still CISC, but the Front End of the processor translates each instruction into one or more *micro-ops*, typically referred to as μops or sometimes just uops. These μops are very similar to RISC instructions, each specialized for a specific task.

Consider the previous example for how CISC and RISC architectures handle an arithmetic operation. The x86 instruction set still supports memory operands for that arithmetic instruction, making it appear CISC to the programmer; however, the Front End might decode that single instruction into three μops. The first, a load μop, might be responsible for loading the contents described by the memory operand. The second μop would then be responsible for performing the actual operation. The third μop would then be responsible for committing the result back to memory.

This hybrid approach gives Intel Architectures the benefits of both approaches. Since memory accesses can be expensive, fetching fewer instructions benefits performance. The CISC nature of the x86 instruction set can be thought of as opcode compression, thereby improving instruction fetch bandwidth. At the same time, by breaking these complex instructions into smaller μops, the execution pipeline can be more agile and flexible, as Section 2.2.3 describes.

The cost of this approach is a more complicated Front End, which requires logic for decoding instructions into μops. In general, this cost is insignificant compared to the performance improvement achieved.

2.2.3 OUT-OF-ORDER EXECUTION

As discussed in Section 2.1.1, prior to the 80486, the processor handled one instruction at a time. As a result, the processor's resources remained idle while the currently executing instruction was not utilizing them. With the introduction of pipelining, the pipeline was partitioned to allow multiple instructions to coexist simultaneously. Therefore, when the currently executing instruction had finished with some of the processor's resources, the next instruction could begin utilizing them before the first instruction had completely finished executing. The introduction of μops expanded significantly on this concept, splitting instruction execution into smaller steps.

Each type of μop has a corresponding type of execution unit. The Pentium Pro has five execution units: two for handling integer μops, two for handling floating point μops, and one for handling memory μops. Therefore, up to five μops can execute in parallel. An instruction, divided into one or more μops, is not done executing until all of its corresponding μops have finished. Obviously, μops from the same instruction have dependencies upon one another so they can't all execute simultaneously. Therefore, μops from multiple instructions are dispatched to the execution units.

Taking advantage of the fine granularity of μops, out-of-order execution significantly improves utilization of the execution units. Up until the Pentium Pro, Intel processors executed in-order, meaning that instructions were executed in the same sequence as they were organized in memory. With out-of-order execution, μops are scheduled based on the available resources, as opposed to their ordering. As instructions are fetched and decoded, the resulting μops are stored in the *Reorder Buffer*. As execution units and other resources become available, the *Reservation Station* dispatches the corresponding μop to one of the execution units. Once the μop has finished executing, the result is stored back into the Reorder Buffer. Once all of the μops associated with an instruction have completed execution, the *μops retire*, that is, they are removed from the Reorder Buffer and any results or side-effects are made visible to the rest of the system. While instructions can execute in any order, instructions always retire in-order, ensuring that the programmer does not need to worry about handling out-of-order execution.

To illustrate the problem with in-order execution and the benefit of out-of-order execution, consider the following hypothetical situation. Assume that a processor has two execution units capable of handling integer μops and one capable of handling floating point μops. With in-order scheduling, the most efficient usage of this processor would be to intermix integer and floating point instructions following the two-to-one ratio. This would involve carefully scheduling instructions based on their instruction latencies, along with the latencies for fetching any memory resources, to ensure that when an execution unit becomes available, the next μop in the queue would be executable with that unit.

For example, consider four instructions scheduled on this example processor, three integer instructions followed by a floating point instruction. Assume that each instruction corresponds to one μop, that these instructions have no interdependencies, and that all three execution units are currently available. The first two integer instructions would be dispatched to the two available integer execution units, but the floating point instruction would not be dispatched, even though the floating point execution unit was available. This is because the third integer instruction, waiting for one of the two integer execution units to become available, must be issued first. This underutilizes the processor's resources. With out-of-order execution, the first two integer instructions and the floating point instruction would be dispatched together.

In other words, out-of-order execution improves the utilization of the processor's resources. Additionally, because μops are scheduled based on available resources, some instruction latencies, such as an expensive load from memory, may be partially or completely masked if other work can be scheduled instead.

Register Renaming

From the instruction set perspective, Intel processors have eight general purpose registers in 32-bit mode, and sixteen general purpose registers in 64-bit mode, however, from the internal hardware perspective, Intel processors have many more registers. For example, the Pentium Pro has forty registers, organized in a structure referred to as a *Physical Register File*.

While this many extra registers might seem like a performance boon, especially if the reader is familiar with the performance gain received from the eight extra registers in 64-bit mode, these registers serve a different purpose. Rather than providing the process with more registers, these extra registers serve to handle data dependencies in the out-of-order execution engine.

When a value is stored into a register, a new register file entry is assigned to contain that value. Once another value is stored into that register, a different register file entry is assigned to contain this new value. Internal to the processor core, each data dependency on the first value will reference the first entry, and each data dependency on the second value will reference the second entry. Therefore, the out-of-order engine is able to execute instructions in an order that would otherwise be impossible due to false data dependencies.

2.3 INTEL® PENTIUM® 4

The P6 microarchitecture was used as the basis for the Intel® Pentium® Pro, Intel® Pentium® II, and Intel® Pentium® III processor families. As a result, each of these generations mostly focused on improving the performance of the previous generation while adding new instructions. On the other hand, the Pentium 4, shown in Figure 2.3, was based on the NetBurst architecture. This new architecture adds new features including IA-32e mode, which extends the processor from 32-bits to 64-bits, and Intel® Hyper-Threading.

2.3.1 IA-32e MODE

The IA-32e processor mode extends Intel Architecture from 32-bit to 64-bit. In order to enter IA-32e mode, the processor must be in protected mode with PAE enabled. Paging is also a requirement for IA-32e mode, so the 64-bit page tables must be be constructed prior to transitioning into the new mode. In IA-32e mode, a fourth level is added to the paging hierarchy, the *page map level 4* (PML4) table. This 4-KB table contains 512 entries that point to PDPTs. Each PDPT is extended from 4 entries to 512 entries. Also, unlike 32-bit paging, where a PDPTE could only reference a page directory table, a PDPTE can map a 1-GB page. Once the *CR*3 register holds the physical base address of the PML4 table, the LME bit in the IA32_EFER MSR is set and then paging is enabled.

Similar to the extension from 16-bit to 32-bit, the extension from 32-bit to 64-bit is handled through the addition of another bit in the code segment descriptor, the L

FIGURE 2.3

Intel® Pentium® 4 (Israel, 2000).

bit. If the L bit is set, then the code within that segment operates in 64-bit mode. If the L bit is not set, but the processor is in IA-32e mode, then the segment operates in compatibility mode. This allows for 16-bit and 32-bit applications to still run while the processor is in 64-bit mode. If the L bit is not set and the D bit is not set, then the code within that segment operates in 16-bit mode. If the L bit is not set and the D bit is set, then the code within that segment operates in 32-bit mode.

In 64-bit mode, the memory address size and the long integer size is increased from 32-bit to 64-bit. While pointers are 64-bit, and are therefore theoretically capable of addressing up to 16 exabytes, 2^{64}, supporting such a large address space introduces extra complexity for little gain. As a result, at the time of this writing, 64-bit processors that support a full 64-bit address space are uncommon. Instead, these processors support a more manageable subset of the full address space. The size of the physical and linear address space supported by the processor can be accessed through /proc/cpuinfo. For example:

```
$ cat /proc/cpuinfo | grep "address sizes" | head -n 1
address sizes   : 36 bits physical, 48 bits virtual
```

In this example, the processor supports a physical address space of 64-GB, and a linear address space of 256-TB. At the time of this writing, 36 physical address pins are common for consumer hardware. On the other hand, server hardware, such as Intel® Xeon® processors, often support a significantly larger physical address space, for example, 46 physical address pins. In order to prevent a 64-bit memory address from exceeding the supported linear address space, the processor will fault on an address that doesn't follow canonical form. The *canonical address form* requires that all bits outside of the implemented address range all have the same value as the most significant bit of the supported linear address space. In the example above, the linear address space supports 48 bits, bits 0 through 47, so bits 48 through 63 must be set to the same value as bit 47.

Additionally, enabling 64-bit mode adds eight more general purpose registers, *R*8 through *R*15, increasing the total from eight to sixteen registers. The SIMD vector registers are also increased from eight to sixteen. Also, aside from the *FS* and *GS* segment registers, which are used for thread-local storage, segmentation is only supported in flat mode.

2.3.2 MULTI-CORE

Until this point, the main granularity of hardware parallelism was the processor die. For the best parallel performance, multiple processors are installed into special motherboards that contain multiple processor sockets. With this configuration, all of the processors can either share the same memory, or each processor socket can be configured to have its own set of corresponding memory DIMM slots. In the case where each processor has a separate set of memory DIMMs installed, memory is divided into two categories. For a given processor, the memory installed in that socket's corresponding DIMM slots are known as *local memory*. On the other hand, all of the other memory is known as *nonlocal memory* or *remote memory*. Memory that is local to a specific processor provides the fastest accesses, while remote memory provides slower accesses, due to the distance between the processor and the memory. Because of this disparity between the memory performance of local and remote memory, this is referred to as a Non-Uniform Memory Access (NUMA) configuration.

In order to best utilize these expensive hardware resources, the operating system needs to be aware of the system topology. For example, without this knowledge, the kernel might inadvertently allocate memory on the slow remote memory while the fast local memory is still available. In Linux, the kernel is configured for NUMA configurations by grouping memory resources into zones. These zones control what regions of memory are given priority, and allow for customization of different memory policies.

While these multiprocessor configurations provide the best performance, and are still popular in the server and workstation segments, these configurations tend to be expensive and require extensive system tuning.

In order to provide better parallel performance than a single processor, without requiring an expensive multiple processor configuration, some of the Pentium 4 models duplicated the processor's execution resources into multiple processor cores. Each core operates as a separate logical processor contained within the processor package.

Within a multi-core processor's die, resources are divided into two categories: core and uncore resources. *Core* resources are duplicated for each logical processor. On the other hand, *uncore* resources are shared between all of the cores present on that processor die. As one would expect, there are tradeoffs in performance between parallel and serial workloads for designing resources to be either core or uncore.

The coordination of multiple cores occurs in an identical fashion to multiple processors. After a hardware #RESET, one of the logical processors, which can be either a core or separate processor, is selected as the boot processor. The boot processor is responsible for performing the system initialization by executing the early BIOS code. All of the other logical processors halt and wait for the boot processor to bring them online. Once the boot processor has completed initialization, it uses Inter-Processor Interrupts (IPIs) to wake the application processors.

2.3.3 INTEL® HYPER-THREADING

Intel Hyper-Threading Technology adds additional parallelism into each processor core by dividing it into multiple hardware threads. Whereas multiple processor cores duplicate all of the core resources for each core, hardware threads only require the duplication of a small subset of execution state. Typically, this subset only includes the registers and APIC.

Since only the execution state is duplicated, but not the execution pipeline, the core's execution pipeline is shared between each hardware thread. As a result, μops from both hardware threads are present within the core's execution pipeline simultaneously. In other words, Hyper-Threading allows the μop scheduler to fill underutilized execution pipeline resources by interleaving the μops of two different processes.

Within Linux, each hardware thread appears as a separate logical processor. For instance, one quad-core processor with Hyper-Threading will register eight logical processors. The CONFIG_SCHED_SMT Kconfig option enables additional logic within the Linux kernel scheduler that makes it aware of hardware threads. Using this information, it can make better decisions when migrating processes between logical processors.

REFERENCES

Intel Corporation, 1996. Pentium® Pro Family Developer's Manual, vol. 1: Specifications.
Intel Corporation, 1997. Pentium® Processor Family Developer's Manual.
Intel Corporation, 2013, 10. Intel 64 and IA-32 Architectures Software Developer's Manual, Computer Hardware Manual.
Israel, J., 1995, 11. Intel pentium pro. Used with permission. http://www.happytrees.org/main-images/chip-v2/ic-photo-Intel--KB80521EX200-(Pentium-Pro-CPU).png, PNG converted to greyscale and EPS.
Israel, J., 1996, 1. Intel pentium. Used with permission. http://www.happytrees.org/main-images/chip-v2/ic-photo-Intel--A80502150--(Pentium-CPU).JPG, JPEG convered to greyscale and EPS.
Israel, J., 2000, 01. Intel pentium 4. Used with permission. http://www.happytrees.org/main-images/chip-v2/ic-photo-Intel--1.8GHZ_256_400_1.75V--(Pentium-4-CPU).png, PNG converted to greyscale and EPS.
Patterson, D.A., Hennessy, J.L., 2007. Computer Organization and Design: The Hardware/Software Interface, third ed. Morgan Kaufmann, Burlington, MA.

Intel® Core™ Processors

3

CHAPTER CONTENTS

In the previous chapter, the Intel® Pentium® lineup of processors was introduced. At that time, mobility wasn't as pervasive as it is today. Of course, there were laptops and mobile users who cared about battery life and power consumption; however, for the majority of computer users, raw computational performance was their primary concern. This trend was reflected in the design of the Pentium processors. While they did introduce new features for reducing power consumption, and there were mobile versions of some Pentiums, more time was spent optimizing their performance.

Once again, the technological landscape was changing, with a new emphasis on reduced power consumption and smaller form factors. At the same time, these mobility needs were compounded by a still increasing demand for raw computational performance. Whereas the Pentium lineup needed to handle intense 3D games, the Intel® Core™ processor family needed to handle blistering 3D games that were being played on battery power while waiting in line at the grocery store.

To accommodate these needs, Intel focused on architecting a series of new processors designed to improve performance while also simultaneously reducing power consumption. The Intel® Xeon® processors are architected to meet the needs of data centers, workstations, HPC supercomputers, and enterprise infrastructure. The Intel® Core™ processors are architected to meet the needs of the consumer and business markets, including both desktop and mobile systems. These chips carry the logo of either Intel® Core™ i3, Intel® Core™ i5, or Intel® Core™ i7. The Intel®

Atom™ processors are architected to meet the needs of smaller form factors, such as phones, tablets, netbooks, and microservers. The Intel® Quark™ microcontrollers are architected to meet the needs of the Internet of Things.

Additionally, Intel adopted a Tick Tock model for processor design. Each tock, which is followed by a tick, introduces a new microarchitecture. Each tick, which is followed by a tock, improves the manufacturing process technology for the previous microarchitecture. Improvements to the manufacturing process reduce the processor's power consumption and thermal output. For example, the Second Generation Intel® Core™ processor family was a tock, manufactured with 32nm manufacturing process technology. The Third Generation Intel® Core™ processor family was a tick, manufacturing the Second Generation microarchitecture with 22nm manufacturing process technology. The Fourth Generation Intel® Core™ processor family is a tock, introducing a new microarchitecture manufactured with the 22nm manufacturing process technology.

This chapter focuses on the power management functionality added to the Intel® Architecture.

3.1 INTEL® PENTIUM® M

The Intel® Pentium® M processor family was introduced in 2003. This family consisted of mobile processors, hence the "M," and exemplifies many of the fundamental power management techniques available for Intel Architecture.

3.1.1 ACPI

The first revision of the Advanced Configuration and Power Interface (ACPI) specification was released in 1996. While ACPI is most commonly associated with power management, the majority of the ACPI specification actually deals with device enumeration and configuration. At boot, UEFI or the legacy BIOS is responsible for creating a series of tables that describe the devices available in the system and their supported configurations.

Additionally, through these ACPI tables, devices expose functions, written in the ACPI Machine Language (AML). The Linux kernel implements an AML interpreter that can parse and execute these functions. This allows for device specific code to be abstracted behind a standardized device interface, and thus for the kernel to control certain devices without requiring a specialized driver.

ACPI also defines a series of processor, device, and system states. The most user-visible of these states are the system S and G states, which include states that most laptop users know as sleep and hibernation. There are three important ACPI processor states to understand.

The first, thermal states, which are often referred to as T states, are responsible for automatically throttling the processor in the case of a thermal trip. In other words, these states are built into the processor to automatically prevent damage caused by overheating. Since a misconfiguration of the T states could result in physical damage, these states are completely independent of software. Obviously, tripping these states should be avoided by ensuring that the processor is cooled by a solution capable of handling its TDP. It is also important to be aware of the fact that thermal throttling will drastically reduce performance until temperatures have returned to safe levels. As a result, this is something to be cautious of when running long benchmarks or tests.

The rest of this section focuses on the other two processor states.

P states and Intel SpeedStep® Technology

The ACPI specification defines the concept of Device and Processor performance states. Performance states, or simply P states, are designed to improve energy efficiency by allowing the processor to reduce performance, and therefore power consumption, when maximum performance is not required. As of the latest ACPI specification, revision 5.1, the performance states are defined as:

P0 "While a device or processor is in this state, it uses its maximum performance capability and may consume maximum power" (Unified EFI, Inc, 2014).
P1 "In this performance power state, the performance capability of a device or processor is limited below its maximum and consumes less than maximum power" (Unified EFI, Inc, 2014).
Pn "In this performance state, the performance capability of a device or processor is at its minimum level and consumes minimal power while remaining in an active state. State n is a maximum number and is processor or device dependent. Processors and devices may define support for an arbitrary number of performance states not to exceed 16" (Unified EFI, Inc, 2014).

Notice that the lower P state numbers correspond to higher power consumption, while the higher P state numbers correspond to lower power consumption. The specification uses `P0` and `P1` to establish the pattern between P states, and then provides each hardware vendor with the flexibility of defining up to sixteen additional performance states. As a result, the number of supported P states for a given system varies depending on the exact processor configuration, and must be detected at runtime through the ACPI tables.

On Intel Architecture, these states are implemented via Enhanced Intel SpeedStep® Technology (EIST). EIST provides an interface for controlling the processor's operating frequency and voltage (Intel Corporation, 2004). This interface consists of various model specific registers for requesting a state transition, `IA32_PERF_CTL_REGISTER`, and for obtaining hardware feedback regarding the state, `IA32_MPERF` and `IA32_APERF`.

It is important to note that these states are requested, as opposed to being set, by software. Many complex factors contribute to the actual P state the processor is put into, such as the states requested by the other cores, the system's thermal state, and so on. Additionally, these MSRs are duplicated per Hyper-Thread, yet prior to the Fourth Generation Intel® Core™ processor family, P states were governed at the granularity of the processor package.

User space applications do not need to worry about explicitly controlling the P state, unless they specifically wanted to. Within the Linux kernel, the CPU frequency scaling driver, `CONFIG_CPU_FREQ`, has traditionally been responsible for controlling the system's P state transitions. This driver supports multiple governors for controlling the desired management policy. At the time of this writing, there are five standard governors:

1. Performance (`CONFIG_CPU_FREQ_GOV_PERFORMANCE`)
2. Powersave (`CONFIG_CPU_FREQ_GOV_POWERSAVE`)
3. Userspace (`CONFIG_CPU_FREQ_GOV_USERSPACE`)
4. Ondemand (`CONFIG_CPU_FREQ_GOV_ONDEMAND`)
5. Conservative (`CONFIG_CPU_FREQ_GOV_CONSERVATIVE`)

The performance governor maintains the highest processor frequency available. The powersave governor maintains the lowest processor frequency available. The userspace governor defers the policy to user space, allowing for an application or daemon to manually set the frequency. The ondemand governor monitors the processor utilization and adjusts the frequency accordingly. Finally, the conservative governor is similar to the ondemand governor but additionally attempts to avoid frequent state changes. Due to the concept of race-to-idle, as introduced in the Introduction chapter, the ondemand governor has typically provided the best power savings on Intel Architectures.

One of the challenges with this driver has been tuning the algorithm for specific hardware generations. In order to remedy this, a new and more efficient P state driver, the Intel® P state driver, was written by Dirk Brandewie. Unlike the previous driver, this one checks the processor generation and then tunes accordingly.

The current frequency driver can be determined by checking the `/sys/devices/system/cpu/` directory. If the older cpufreq driver is active, a `cpufreq/` directory will be present, whereas if the Intel P state driver is active, an `intel_pstate` directory will be present. Within these sysfs directories are the tunables exposed to user space by these drivers.

C states

While lowering the core's frequency reduces power consumption, dropping the frequency to zero provides significantly greater savings. C states are the result of the observation that the processor cores in client systems sit idle most of the time. Therefore, while running the core at its lowest possible frequency is better than running it at its highest, it's even better to simply turn it off.

The ACPI specification also defines the concept of processor power states. As of the latest ACPI specification, the states are defined as:

C0 "While the processor is in this state, it executes instructions" (Unified EFI, Inc, 2014).

C1 "This processor power state has the lowest latency. The hardware latency in this state must be low enough that the operating software does not consider the latency aspect of the state when deciding whether to use it. Aside from putting the processor in a non-executing power state, this state has no other software-visible effects" (Unified EFI, Inc, 2014).

C2 "The C2 state offers improved power savings over the C1 state. The worse-case hardware latency for this state is provided via the ACPI system firmware and the operating software can use this information to determine when the C1 state should be used instead of the C2 state. Aside from putting the processor in a non-executing power state, this state has no other software-visible effects" (Unified EFI, Inc, 2014).

C3 "The C3 state offsets improved power savings of the C1 and C2 states. The worst-case hardware latency for this state is provided via the ACPI system firmware and the operating system can use this information to determine when the C2 state should be used instead of the C3 state. While in the C3 state, the processor's caches maintain state but ignore any snoops. The operating system is responsible for ensuring that the caches maintain coherency" (Unified EFI, Inc, 2014).

Notice that similar to P states, a lower C state number corresponds to higher power consumption, while a higher C state number corresponds to lower power consumption. While only four C states are defined in the specification, processors are capable of supporting deeper sleep states, such as *C*6 and *C*7. Also notice that each sleep state has an entrance and exit latency, which is provided to the operating system through an ACPI table.

With each P state, the core is constantly executing instructions. On the other hand, with C states, once the core exits C0, it is halted, that is, it completely stops executing instructions. As a result, a core's P state is only valid when the core is in C0. Otherwise, the frequency is or is almost zero.

When all of a processor's cores are in the same, or deeper, sleep states, additional uncore resources can also be powered off, providing even greater savings. These processor-wide states are referred to as *package C states*, since they are a C state for the entire processor package.

Similar to P states, user space applications don't need to worry about requesting C states, as this is handled by the kernel. The Linux kernel has both a generic ACPI idle driver and also a more advanced Intel® Idle driver, CONFIG_INTEL_IDLE, specifically designed and tuned for Intel® processors. One of the advantages of the Intel Idle driver is that it includes the estimated entrance and exit latencies for each C state for each supported hardware generation. This is especially beneficial for users whose firmware provides an incorrect or incomplete ACPI table for C state latencies, since the driver will default to using the correct values.

As deeper sleep states are entered, additional resources are powered down when the core enters the C state and then must be powered up when the core exits the C state. In other words, the lower C states provide smaller power savings, but are quicker to enter and exit, while the deeper C states provide more power savings, but are slower to enter and exit. As a result, when selecting a C state, the kernel considers how long the processor can sleep, and then chooses the deepest C state that meets that latency requirement. In other words, while user space applications aren't responsible for manually selecting C states, their behavior must be tuned in order to allow the core to stay in deep sleep for as long as possible.

3.2 SECOND GENERATION INTEL® CORE™ PROCESSOR FAMILY

Launched in early 2011, the Second Generation Intel® Core™ processor family, shown in Figure 3.1, introduced significant improvements to a wide range of components. For example, the Front End was updated with a new cache for storing decoded μops. The instruction set was updated with the introduction of Intel® Advanced Vector Extensions (Intel® AVX), which extended the SIMD register width.

FIGURE 3.1

Intel® Xeon® processor (van de Ven, 2014).

3.2.1 INTEL® HD GRAPHICS

Prior to the Second Generation Intel Core processor family, Intel® integrated graphics were not part of the processor, but were instead located on the motherboard. These graphics solutions were designated Intel® Graphics Media Accelerators (Intel® GMA) and were essentially designed to accommodate users whose graphical needs weren't intensive enough to justify the expense of dedicated graphics hardware. These types of tasks included surfing the Internet or editing documents and spreadsheets. As a result, Intel GMA hardware has long been considered inadequate for graphically intensive tasks, such as gaming or computed-aided design.

Starting with the Second Generation Intel Core processor family, Intel integrated graphics are now part of the processor, meaning that the GPU is now an uncore resource. While the term "integrated graphics" has typically had a negative connotation for performance, it actually has many practical advantages over discrete graphics hardware. For example, the GPU can now share the Last Level Cache (LLC) with the processor's cores. Obviously, this has a drastic impact on tasks where the GPU and CPU need to collaborate on data processing.

In many ways, the GPU now acts like another core with regards to power management. For example, starting with the Second Generation Intel Core processor family, the GPU has a sleep state, *RC6*. Additional GPU sleep states, such as *RC6P*, were added in the Third and Fourth Generation Intel Core processors. This also means that for the processor to enter a package C state, not only must all the CPU cores enter deep sleep, but also the GPU. Additionally, the GPU is now part of the processor's package's TDP, meaning that the GPU can utilize the power budget of the cores and that the cores can utilize the power budget of the GPU. In other words, the GPU affects a lot of the CPU's power management.

3.2.2 INTEL® FLEX MEMORY TECHNOLOGY

Unfortunately, while processor technology has been advancing rapidly, memory speeds have not kept pace. One technique for improving memory throughput has been the addition of parallel channels. Since these channels are independent, the memory controller can operate in an interleaved mode, where addresses can alternate between the channels. This technique effectively multiplies the potential memory bandwidth by the number of available channels. At the time of this writing, dual-channel memory is the most prevalent, although triple-channel and quadruple-channel systems are available.

In order to utilize interleaved mode, three prerequisites need to be met. First, the amount of memory in each channel must be equal. Second, the size of the memory modules installed in each of the paired memory slots must be identical. Finally, the memory modules need to be installed in the correct channel slots on the motherboard, which are typically color-coded so that alternating pairs share the same color. Failure to meet any of these requirements would result in the memory controller falling back to asymmetric mode. As a result, two 2-GB memory modules, correctly configured, will be faster than one 4-GB memory module.

Whereas symmetric, that is, interleaved, or asymmetric mode has traditionally been all or nothing, Intel Flex Memory Technology allows for finer-grain control over the access mode. In other words, memory accesses to regions where both channels have physical memory are performed in interleaved mode, while memory accesses to regions where only one channel has physical memory are performed in asymmetric mode. This provides a performance boost even when the memory configuration is less than ideal.

For example, consider the situation where one 4-GB and one 2-GB memory module are installed. For the bottom 4-GB, memory accesses occur interleaved between the bottom 2 GB of the 4-GB module, and the 2-GB module. On the other hand, higher memory accesses will occur in asymmetric mode, since all requests will need to access the top 2 GB of the 4-GB module. This type of memory configuration is often referred to as a *L-shaped memory configuration*. This is because the interleaved portion resembles the lower part of the letter L, while the asymmetric portion resembles the upper part of the letter.

The result of a L-shaped memory configuration is similar to a Non-Uniform Memory Access (NUMA) configuration, typically seen in the server space. This is because some memory accesses will be faster than others. While it may be tempting to use the NUMA infrastructure to inform the kernel about these discrepancies in performance, the existing techniques for handling NUMA are a bit too heavy handed for this kind of situation.

While Intel Flex Memory Technology reduces the performance impact of L-shaped memory configurations, they should still be avoided. Since Intel integrated graphics, except for the Iris™ Pro brand, have no dedicated memory, and therefore utilize the system's memory, L-shaped memory configurations can also adversely affect graphics performance.

3.2.3 INTEL® TURBO BOOST TECHNOLOGY

One of the challenges involved in optimizing a processor architecture is balancing the tradeoffs in performance between optimizing for serial and parallel workloads. While providing excellent parallel performance is a priority to Intel, neglecting serial workloads would be significantly detrimental to many common workloads.

While modern processors provide multiple cores on the package, outside of parallel workloads, most of the cores in client systems are often idle, either in deep sleep states, or operating at a reduced frequency in order to conserve power. At the same time, the processor package must be designed to handle the thermal and power requirements of each of the cores, and the GPU, operating under sustained heavy load. As a result, the processor is often operating well below the power and thermal levels at which it was designed to operate. This value, the amount of power the processor package requires to be dissipated in order to prevent overheating, is referred to as the *Thermal Design Power* (TDP). The TDP is also sometimes referred to as the processor's *power budget*. It is important to note that TDP is *not* the maximum amount of power the processor can pull.

Intel Turbo Boost technology leverages this observation in order to significantly boost single-threaded performance. When the processor detects that it is operating below the TDP, it uses the extra, currently unutilized, power to increase the frequency of one or more of the active cores, or GPU, beyond its normally available frequency. This continues, typically for a very short period of time, until the conditions for boosting are no longer met, at which point the core, or cores, return to normal frequencies.

One common misconception is that Intel Turbo Boost is a form of automated overclocking. It's important to emphasize that Turbo Boost does not push the processor beyond its designed limitations.

3.2.4 INTEL® RAPL

The Running Average Power Limit (RAPL) interface provides the ability to deterministically monitor and enforce power management policies. This interface provides the administrator or operating system detailed control over how much power can be consumed by the specified components. As a result, RAPL can be utilized in order to avoid thermal throttling, conserve battery life, or lower the electricity utility bill.

The RAPL interface partitions the system into hierarchical domains. There are currently four supported domains, although not all processors support every domain. These four are:

Package (PKG) Processor Package (Core and Uncore)
Power Plane 0 (PP0) Processor Core Resources
Power Plane 1 (PP1) Processor Uncore Resources
DRAM (DRAM) Memory

For each supported domain, a series of two to five model-specific registers (MSRs) is available. These MSRs, along with the RAPL concept, are nonarchitectural. This means that their presence and behavior is not guaranteed to remain consistent throughout all future processor generations. At the time of this writing, the Second, Third, and Fourth Generation Intel Core processor families support RAPL.

Each of the MSRs corresponds to a RAPL domain and capability, and therefore follows the naming convention of MSR_x_y, where x is the domain name, as shown in parenthesis above, and y is the capability name. For example, the register exposing the energy status capability of the package and PP0 domains would be MSR_PKG_ENERGY_STATUS and MSR_PP0_ENERGY_STATUS, respectively.

The power limit capability, controlled through the registers named with the MSR_x_POWER_LIMIT pattern, allows for the average power consumption over a specified time window to be capped for the relevant domain. Note that this is the average power usage for the component, *not* the maximum power usage. Some domains, such as the processor package, support two independent power caps, each with their own average power limit and designated time window. This is often useful for specifying one short term goal for controlling the component's temperature, and one long term goal for controlling battery life.

The energy status capability, controlled through the registers named with the `MSR_x_ENERGY_STATUS` pattern, provides the total energy consumption, in joules.

Because the RAPL interface is exposed through MSRs, any application with sufficient privileges can utilize this interface without any kernel support. For example, the PowerTOP tool, described in further detail in Section 11.3, manually accesses the power consumption data from RAPL for some of its power estimates. Aside from manually accessing the MSR registers, the Intel® RAPL powercap Linux kernel driver, `CONFIG_INTEL_RAPL`, exposes the MSRs through the sysfs filesystem. This sysfs interface is utilized by the Linux Thermal Daemon, `thermald`. By default, the `thermald` daemon monitors the system's temperatures and uses RAPL power capping, along with the Intel P state driver, `CONFIG_X86_INTEL_PSTATE`, in order to prevent thermal throttling with T states. More information on the Linux Thermal Daemon can be found at https://01.org/linux-thermal-daemon.

REFERENCES

Bohr, M., Mistry, K., 2011, 05. Intel's Revolutionary 22nm Transistor Technology. http://download.intel.com/newsroom/kits/22nm/pdfs/22nm-details_presentation.pdf. Linux Kernel Source.

Brandewie, D., 2012. intel_pstate.c. ${LINUX_SRC}/drivers/cpufreq/intel_pstate.c. Linux Kernel Source.

Brown, L., 2013. intel_idle.c. ${LINUX_SRC}/drivers/idle/intel_idle.c. Linux Kernel Source.

Intel Corporation, 2004 ,03. Enhanced Intel SpeedStep® Technology for the Intel Pentium® M Processor.

Intel Corporation, 2012, 01. "Making of a Chip" Illustrations: 22nm 3D/Trigate Transistors – Version. http://download.intel.com/newsroom/kits/chipmaking/pdfs/Sand-to-Silicon_22nm-Version.pdf.

Unified EFI, Inc, 2014, 07. Advanced Configuration and Power Interface Specification 5.1. http://www.uefi.org/sites/default/files/resources/ACPI_5_1release.pdf.

van de Ven, A., 2014, 09. Intel Xeon® E5-2403.Used with Permission.

Performance Workflow

4

CHAPTER CONTENTS

Performance work rarely exists in a vacuum. Instead, it will often be necessary to provide feedback to other developers, to have results reproduced by others, and to influence the decisions of others. This last goal, to influence, is frequently a crucial part of any performance task. Performance gains are for naught if no one is convinced to utilize them. This challenge is further compounded by the skeptical nature many hold toward the area of performance. Some of this skepticism results from a misunderstanding of "premature optimization" and why performance is important; however, the majority of skepticism is steeped in the reality that performance analysis and optimization can be difficult and complex.

Subtle mistakes, which can propagate and sway results drastically, are often very easy to overlook. Some bottlenecks are only caused by certain architectural details, making results hard to verify. As such, if one intends to be successful in performance craft, one must strive to reduce these issues by rigorously maintaining discipline in one's methodologies. This chapter outlines a general workflow for performance optimizations, designed to help avoid common pitfalls. A flowchart describing the progression between steps can be found in Figure 4.1.

4.1 STEP 0: DEFINING THE PROBLEM

As Einstein so eloquently stated, "the mere formulation of a problem is far more often essential than its solution." While creating an explicit problem statement might seem like busy work, it actually has tangible benefits, including helping to keep the project scope limited, ensuring that expectations for the work are set appropriately, and providing a reminder regarding the larger picture, that is, the real purpose, of the work. In the author's personal experience, it is very hard for a project to succeed without an unambiguous goal and measure of success.

When defining the goal, aim for something that is clearly desirable and meaningful. Instead of focusing on the technical details or implementation, focus on the impact to the end user. The benefits of this are twofold. First, the goal can be easily explained and justified to a nontechnical individual through the high-level impact. Secondly, it helps the project avoid becoming so engrossed in the implementation, that the bigger picture is lost.

For example, consider the following goal:

"To reduce latency in the input stack."

While this is a worthwhile technical goal, it lacks the relevant motivation as to why this task is important. This example could be fixed by expanding on the impact:

"To improve user experience by reducing latency within the input stack in order to provide smooth scrolling of the graphical interface."

Another important aspect of a goal is the definition of success, including how it should be measured, on what metric, for which workload, and for what platform. The author considers it prudent to specify multiple levels of success, such as an ideal target, an acceptable target, and a minimum target. This provides an easy method to grade the task's current progress, provides slack in case of unforeseen difficulties, and also prevents the project from dragging on for too long.

For instance, if an engineer is currently working on two projects, one that has already reached its acceptable target, and one that has not, its probably safe for that engineer to prioritize the project that has not reached its acceptable target. This is especially important as performance projects do not always have clear stopping points.

Continuing our earlier example, we might improve the goal to:

"To improve user experience by reducing latency within the input stack in order to provide smooth scrolling of the graphical interface. The latency is most noticeable

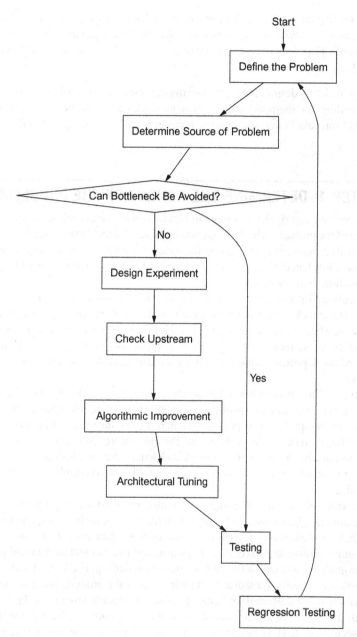

FIGURE 4.1

Performance workflow.

while swiping the home screen interface, workload α, which is automated via our testing tool T_α. Our usability testing has identified that input latency, calculated by formula TL(x), should on average be faster than P_{ideal}, and never be slower than $P_{minimum}$."

This goal clearly defines the high-level impact, user experience issues experienced during scrolling, the method for measurement, workload α via the automated testing tool T_α and formula $TL(x)$, and also the measures for success, P_{ideal} and $P_{minimum}$.

4.2 STEP 1: DETERMINE THE SOURCE OF THE PROBLEM

Now that we have clearly defined an unambiguous problem statement, we must isolate the source of the problem. This will be code that overutilizes some expensive or scarce architectural resource, thus limiting performance. We refer to this limiting resource as a *bottleneck*. Bottlenecks can take many different forms, such as network bandwidth, CPU execution units, or disk seek time.

As mentioned previously, modern systems are far too complex for guesswork regarding bottlenecks. Instead, monitors are used to capture data regarding hardware and software state during execution. This data is then analyzed and interpreted to determine the bottleneck. This process is referred to as *profiling*. Part 2 of this book focuses on how to profile with some of the more common software monitors available for Linux.

When profiling, it is important to analyze the data objectively. There can be a temptation, before conducting profiling, to prematurely conclude what the bottleneck must be. This temptation is especially dangerous, because it can bias the profiling outcome. Regardless of the validity of the premature conclusion, it is usually possible to contrive a situation and workload where the conclusion can be cast as true. Keep in mind what Mark Twain once said, "Facts are stubborn. Statistics are more pliable."

Aside from objectivity, thoroughness is also required when profiling, because subtle details can often have a large impact on results, and their subsequent meaning. Notice that the definition of profiling involves both data collection *and* analysis. A very common mistake is to collect an insurmountable amount of data and perform very little analysis, a situation the author refers to as flailing. Flailing typically occurs due to nothing obvious immediately standing out to the analyst, because either the wrong data is being collected, or because an unmanageable amount of data is being collected. If this kind of situation arises, where a lot of data is collected, but the data doesn't seem to be leading anywhere, slow down and really concentrate on what the existing data means.

Working at Intel, the author has the privilege of working with some of the best performance analysts, and one of the first things the author noticed was how thoroughly they interrogate each data point.

4.3 STEP 2: DETERMINE WHETHER THE BOTTLENECK CAN BE AVOIDED

At this point, we should understand the interaction between the code and the limiting resource, which manifests itself as the problem. Before moving further, verify that the problematic work is really necessary and unavoidable. This is especially important when dealing with large or old codebases, which are often heavily modified from their original design and operate on systems that may violate older assumptions.

For instance, an older codebase for a disk I/O intensive application may have been heavily optimized to minimize the hard drive's spinning-platter seek times. This application might now be run on systems consisting of solid-state drives, thus rendering the cycles needed for scheduling reads and writes wasteful. If the problem from Step 1 was caused by this scheduling overhead, a solution would be to simply disable the seek-time optimizations when running on flash storage.

Another way to potentially avoid performance issues is through the tunable parameters exposed via the software. Many applications provide some configurability in terms of buffer and cache sizes, timeouts, thresholds, and so on. A prime example of this is the `sysctl` interface for the Linux kernel, exposed through `/proc/sys` and often configured at boot by `/etc/sysctl.conf`. This interface allows the user to change runtime parameters that affect the Linux kernel's behavior, and thus its performance.

If the work is deemed necessary, it may still be possible to avoid a significant portion of it by utilizing caching. Expensive computations can be precomputed into a lookup table, trading memory usage for processing power. Computations that are computed frequently can also be cached via memoization, where the result of the computation is cached after its first evaluation.

For expensive calculations, also consider the precision required by the application. Sometimes it is possible to replace an expensive and precise calculation with a cheaper but less precise estimation.

4.4 STEP 3: DESIGN A REPRODUCIBLE EXPERIMENT

At this point, we should design an experiment to demonstrate the problem. The goal here is to isolate the problem in such a way that it is easy to verify and share. A well designed experiment should meet the following criteria.

First, the experiment must clearly display the current performance numbers in an automated fashion. Neither the calculations nor the actual experiment should require any human interaction. This will save time otherwise spent verifying that everyone is computing things properly. The performance numbers should be calculated exactly as described in the problem statement. Also, make sure to keep output formatting consistent and unambiguous. Aside from always labeling units, it may be helpful to mark whether metrics are higher-is-better (HIB), lower-is-better (LIB), or nominal-is-better (NIB).

While it may be tempting to display a lot of extra data, this can often lead to confusion when others need to interpret the results. If the extra data is really useful, consider only printing it in a "verbose mode," and keeping the default output clean, simple, and straightforward. Remember, these experiments may be run by others, perhaps even when you aren't available for clarifications, and decisions might be influenced by the misinterpreted results, so always aim to keep things simple and straightforward.

Second, the experiment should be designed to allow others to easily reproduce the problem and validate progress. Ideally, this involves stripping out code and dependencies that are not relevant to the problem. For instance, if optimizing a mail client's search functionality, there is no point keeping the code to handle the IMAP protocol as part of the experiment. Instead, pull out just the necessary search code and write a separate program to benchmark that algorithm on a fixed workload.

Third, the experiment should aim to reduce unnecessary variables that could affect performance or variance. Chapter 5 covers how to remove common variables such as disk and network I/O costs. These, and other variables, have the potential to increase variance and can therefore lead to misleading results. Remember, the goal is to clearly show the current performance in a reproducible way. By reducing external variables, time is saved that would otherwise be spent debugging disparities between different hardware and software configurations.

The author imagines that some readers are wondering how these variables can be removed; after all, aren't they part of the code's performance characteristics? The answer to this question lies in what aspect of the system is being measured and optimized.

For example, consider a comparison of the throughput of two algorithms A_α and A_β for a given CPU. Assume that fetching data from memory, algorithm A_α achieves a throughput of 2500 MB/s, while algorithm A_β achieves a throughput of 3500 MB/s. Now consider if both algorithms are required to fetch data from a hard drive that only can provide data at about 150 MB/s.

For a comparison of which algorithm was capable of the higher throughput, the presence of the disk in the experiment would providing misleading results, as both algorithms would have a throughput of about 150 MB/s, and thus the disk I/O bottleneck would mask the performance difference. On the other hand, for a comparison of which algorithm made the best usage of the limited disk throughput, the disk would be a needed part of the experiment.

For every test, each component under test needs to be placed in a reproducible state, or at least as close as possible. This needs to be a careful decision, one with planning on what that reproducible state is, how to enter it, and an understanding of the potential impact on the meaning of the test results.

Fourth, the experiment must accurately represent the actual performance characteristics. This is something to be especially careful of when writing microbenchmarks, because subtle differences in cache state, branch prediction history, and so on, can drastically change performance characteristics. The best way to ensure this remains true is to periodically validate the accuracy of the models against the real codebase.

Fifth, at this stage, workloads are selected for exercising the problematic algorithms. Ideally, these workloads should be as realistic as possible. However, as more and more software deals with personal information, care must be taken to avoid accidentally leaking sensitive data. Consider the ramifications if an email provider published a performance workload containing the private emails of its customers. The author imagines that upon reading this, some are thinking, "I'll remember not to publish that data." The flaw in this logic is that the entire purpose of creating these kinds of experiments is to share them, and while you might remember, a colleague, years later, may not.

To avoid this entire problem, the author recommends studying real workloads, extracting the important patterns, and substituting any sensitive content with synthetic content, taking care to ensure that the data is similar. Going back to the email workload example, perhaps create a bunch of emails to and from fictitious email addresses, replacing the English text message bodies with excerpts from Shakespeare.

Finally, while not an absolute requirement, the author likes to also keep a unit test suite along with the benchmark to provide a method for verifying correctness. This is a very convenient time to handle early testing, because the old and new implementations are both present, and thus they can be run on the same input and tested on having identical outputs.

4.5 STEP 4: CHECK UPSTREAM

As mentioned earlier, performance work rarely exists in a vacuum. Interacting with others is even more important when working on, or interacting with, open source projects.

The main objective of this step is to gather information about possible solutions. Whether that simply involves checking out the source tree history, or chatting up the project developers is completely up to the reader's discretion. As such, when, or whether, to communicate with the project upstream can occur at any phase. Some developers tend to prefer submitting fully tested patches, and thus hold off any communications until the performance work is complete. Others prefer communicating early, getting other developers involved in the effort. Projects typically have preferences themselves.

Regardless of the development method chosen, the author considers it crucial to contribute changes back to the upstream project. This consideration doesn't stem from an ideological position on open-source software. In fact, the author is pragmatic about using the proper tools for the job, regardless of their development model. Instead, this suggestion comes from the realization that maintaining separate code, divergent from the project's official codebase, can quickly become a significant maintenance burden.

One of the powerful advantages of open source, although proprietary code is starting to move in this direction as well, is the rapid development model. As a result, maintaining a separate out-of-tree code branch will require keeping up with that rapid development model, and will require a significant investment in frequently rebasing the code, handling conflicts that are introduced by other patches, and performing separate testing. The consequences of not fulfilling this investment is bit rot, leading to code abandonment.

On the other hand, patches integrated upstream benefit from all the testing of the developers and other users, as well as any further improvements made by the community. Any future patches that introduce conflicts with the upstreamed code are a regression, and the burden of resolving them would lie with the author of the offending patchset, rather than with the reader's patches. So while upstreaming code may seem to be more work, it's an up-front cost that definitely saves time and effort in the long run.

While every open source project is run differently, with its own preferences, the rest of this section provides some general hints for getting results.

4.5.1 WHO

Consider the analogy of open source project releases to a river. The "source" of the river, that is, its origin, is the original project. This includes the project's developers, who write the actual code, and produce releases. These releases "flow" down the river, being consumed and modified by each interested party before making their way to the "mouth" of the river, the end user. At any point in the river, upstream refers to any point closer to the "source," while downstream refers to any point closer to the "mouth."

The majority of open source code consumed by the end user doesn't come from the original project, but rather is the version packaged, in formats like RPM and ebuild, by their Linux distribution. Linux distributions consume projects from upstream and integrate them together to produce a cohesive deliverable, which then flows downstream.

As a result of these modifications, the same version of a project on two different distributions might be drastically different. Things become even more complicated, because some distributions, notably enterprise distributions, backport new features and bugfixes into older stable releases, making software release numbers potentially misleading.

Due to all of this, it is important, when attempting to reach out to a project, to determine the proper community to contact. Typically, the first step is to determine whether the problem is reproducible with the original project release, that is, checking at the "source" of the river. If so, the project would be the correct party to contact. If not, further investigation is required into where the offending change was introduced. This process is simply a matter of working downstream until finding the first codebase that reproduces the problem.

4.5.2 WHERE AND HOW

So now that problem has been isolated to a specific release, it's time to determine where to contact the owner. While each project has a unique setup, there are common modes of communication utilized by many projects. These typically are mailing lists, bug trackers, and IRC channels. The links to these, or the desired communication method, along with any guidelines for their usage, can typically be found on the project's website.

Here are some tips for getting results:

1. *Check the project's mailing list archives and bug tracker* to see whether the issue being reported is already known. If so, use this information to determine what further steps should be taken.
2. Since each community is unique, the author sometimes finds it helpful to examine prior communications, such as the mailing list archive, in order to *gain a better understanding of the community and how it operates.* If archived communications aren't available, or if communicating via a real-time format, such as IRC, the same effect can be achieved by lurking on the channel before asking your question. Taking the time to understand the community's dynamic will typically yield helpful insights on how to tailor your communication for getting results.
3. If communicating by email, *ensure that your email client produces emails that adhere to any project requirements.* When in doubt, a safe configuration is the one described in the Linux kernel documentation, under `${LINUX_SRC}/Documentation/email-clients.txt`.
4. *Avoid HTML emails* at all costs. Many mailing lists will reject HTML emails, and many developers, including the author, maintain `procmail` rules classifying all HTML email as spam.
5. *Avoid Top-Posting.* Instead, type your responses inline. This simplifies code reviews and makes it much easier to follow the conversation.
6. When possible, use `git send-email` for emailing patches.
7. Strive to *use proper spelling and grammar.* It doesn't have to be perfect, but at least make an effort. Spelling and grammar reflect back on the writer's education and level of maturity.
8. *Avoid attempting to communicate in a language other than the project's default.* Some projects have special mailing lists or channels for different languages.
9. *Verify your communications were received.* If the mailing list archives are available, after sending an email, check to ensure that your email appears in the archive. If not, don't immediately resend. Sometimes emails require moderation before appearing, or perhaps the archives take a while to update. At the same time, mailing lists occasionally will drop emails.
10. *Be polite.* Remember, that while many open source contributors are paid, many do this as an enjoyable hobby. Keep in mind that no project or developer owes you anything.
11. *Understand the terms of popular open source licenses,* such as the GPL, LGPL, and BSD license. When in doubt, seek professional legal counsel.
12. *Always label untested or experimental code.* The author typically prefaces these communications with "RFC," that is, Request For Comments.

13. *Support your code.* Just because your code has been accepted upstream doesn't mean your job is over. When questions or bugs appear, take responsibility for your work.

14. *Follow the project's coding style guidelines.* This includes configuring your text editor for preferences such as spaces versus tabs or the number of characters in an indentation. This also includes following any formatting around bracket placement and spacing. When in doubt, follow the style of the existing code.

15. *When submitting a patchset, ensure that every patch builds without later patches.* Often when creating a series of interrelated patches, there are dependencies between the patches. This can lead to situations where one patch relies on something introduced in a later patch to compile. In this situation, the build is temporarily broken, but then immediately fixed by a later patch in the same patch series. While this might not appear to be a problem, it becomes one whenever attempting to perform a bisection; see Section 4.5.3 for more information. Instead, organize the patches so that any infrastructure is introduced before its use, and thus the tree will build after each patch is applied.

4.5.3 WHAT

Obviously, what can be communicated depends on the progress made and the environment of the open source project. Some projects are very receptive to bug reports, while some projects aren't interested in bug reports without patches.

This section will cover how to leverage some helpful features of Git in order to simplify the work required to contribute.

Git bisect

Tracking down a regression, performance or not, is much easier once the offending commit, that introduced the issue, is discovered. When reporting a regression, including this information can help accelerate the process of determining the next course of action. Git makes this process simple through the `git bisect` command, which performs a binary search on the commit range specified by the user. This search can occur interactively, with the user marking each commit suggested by Git as either good or bad, or automatically, with a script that communicates with Git via the exit status.

If not using Git, for some odd reason, there are two options. The first option is to leverage one of the existing tools that allows Git to interact with other SCM systems, such as `git-svn`. The second option is to write an equivalent tool or to manually perform the search of the commit history for the SCM system.

An interactive bisection session begins by executing `git bisect start`, which initializes some state in the `.git` directory of the repository. At any time, the history of bisection commands can be printed by executing `git bisect log`, or looking at the file `.git/BISECT_LOG`. It is possible to execute a list of bisect commands, such as the log file, via `git bisect replay`.

At this point, Git expects the user to define the bounds for the search. This occurs by marking the first good commit, and the first bad commit, via the `git bisect good` and `git bisect bad` commands. These commands each take a list of Git refs as arguments. If no arguments are given, then they refer to `HEAD`, the current commit.

Once both endpoints are marked, Git will check out a commit to test, that is, the current node in the binary search. The user must then perform the required testing to determine whether or not the current node suffers from the same regression. If so, mark the commit as bad, using `git bisect bad`, or if not, mark the commit as good, using `git bisect good`. It is also possible to skip testing the current commit, using `git bisect skip`, or by manually removing the commit from the current tree, via `git reset --hard HEAD~`. Be aware that normally `git reset --hard HEAD~` will delete a commit from the branch. During bisection, once the bounds have been established and Git begins suggesting commits for testing, Git checks out individual commits and their history, so deleting a commit won't delete it from the original branch.

This cycle will continue until the first bad commit is found. Git will print the SHA1 of this commit, along with the commit information. Examining this commit should provide insight into what caused the regression. The bisection session can now be terminated via `git bisect reset`, which will remove any bisection state, and return the tree to the original state from which the bisection was started.

The manual testing above can be alleviated via the use of `git bisect run`, which will execute a script and then use the return value to mark a given commit as good, a return value of 0, or bad, any return value between 1 and 127, excluding 125. The script returning a value of 125 indicates that the current tree couldn't be tested and should be skipped.

Cleaning patches with git

A patch represents a logical change, expressed as the addition and subtraction of file lines, to a source code tree. In the open source community, patches are the means of progress, so learning how to properly generate and structure patches is important for contributing.

Typically, the process of writing code is messy and imperfect. When submitting patches, the patches need to present the solution, not the process, in a logical and organized manner. To accomplish this, the author typically keeps at least two branches for each endeavor, a messy development branch and a clean submission branch. The messy development branch will contain commits as progress is made, such as adding new code or fixing typos. The clean submission branch will rewrite the commit history of the development branch to separate the commits into logical changes. This can involve combining multiple commits into a single commit, removing unnecessary commits, editing commits to remove extra whitespace and newlines and ensuring that the formatting complies with the project's formatting standards.

The author imagines that some readers are concerned by the concept of rewriting their commit history. Some of this concern stems from the fact that changing the commit history of a public branch is annoying to those who have based code on top of the history that has now changed. This concern is alleviated by the developer ensuring that the development branch isn't publicly shared, and that only the clean branch is visible. If the development branch must be shared publicly, provide a disclaimer to those you're working with that the history of that given branch may change. Another area of concern is the possibility of introducing errors into the code while modifying the commit history. This is why the author recommends keeping two separate branches. The benefit of keeping the two branches separate is that a simple `git diff` between the two will ensure no changes are accidentally introduced in the cleaning process.

Once the development branch is at a point where the developer would like to submit the work, the clean branch is created by copying the development branch to the new branch. Now it's time to rewrite the commit history for the clean branch. This is accomplished by performing an interactive rebase, via the `git rebase -i` command, with the earliest Git ref to modify passed as a command-line argument. At this point, `$GIT_EDITOR` will open, containing a list of commits and the actions to perform on them. An example of this interface can be seen in Figure 4.2. The order of the commit lines is the commit history, with the earliest commit listed on the top line, and the later commits listed downwards. Commits can be reordered by reordering the commit lines. Commits can be deleted by removing the associated commit line.

By default, the action for each commit will be "pick." Picking a commit simply keeps the commit at it's current location in the history list. Other actions are performed by changing the text before the commit SHA1 from "pick" to the associated action name, or letter shortcut. The "reword" action, with letter shortcut "r," keeps the commit, but will open `$GIT_EDITOR` with the current commit message, allowing the user to change the commit message. The "squash" action, with letter shortcut "s," combines the commit with the previous commit, and opens `$GIT_EDITOR` with both commit messages, allowing the user to merge them accordingly. The "fixup"

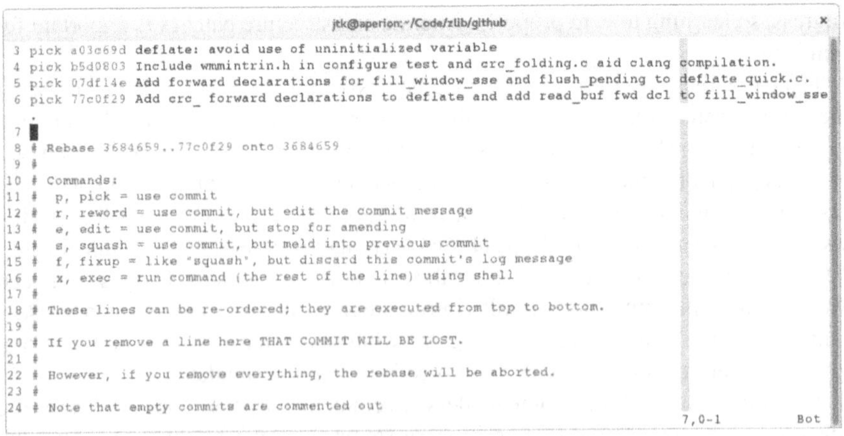

FIGURE 4.2

Git interactive rebase.

action, with letter shortcut "f," combines the commit with the previous commit, and discards the fixed-up commit's log message. This action is especially useful for merging commits that fix typos with the commit that introduced the typo. The "edit" action, with letter shortcut "e," will stop Git before applying this commit, allowing the user to modify the content of the commit manually. This action can be used for splitting a commit into multiple commits. Finally, there is the "exec" action, with letter shortcut "x." This action is different from the previous actions in that it doesn't modify a commit, but rather executes the rest of its line as a shell command. This allows for executing commands for sanity checking at certain stages of the rebase process.

After all of the actions are selected and all of the commits are in the desired order, save and quit from the editor. If the rebase should be canceled, delete *all* of the lines from the file, and then save and quit from the editor. At this point, Git will begin performing the actions in chronological order.

When Git stops to edit a commit, the changes of that commit are already added to the current index, that is, the changes are already staged for committing. In order to unstage the changes, run `git reset HEAD^`. Now the changes introduced in the commit can be modified, or partially staged to create multiple commits.

Splitting changes to a single file can be performed with an interactive add, via `git add -i`. This will launch an interactive interface for controlling what content hunks are added to the index. To stage hunks, select command five, with the text label "patch." Now select the number corresponding to the file with the desired changes. Once all of the files have been selected, press Enter without a number to begin iterating each hunk present in each of the selected files.

For each change, the user is prompted whether they want to stage the change, option "y," skip the change, option "n," edit the hunk, option "e," stage this hunk and all later hunks in the file, option "a," split the hunk into smaller hunks if possible, option "s," or skip the current change and all other changes, option "q." Once all the changes have been staged, commit as normal. Repeat the process until all the desired commits have been created, and then continue the rebasing process with `git rebase --continue`.

Depending on the interdependence of the commits, occasionally the rebase will be unable to automatically apply the change, and will require manual intervention from the user.

Now it's time to generate patches and submit our code.

Sending patches with git

Traditionally, patches are generated via the `diff` utility, applied via the `patch` utility, and communicated via attaching the patch file inline into an email. Git was designed with this workflow in mind, and therefore it provides tools to simplify working with patches.

Patches can be created for a series of commits by utilizing `git format-patch`, which creates a patch file, in the mbox mail format, for each specified commit. The first line of the commit message is designated as a short summary for the patch, and is used as the subject line for the corresponding email. The `From` header is populated

Table 4.1 SMTP Configuration Options for `git send-email` (git-send-email - Linux Manual Page, 2014)

Command Argument	Config	Description
--smtp-server	sendemail.smtpserver	Network address of the SMTP server, or file path to sendmail-like program
--smtp-server-port	sendemail.smtpserverport	SMTP server port
--smtp-server-option	sendemail.smtpserveroption	SMTP option to use. Repeat command-line argument or configuration field for multiple options
--smtp-encryption	sendemail.smtpencryption	SSL or TLS. If not set, none
--smtp-ssl-cert-path	sendemail.smtpsslcertpath	Path to certificates. If empty, disables certificate verification
--smtp-pass	sendemail.smtppass	SMTP password, if applicable
--smtp-user	sendemail.smtpuser	SMTP username, if applicable
--smtp-domain	sendemail.smtpdomain	Fully Qualified Domain Name given to SMTP server

from the commit author's name and email address, and the `Date` header is populated from the commit's date.

On top of formatting patches, Git can also email patches directly with the `git send-email` command. Before this is possible, it is necessary to configure Git in order to utilize the SMTP server. While it is possible to specify the server configuration at each invocation of `git send-email`, it's much simpler to add these options to the global git configuration. Regardless of the method chosen, Table 4.1 lists the configuration options for configuring Git for SMTP.

This command accepts patch files in the mbox format produced by `git format-patch`. More conveniently, it accepts the specified commits via their Git ref and will invoke `git format-patch` automatically. The recipients are controlled via the `--to`, `--cc`, and `--bcc` arguments, each of which can appear multiple times for multiple recipients. Conveniently, Git supports email alias files, saving the user from typing in full email addresses. This is configured by setting `sendemail.aliasesfile`, in the Git configuration, to the alias file path, and setting `sendemail.aliasfiletype` to the format of the file, one of `mutt`, `mailrc`, `pine`, `elm`, or `gnus`.

So for instance, rather than typing `--to linux-kernel@vger.kernel.org`, Git can be configured to recognize `--to lkml` with the following configuration:

```
$ cat ~/.mutt/contacts
alias lkml      Linux Kernel    <linux-kernel@vger.kernel.org>
$ git config --global sendemail.aliasesfile ~/.mutt/contacts
$ git config --global sendemail.aliasfiletype mutt
```

Git can automatically add email addresses within the commit to the CC. The extent of this behavior can be controlled via the `--suppress-cc` command argument, or

Table 4.2 Git Values for `sendemail.suppresscc` and `--suppress-cc` (git-send-email - Linux Manual Page, 2014)

Value	Effect
author	Avoid auto-cc'ing patch author
self	Avoid auto-cc'ing patch sender
cc	Avoid auto-cc'ing anyone mentioned in Cc lines of patch header
bodycc	Avoid auto-cc'ing anyone mentioned in Cc lines of patch description
sob	Avoid auto-cc'ing anyone mentioned in Signed-off-by lines
cccmd	Skip running `--cc-cmd`, which runs once per patch and generates additional Cc's.
body	sob + bodycc
all	disable auto-cc

through the `sendemail.suppresscc` configuration value. Table 4.2 contains the list of acceptable values. Personally, the author prefers to disable the auto-cc feature, and manually select the recipients.

Using the `--compose` argument will open `$GIT_EDITOR`, in which a cover letter can be written, that is, the first email in the series, which can provide some background information for the patch series. During composing, the cover letter `Subject` header can be set by filling in the line beginning with `Subject:`, or with the `--subject` command-line argument. Also, the emails can be send as a reply to an existing email, by filling in the `In-Reply-To:` line during composing, or with the `--in-reply-to` command-line argument, with the corresponding `Message-ID` header.

When in doubt, the author recommends first emailing the patches to yourself, and then validating that the results were exactly as expected, before sending them publicly.

4.6 STEP 5: ALGORITHMIC IMPROVEMENT

A common mistake after profiling is to jump directly into architectural tuning. The problem with skipping this phase is that the largest performance improvements typically come from selecting a better algorithm, as opposed to tuning that algorithm for a specific architecture. Remember, no matter how much time is spent tuning a bubblesort implementation, a quicksort implementation will be faster.

When searching for algorithmic improvements, profile the CPU time to determine what operations occur frequently, and what operations occur infrequently. Using this information, look for data structures that can perform the frequent operations cheaply and trade the costs over to the less-frequent operations.

Coverage of specific algorithms and general algorithmic techniques, such as divide and conquer or dynamic programming, is out of the scope of this book, as there are already many excellent resources on these topics. A few of the author's favorites include:

1. *The Algorithm Design Manual* by Steven Skiena
2. *Algorithms in C* by Robert Sedgewick
3. *The Design of Data Structures and Algorithms* by J.J Van Amstel and J.J.A.M. Porters
4. *The Design and Analysis of Algorithms* by Anany Levitin
5. *Algorithms* by Sanjoy Dasgupta, Christos Papadimitriou, and Umesh Vizirani

When evaluating algorithms at this level, algorithms are classified by their order of growth as the input size grows. This provides insight into how well the algorithm will scale across input sizes, but disregards potentially significant disparities in performance.

For instance, consider two algorithms $A_0(n) \in O(n)$ and $A_1(n) \in O(n)$, that is, two algorithms who both belong to the linear asymptotic efficiency class. By definition, the cost of both algorithms, in the worst case, is bounded by $c,d \exists \mathbb{N}_{\neq 0}$ such that $A_0(n) \leq c * n$ and $A_1(n) \leq d * n$. Despite being in the same class, the difference between the two factors, c and d, can be significant.

As a result, never rely on asymptotic classes alone to judge performance. As with all other things, measure and verify.

4.7 STEP 6: ARCHITECTURAL TUNING

Once the best-performing algorithm has been selected, further performance can typically be achieved by tuning the algorithm to best utilize the architectural resources. This includes optimizations such as restructuring the code to improve branch prediction, to improve data locality, and leveraging instruction set extensions, such as SIMD.

This begins with profiling to determine what resources are over or underutilized. Part 2 goes into more details on the profilers available and how to use them, with Chapter 6 explaining the profiling process. Once opportunities for further performance are identified, Part 3 dives into some optimization techniques for exploiting them.

It's important to note that architectural tuning doesn't necessarily require rewriting everything in assembly. Typically, it's possible to coax better code from the compiler through restructuring the code and providing the compiler with more information about the context. Modern compilers, at least the serious ones, are able to produce heavily optimized code, and out-of-order CPU pipelines are forgiving to instruction scheduling.

However, this doesn't mean that there aren't situations that require handcrafted assembly in order to achieve the best performance. In the common case, assembly is required because the compiler doesn't pick up on the potential for leveraging certain special instructions, such as SSE or Intel® AVX. Chapter 12 introduces the techniques for utilizing assembly with C code. Chapters 15 and 16 explain the types of special instructions that can drastically improve performance.

Considering the almost legendary regard many hold about writing assembly, the author considers it prudent to debunk or clarify a couple of popular myths about the use of assembly.

Myth 0: Assembly is fast

This is a common misconception that the author believes was born from decades of engineers seeing assembly-optimized routines vastly outperform other implementations. While writing assembly does provide the developer with the most freedom to express their code in an optimal way, there is no magical performance element. Regardless of the programming language used, all the processor sees is opcodes.

Writing fast and efficient code, regardless of the programming language or system, requires measurement. *Measure everything.* The author can't emphasis this point enough. If this is the only point the reader takes away from this book, the reader will be far better off than the reader who takes away every other point, because measurement will lead the reader to the correct questions. Without measurement, performance work devolves into unproductive guesswork.

The only way to write fast assembly, or fast C, is to measure the current code, determine what parts are slow, and then improve them.

Myth 1: Assembly is not portable

Portability can take many different formats, such as portability across architectures, portability across processor generations, portability across operating systems, and so on. Writing assembly requires following certain specifications, whether the hardware's instruction set specifications, the Application Binary Interface (ABI) specifications, or the executable file format specifications. Whatever specifications are used, limits the portability of the code to systems that follow that specification.

For example, a vectorized SIMD numerical calculation might be written without any ABI specifics, except for perhaps the function calling conventions, and even this can be hidden with inline assembly. As a result, even though this code is written in assembly, it will be portable across different operating systems and executable file formats. Additionally, this assembly will provide consistent performance across multiple compiler versions.

Providing consistent performance is another benefit of writing assembly. Often, software needs to be supported across a wide range of Linux distributions, each with their own compiler versions. While some distributions provide recent compiler versions capable of more optimizations, other distributions provide older compilers, which aren't capable of optimizing as well, leading to inconsistent performance across the install base.

Myth 2: Assembly is hard

Another common myth is that writing assembly is immensely difficult; a task reserved only for processor architects and software rockstars. While assembly does expose the developer to more complexity than high level languages, assembly is in many ways more logically straightforward. A processor is simply a state machine, comprised of a current state, such as the values of the registers, and various well-documented methods for transitioning from the current state to another state, the instruction set.

Writing assembly requires a bit more of an initial investment in learning the required concepts and becoming familiar with the techniques, but that investment pays significant dividends, because the low level technical details shed light into the design and architecture of the software layers.

Many developers are taught in school that assembly, or even C, is too difficult and that it is better to focus on learning at a higher level of abstraction. In fact, the discipline of computer science tends to solve problems of complexity through the layering of abstractions. However, time and time again, it has been shown that abstractions are often leaky, forcing engineers to understand the very complexities the abstractions were designed to hide. For instance, the Java programming language attempts to hide the complexity of memory management from the developer, and yet many Java developers spend a significant amount of time worrying about memory management, and how to handle it properly within the constraints imposed by the abstraction.

The author submits that it is significantly harder to debug problems without understanding the underlying details than it is to learn the underlying details in the first place.

Myth 3: Assembly is a relic of the past

As compilers continue to improve at optimizing code, the question becomes whether software developers can actually produce better code than the compiler. Many developers look at the advancements in compiler technology and the inherent complexity of modern processor technology and decide that they aren't capable of improving performance further.

On the contrary, it is important to remember that compilers are capable of performing transformations on the code in order to improve performance, but they aren't capable of thinking. Compiler optimizations save the developer from worrying about small inefficiencies, such as whether a multiplication can be performed faster by a bitwise shift. Gone are the days where tons of small code tweaks are required to obtain acceptable performance. This frees the developer to focus solely on the large performance bottlenecks identified by profiling.

As a general rule of thumb, the author recommends never "optimizing" code that doesn't show up on the profile.

4.8 STEP 7: TESTING

At this stage, an optimized version of the code exists and performance benchmarking has shown this version to be a performance win. Before releasing these changes, it is first necessary to ensure that the correctness of the optimized code has not been compromised.

Depending on the testing infrastructure of the codebase, this step can be as simple or as complex as required. Some codebases maintain a significant number of unit tests for ensuring correctness. In this case, depending on the test coverage and level of detail, it may be enough to leverage the existing tests. Other codebases do not have such elaborate testing practices, so it may be necessary to write custom test cases. When in doubt, the author recommends always favoring overtesting, and perhaps being overly cautious, to not being cautious enough and potentially introducing functionality or, even worse, security bugs.

One advantage of the setup described in Section 4.4 is that the conditions for designing reproducible performance experiments, such as isolating the code of interest, removing unnecessary dependencies, and having both versions together, yields itself very well to functionality testing.

What the author prefers to do, if possible, is write two programs when creating the reproducible experiment. The first program evaluates the current performance while the second program evaluates the current correctness. Once these programs have been written, both performance and correctness can be checked by simply running each program, and regressions with regards to correctness can hopefully be found quickly.

In order to ensure that both the testing program and performance program are leveraging exactly the same code, the author recommends keeping the implementations in separate source files, which are built into separate object files. Each of the previously mentioned two programs uses the symbols exported within each implementation's object file.

4.9 STEP 8: PERFORMANCE REGRESSION TESTING

What was once problematic may become problematic again. In order to recognize this early, the reproducible experiment should be run periodically to ensure that the performance doesn't regress back to where it was before the performance work was conducted. This parallels unit testing, where once a bug is discovered, it should be added to the test suite to ensure that the functionality never regresses.

Another advantage of lower level performance tests, such as the reproducible experiment from Section 4.4, is how well they complement higher level performance tests. The higher level tests function as the canary in the coal mine, detecting performance regressions, while the lower level tests help isolate which aspect of the code regressed.

REFERENCES

Del Vecchio, P., 2011, 05. De-Mystifying Software Performance Optimization. https://software.intel.com/en-us/articles/de-mystifying-software-performance-optimization.

Dunlap, R., n.d., Email clients info for Linux. ${LINUX_SRC}/Documentation/email-clients.txt.

git - Linux Manual Page. 2014. git-scm.com/documentation.

git-bisect(1) - Linux Manual Page. 2014. git-scm.com/documentation.

git-rebase(1) - Linux Manual Page. 2014. git-scm.com/documentation.

git-send-email(1) - Linux Manual Page. 2014. git-scm.com/documentation.

Jain, R.K., 1991. The Art of Computer Systems Performance Analysis: Techniques for Experimental Design, Measurement, Simulation, and Modeling. Wiley.

Designing Experiments

5

CHAPTER CONTENTS

Performance analysis and optimization is a data-driven endeavor. It then follows that the work's success or failure depends on its ability to collect accurate data. Just as the correct data will lead the project to the correct conclusions, incorrect or misleading data will lead the project to incorrect conclusions. Therefore, it is crucial to understand how to design experiments that produce accurate data.

Unfortunately, errors in data collection are very easy to overlook and may not manifest themselves until much later in the project. These issues often are a result of the inherent complexity of modern computing, such as the complex interactions between hardware and software or between shared resources utilized by multiple processes simultaneously. While it isn't possible to always mitigate these issues, it is still important to quantify and understand their impact on the data.

5.1 CHOOSING A METRIC

In Chapter 4, the importance of measurement was highlighted throughout the performance workflow. In the early stages, such as defining the problem, the focus rests on choosing the proper measure of performance. These measures are referred to as *metrics*.

Many different metrics exist, but there are two popular categories for performance metrics, either metrics that measure the cost of performing an operation once or metrics that measure how often that operation can occur during a given interval. Metrics in the first category, when measuring time, are often referred to as measuring *latency*. Metrics in the second category are often referred to as measuring *throughput*.

To illustrate this point, consider two metrics for measuring graphics rendering performance, frame time and frame rate. Since the frame time metric measures the cost, in time, of performing one operation, rendering a frame, it would fall into the first category. Since the frame rate, measured in frames per second, measures how many operations, frame renders, can occur for a given interval, one second, it would fall into the second category.

When selecting a metric, it is important to choose a metric at an appropriate level of detail, which is dictated by the component being measured. For example, when comparing the performance of two algorithms for a given CPU pipeline, clock cycles is an appropriate level of detail. On the other hand, when comparing graphics rendering performance, clock cycles would probably be too low-level of a detail.

All metrics fall into one of three categories in terms of their interpretation, higher is better (HIB), lower is better (LIB), or nominal is better (NIB). As the reader might expect, when comparing two measurements for an HIB metric, the higher value is the better performing. HIB and LIB metrics are far more common than NIB metrics, in which neither too high of a value nor too low of a value is ideal.

5.2 DEALING WITH EXTERNAL VARIABLES

As mentioned in Section 4.4, it is important when benchmarking to reduce exposure to external variables that can impact performance. When designing an experiment, there are two types of external variables to consider, the controllable and the uncontrollable.

5.2.1 CONTROLLABLE EXTERNAL VARIABLES

Controllable external variables are simply variables whose effects can be completely mitigated, and thus won't affect performance measurements. The effects of some external variables can be discarded by controlling when data collection begins and ends. Other effects require engineering small controlled scenarios, often referred to as *microbenchmarks*.

For example, consider how to accurately measure the time required for a web browser to render a HTML page. First, let's define our operation, "rendering an HTML page," to include parsing an HTML file into the necessary internal data structures, and then producing a rendered image. The real-world use case for this feature most likely involves:

1. Handle user input
2. Network initialization (DNS host lookup, TCP handshake, and so on)
3. Retrieve multiple remote resources
4. Parse resources into internal data structures
5. Render data structures into rendered webpage
6. Displaying rendered webpage to user

As described in Section 4.4, experiments should be fully automated, requiring no human interaction, and thus Item 1 should be eliminated from the experiment. This can be achieved by programmatically invoking the next steps for a fixed workload, or by starting the data collection after the user has submitted a query. The first controllable external variable, the human, has been mitigated.

Now consider the next two steps, which retrieve the remote resources. Each of these steps requires interaction with networked computers, thus exposing the experiment to variance from the network. For instance, one run of the experiment might occur while the network is suffering from heavy congestion, thus elongating measured time. Or perhaps after the first fetch, the resources will be cached, making their subsequent retrievals faster, and thus reducing measured time. Depending on what aspects of this use case are being measured, there are a couple different ways to avoid introducing this variance.

One potential method for shielding our experiment from these disparities is to create a private closed network for testing. This allows for significant control over network bandwidth, congestion, and other network variables. In fact many complex situations, such as heavy congestion, can be simulated on such a network. However for our specific example, our measurements aren't dependent on exact network interactions, therefore this type of setup is overkill.

Another method for avoiding the network variance is to only start data collection after all the network resources have been downloaded. Unfortunately for our example, parsing the HTML file can trigger other resources to be downloaded. As a result, the solution is to bypass the network and serve all the content locally from the disk. The second controllable external variable, the network, has been mitigated.

While the variability of disk performance is significantly less than than the variability introduced by the network, it still can have a large impact on results. Both spinning platter and solid state drives are huge sources of variability. One reason for this is the amount of buffering and caching utilized at both the software and hardware layers. Assuming the dataset is small enough, the disk can be removed from our measurements by serving them from memory.

There are two primary techniques for accomplishing this, either copying the files into a RAM-backed filesystem, like `tmpfs`, or by leveraging the `mmap(2)` system call.

An advantage of the first technique, using `tmpfs`, is that no code modifications are required. This is because `tmpfs` files are accessed through the normal VFS operations, such as `open(2)` and `read(2)`, just like a disk-backed filesystem. In order to utilize `tmpfs`, a mount point must be created, the files must be copied to that location, which effectively loads the files into memory, and then the application can interact with the files stored at that mount point.

Many Linux distributions maintain a `tmpfs` mount at `/dev/shm/`. Some distributions also use `tmpfs` for `/tmp/`. This can be easily verified by running:

```
$ mount | grep tmpfs
```

Adding a `tmpfs` mount point is as simple as running:

```
# mkdir tmp_dir
# mount -t tmpfs tmpfs tmp_dir
```

The second technique, using the `mmap(2)` system call, allows an application to map files or anonymous pages into the process's address space. This then returns a pointer to the beginning of the file's memory address, allowing for the application to manipulate it, like it would any data in memory. Paging in Linux is performed lazily, that is, the page mappings are added to the process's page tables, but the data isn't retrieved from disk until the first page fault to that page. To avoid this page fault overhead from occurring during the measurements, use the `MAP_POPULATE` flag for `mmap(2)`, which causes the pages to be loaded immediately.

Serving our HTML resources from memory, as opposed to the network or disk, will greatly decrease the variance present in our experiments. If the resources are small enough to fit into the LLC, it's possible to go even further, by iterating the data to warm the cache. This ensures that memory accesses never actually hit memory during the measurements. Of course, this assumes that the measurement is focusing on the processor pipeline efficiency, for an algorithm that is invoked with cache warm data. Data can still be served cache cold from memory by ensuring cache line alignment and using the clflush or nontemporal store instructions.

Now that our microbenchmark has accounted for variance in Items 1 through 4, it's time to look for controllable sources of variance during the actual rendering measurement. Variance can be introduced by CPU power-saving features, such as P and C states, as well as some features designed to improve CPU performance, for example, Intel® Turbo Boost and Intel® Hyper-Threading Technology. Often these features can be temporarily disabled in the BIOS. The author doesn't recommend disabling them for any longer than the test duration.

The variance introduced via P states and Intel Turbo Boost stem from the possibility of varying clock frequencies between measurement runs. For instance, the clock frequency could be 800 MHz for one run, and 1.6 GHz for another. In the deeper C states, such as C6, the caches are powered down and thus invalidated, causing previously warm caches to turn cold. If P states can not be disabled, the Linux kernel's cpufreq frequency scaling driver, `CONFIG_CPU_FREQ`, can be used in conjunction with the performance governor. This will keep the CPU frequency constant between tests.

Another source of variance is CPU migrations, where the process moves from executing on one processor to another, again leading to situations where the cache state suddenly changes. Migrations can be avoided by pinning the process to an individual CPU. This can be done either with the `taskset` command or programmatically via the `sched_setaffinity` system call.

Variance can also be introduced by running the benchmark on a system running other processes that are consuming significant amounts of resources. This type of system is often referred to as a *noisy system*. These other processes can lead to issues such as increased CPU migrations or thermal issues. One way to mitigate this issue is to boot the Linux kernel in single user mode, by adding "*single*" to the kernel command-line, or setting the init program to a shell, by adding *init=/path/to/shell* to the kernel command-line. Once the system has booted to this minimal configuration, the benchmark can be run without interference from other processes. If the benchmark requires other programs to run, such as a graphical application requiring an instance of `Xorg` running, those will need to be started manually.

5.2.2 UNCONTROLLABLE EXTERNAL VARIABLES

As mentioned in Section 4.4, it is important, when benchmarking, to reduce exposure to external variables that can affect performance. However, when designing experiments, it is also necessary to recognize that many external factors are outside of our immediate control.

Since these factors cannot be mitigated, they must be accounted for in the design of the experiment. To accomplish this, the benchmark should be run multiple times, and then these multiple data points should be analyzed to quantify the effects of the external variables on the results.

The number of data points required to be collected, in order to provide an accurate measurement, depends on how significantly the benchmark is affected by the uncontrollable variables. As a general rule of thumb, measurements at a smaller level of granularity will require more runs than measurements at a higher granularity. When in doubt, the author recommends erring on the side of collecting too many data points, which wastes time but provides a more accurate measurement, rather than too few, which saves time but provides a potentially misleading measurement.

As an aside, in statistics the distinction is made between calculations involving the population and calculations involving samples. The population represents the entire set of elements, whereas samples involve a subset of the population. To calculate the population mean of a benchmark would require averaging the result of every single run ever, an infinite set. Due to the impossible nature of this task, a sampling of the population set is used. Statistics are calculated from the sample set in order to reason about the properties of the population. The law of large numbers dictates that as the number of data points within the sample set increases, the sample's behavior approaches the behavior of the total population (Renze and Weisstein, 2014).

The most common statistic for summarizing performance samples is the mean. The population mean is denoted μ, whereas the sample mean is denoted as $\bar{x}$. While most readers will be familiar with the algorithm for calculating the mean, the author includes it in Equation 5.1 for completeness.

$$D = [d_0, \ldots, d_{n-1}] : \bar{D} = \frac{1}{n} \sum_{i=0}^{n-1} d_i \qquad (5.1)$$

However, it's important to understand that the sample mean only estimates the population mean, given the snapshot of samples available. Different samples, representing the same population, may have significantly different means. In order to determine the accuracy of the sample mean's estimation of the population mean, it is necessary to also calculate the sample variance. The sample variance estimates the dispersion of the population's distribution. As the sample variance approaches zero, the members of the population move closer to one another, thus instilling more confidence in how well the sample mean estimates the population mean. As such, when reporting a mean, always also report the corresponding variance. Variance is typically expressed as its root, the standard deviation. The reason for reporting the standard deviation, as opposed to the variance, is that the standard deviation is in the same units as the mean, making it easier to reason about (Miller and Miller, 1998). The population variance is denoted σ^2, whereas the sample variance is denoted as S^2. Equation 5.2 is the formula for calculating the variance, while the standard deviation is simply the square root of the variance.

$$D = [d_0, \ldots, d_{n-1}] : S^2 = \frac{1}{n-1} \sum_{i=0}^{n-1} (d_i - \bar{D})^2 \qquad (5.2)$$

As an aside, the reader may be wondering why the dividend in Equation 5.2 is $n-1$ rather than the intuitive value of n. The key insight here is that the sample variance estimates the population variance. Estimators can be categorized as unbiased, that is, the expected value of the statistic equals the estimated value, or biased. Obviously a statistic with the unbiased property is preferable to a statistic with the biased property (Miller and Miller, 1998). Because the sample mean, not the population mean, is used for calculating the variance, dividing the sample variance by n yields a biased estimator, whereas dividing by $n-1$ yields an unbiased estimator. For more information, see "Bessel's Correction" (Weisstein, 2014).

Note that in the variance formula, Equation 5.2, that each value is subtracted by the mean. This makes the calculation susceptible to floating point catastrophic cancelation, when a datum and the mean are very close. As the two close numbers are subtracted, the valid bits are essentially canceled out, leaving the number to be dominated by rounding errors (Goldberg, 1991). In order to prevent this, the author typically uses a different formula, first introduced by Welford(1962), which is less susceptible to catastrophic cancelation. An example implementation can be found in Listing 5.1.

```
1   void calc_mean(double *const restrict avg, double *const restrict
                   std_dev)
2   {
3          size_t i;
4
5          *avg = 0.0;
```

```
6              *std_dev = 0.0;
7              for (i = 0; i < NUM_RUNS; i++) {
8                      double tmp, measure;
9
10                     measure = measure_once();
11
12                     tmp = measure - *avg;
13                     *avg += tmp / (i + 1); /* i + 1 because i is
                        zero-based */
14                     *std_dev += ( tmp * (measure - *avg));
15             }
16             *std_dev = sqrt(*std_dev / (NUM_RUNS - 1));
17      }
```

LISTING 5.1

Online algorithm for computing mean and standard deviation.

This then raises the question of how to determine whether the difference between two samples, say one sample containing experiment runs for one algorithm and one sample containing experiment runs for a different algorithm, is caused by the variance within the data, or by an actual change in the population, that is, whether the change is statistically significant. To make this distinction, hypothesis testing is performed.

5.3 TIMING

In order to write benchmarks, it is necessary to understand how to take accurate measurements. One of the most commonly taken measurements is that of time, that is, how long a snippet of code takes to execute a given workload. While the process for measuring time might seem like it should be fairly straightforward, computer timers are actually a fairly complex subject.

When using timers, or taking any other measurement, it is necessary to always be aware of the measurement resolution, that is, the smallest measurable element. For instance, if two algorithms are being measured, and the first algorithm runs for 1 ms and the second runs for 100 ms, but the timer used for measurement only has a resolution in seconds, then both algorithms will be recorded as taking zero seconds and the significant differences between the two algorithms will be lost.

Another important aspect to consider is whether the timer is monotonically increasing. A *monotonically increasing* timer always returns a result that is greater than or equal to previously returned results, and thus ensures that the timer never moves backwards. A timer without this guarantee could yield misleading results. In the best case, the backwards movement would lead to an arithmetic underflow when comparing the second reading against the first, and thus the results would be obviously wrong. In the worst case, the backwards movement would be slight enough to not cause an underflow, but would still provide an inaccurate reading, and thus the results would be silently corrupted.

It is also important to determine whether the timer measures wall time or process time. The *wall* time measures the total time that has elapsed during the measurement period. On the other hand, the *process* time only measures time accounted to the process being measured. For instance, if the execution of one process takes a total of 30 seconds, with 10 seconds of that time spent with the core executing a different process, the wall time would be 30 seconds, and the per-process time would be 20 seconds.

5.3.1 CPU CYCLES

At the processor level, the CPU keeps track of time by counting the number of clock cycles. A *cycle* represents one iteration of the CPU core's loop for fetching, decoding, executing, and retiring instructions. Because the CPU is a pipeline, each of these phases occur concurrently. So during one cycle, 16 bytes worth of instructions are fetched, instructions from the previous cycle's fetch are decoded, or continue decoding, instructions decoded from an earlier cycle are executed, or continue executing, and instructions executed from an even earlier cycle are retired. The *frequency* of a processor estimates the number of these cycles that can occur per second, that is, a hertz. For example, a processor that operates at a frequency of 1.0 GHz, would perform one billion clocks each second.

The cycle count can be accessed either through the time-stamp counter or via PMU events. This section focuses on the time-stamp counter. For more information on the PMU events, see Chapter 6.

The time-stamp (TSC) counter is a MSR, IA32_TIME_STAMP_COUNTER_MSR, that holds the 64-bit number of clock cycles since the processor was booted. Originally, the TSC incremented at the actual CPU frequency, however on modern Intel® processors the TSC is invariant. Unlike the other methods for accessing the cycle count, the TSC *does* increment while the processor is halted. The TSC is also monotonically increasing, except in the case of 64-bit overflow.

Access to the TSC is provided via the RDTSC and RDTSCP instructions. Since the behavior for these instructions is the same for both 32- and 64-bit, the top 32 bits of the 64-bit counter are stored in the *EDX* register, while the lower 32 bits are stored in the *EAX* register. The RDTSCP instruction also returns the contents of the current hardware thread's 32-bit IA32_TSC_AUX_MSR in the *ECX* register. Linux sets this MSR to the hardware thread's logical id number, allowing for the code to also detect CPU migrations.

Due to the out-of-order execution of modern CPU pipelines, it is necessary to verify that reads to the TSC only count the instructions that are being benchmarked. In order to accomplish this, it is necessary to add two serialization points into the pipeline. A serialization point, in the form of a serializing instruction, will flush the pipeline and enforce that all previous instructions have finished executing, and that all future instructions haven't started executing.

The RDTSC instruction performs no serialization, while the RDTSCP instruction verifies that all prior instructions have finished executing, but makes no guarantee about future instructions. In order to ensure accurate results, a fully serializing instruction, typically CPUID, is used. Listing 5.2 demonstrates two small inlined functions for accessing the TSC, along with their serializing CPUID instructions on lines 8 and 26. Note that line 9 uses a regular RDTSC instruction, since it is fully protected by the prior CPUID, whereas line 23 uses a RDTSCP instruction to ensure that the benchmarked code has finished executing before making the measurement. The final CPUID instruction on line 26 ensures that no later instructions begin executing before the TSC has been read.

Notice that since the TSC is a MSR, and therefore duplicated per hardware thread, and increments at a fixed rate regardless of the core state, the cycle count corresponds to the wall time, not the process time.

```
1   #include <inttypes.h>
2
3   static inline uint64_t start_cycle(void)
4   {
5           register unsigned a, d;
6
7           __asm__ __volatile__ (
8                   "cpuid\n\t"
9                   "rdtsc\n\t"
10          : "=a" (a),
11            "=d" (d)
12          :
13          : "ebx", "ecx"
14          );
15          return (((uint64_t)d << 32) | a);
16  }
17
18  static inline uint64_t stop_cycle(void)
19  {
20          register unsigned high, low;
21
22          __asm__ __volatile__ (
23                  "rdtscp\n\t"
24                  "movl    %%eax, %[low]\n\t"
25                  "movl    %%edx, %[high]\n\t"
26                  "cpuid\n\t"
27          : [high] "=r" (high),
28            [low]  "=r" (low)
29          :
30          : "eax", "ebx", "ecx", "edx"
31          );
32          return (((uint64_t)high << 32) | low);
33  }
```

LISTING 5.2

Functions for measuring cycle count.

Combining the functions defined in Listing 5.2, and the technique for computing the average and standard deviation from Listing 5.1, it would be possible to count the number of cycles for a given workload with the following code snippet:

```
1   #include <stdio.h>
2   #include <math.h>
3   #include <inttypes.h>
4
5   static void run_bench(double *const avg, double *const std_dev)
6   {
7           size_t i;
8
9           *avg = 0.0;
10          *std_dev = 0.0;
11          for (i = 0; i < NUM_RUNS; i++) {
12                  uint64_t start, end;
13                  double t, measure;
14
15                  start = start_cycle();
16                  /* do benchmarked code */
17                  end = stop_cycle();
18
19                  measure = (double)(end - start);
20                  t = measure - *avg;
21                  *avg += t / (i + 1);
22                  *std_dev += (t * (measure - *avg));
23          }
24          *std_dev = sqrt(*std_dev / (NUM_RUNS - 1));
25  }
```

5.3.2 CLOCK TIME AND UNIX TIME

As mentioned previously, the processor has no concept of time outside of clock cycles. Therefore, all of the interfaces for accessing time in the normal human units of time, such as seconds, are provided by the operating system, rather than the instruction set. The Linux kernel has a few different options for a clock source.

Traditionally, the Linux kernel ticked, that is, it would program the hardware timer to generate an interrupt at a given frequency, representing one tick. Each of these interrupts would cause the kernel to pause the current user space program, perform some accounting, and then choose the next process to run. This tick would occur at an interval selected at compile time, via the CONFIG_HZ Kconfig option. The possible configuration options for x86 were 1000, 350, 250, and 100 Hz. For instance, a kernel configured with HZ = 1000 would receive 1000 tick interrupts every second, limiting the resolution of the timers to 1 ms.

Selecting this frequency was a tradeoff between the number of interrupts generated, which keeps waking the processor up and therefore reduces the effectiveness of deep sleep states, and the ability to respond quickly to interactive tasks, due to the scheduler's smaller time quantum. Each tick would increment the jiffies kernel variable. Since a tick corresponds to a precise time, that is, the value of a jiffy is equal to $\frac{1}{CONFIG\_HZ}$ seconds, the number of jiffies could be used as a clock source.

Nowadays, users who care about power consumption configure the Linux kernel to be tickless, that is, CONFIG_NO_HZ=Y. In a tickless kernel, interrupts only occur when needed, as opposed to a fixed interval. This prevents the tick interrupts from waking the CPU out of deeper sleep states as frequently, and thus saves power.

The available clock sources for the system can be queried through sysfs by reading available_clocksource and current_clocksource in /sys/bus/clocksource/devices/clocksource0/. For instance:

```
$ cat /sys/bus/clocksource/devices/clocksource0/available_clocksource
tsc hpet acpi_pm
$ cat /sys/bus/clocksource/devices/clocksource0/current_clocksource
tsc
```

The default clock source in the Linux kernel is now the TSC register described above in Section 5.3.1. The kernel uses a scale factor to convert cycles into nanoseconds. The exact scaling formula can be seen in the cycles_2_ns() function in ${LINUX_SRC}/arch/x86/kernel/tsc.c. In the case where the system TSC is not invariant, or demonstrates that it is not reliable, the High Precision Event Timer (HPET) is used instead.

The clock source is then exposed to user space through a series of time system calls, including time(2), gettimeofday(2), and clock_gettime(2).

The time(2) system call returns UNIX time, that is, an integer representing the number of seconds since the UNIX Epoch, midnight, January 1, 1970. Because UNIX time is a single integer, it is very easy to work with. Unfortunately, it counts seconds, and therefore has a resolution of 1 second, making it impractical for exact measurements.

The clock_gettime(2) system call, provides access to a number of different clocks, each with a slightly different behavior with regards to what they measure. The resolution of each available clock can be measured with clock_getres(2). The following clocks are available:

CLOCK_REALTIME Measures wall time. Affected by changes to the system clock.
CLOCK_REALTIME_COARSE Similar to CLOCK_REALTIME, but trades precision for better performance.
CLOCK_MONOTONIC Measures the uptime of the system. Unaffected by manual changes to the clock, but is affected by updates via adjtime(3) and NTP. Does not include time in sleep state.
CLOCK_MONOTONIC_COARSE Similar to CLOCK_MONOTONIC, but trades precision for better performance.

CLOCK_MONOTONIC_RAW Similar to CLOCK_MONOTONIC, but unaffected by changes to changes in the system clock.
CLOCK_BOOTTIME Similar to CLOCK_MONOTONIC, but includes sleep states.
CLOCK_PROCESS_CPUTIME_ID Per-process CPU timer
CLOCK_THREAD_CPUTIME_ID Per-thread CPU timer.

The gettimeofday(2) system call is essentially identical to clock_gettime(2) using CLOCK_REALTIME. The timezone parameter is deprecated, and should be set to NULL.

```
1   #include <stdio.h>
2   #include <math.h>
3   #include <sys/time.h>
4
5   static inline double time_diff_ms(const struct timeval *const s,
6                    const struct timeval *const e)
7   {
8           double s_ms, e_ms;
9
10          s_ms = (s->tv_sec * 1000) + (s->tv_usec / 1000);
11          e_ms = (e->tv_sec * 1000) + (e->tv_usec / 1000);
12          return e_ms - s_ms;
13  }
14
15  static void run_bench(double *const avg, double *const std_dev)
16  {
17          size_t i;
18
19          *avg = 0.0;
20          *std_dev = 0.0;
21          for (i = 0; i < NUM_RUNS; i++) {
22                  double measure, t;
23                  struct timeval s, e;
24
25                  gettimeofday(&s, NULL);
26                  /* do benchmarked code */
27                  gettimeofday(&e, NULL);
28
29                  measure = time_diff_ms(&s, &e);
30                  t = measure - *avg;
31                  *avg += t / (i + 1);
32                  *std_dev += (t * (measure - *avg));
33          }
34          *stddev = sqrt(*std_dev / (NUM_RUNS - 1));
35  }
```

LISTING 5.3

Functions for measuring milliseconds.

5.4 PHORONIX TEST SUITE

Aside from running one of the most popular websites dedicated to Linux performance news, http://www.phoronix.com, Phoronix Media also produces a framework designed specifically for benchmarking. This framework, known as the Phoronix Test Suite, provides a flexible architecture that is easily extendable through custom modules and benchmarks. While Phoronix typically focuses on Linux performance, the Phoronix Test Suite is cross-platform.

Leveraging the Phoronix Test Suite provides a significant number of advantages over writing a custom benchmark manager. One of these advantages is the presence of advanced benchmarking features, such as the ability to automatically rerun test runs with a high variance or the ability to leverage Git bisection in order to automatically pinpoint the source of performance regressions.

Another one of these advantages is the ability to generate publication-ready graphs for plotting results and displaying system information. These graphs are of considerable quality, highlighting not only the results, but also the relevant test and system configurations, as well as clearly labeling the metrics. The attention paid to producing high quality graphics for summarizing the benchmarking data highlights the fact that the Phoronix Test Suite is used for generating content for Phoronix news articles.

For instance, Figures 5.1–5.3 depict examples of the graphs created for displaying results. In this case, two different software configurations, "Version 0" and "Version 1" were tested with a single benchmark, "Unpacking the Linux Kernel." For each benchmark that is run, one bar graph, such as the one in Figure 5.1, and one graphical table, such as the one in Figure 5.2, are generated. Depending on the test configuration, some of these graphs may be annotated at the bottom with relevant configurations, such as the compiler flags used to build the benchmark. Also, two summary graphics are created, one displaying the system configuration, shown in Figure 5.3, and one displaying a table summarizing all of the individual results.

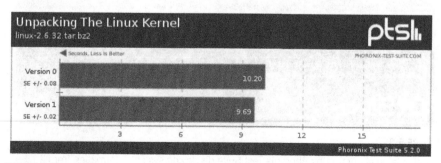

FIGURE 5.1

Graph generated by Phoronix Test Suite comparing two results.

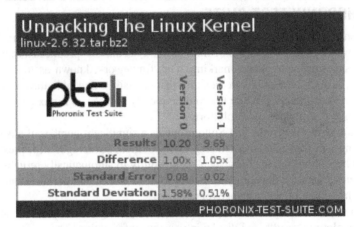

FIGURE 5.2

Graphic table generated by Phoronix Test Suite comparing two results.

lpaex2

Intel Core i7-2760QM @ 3.50GHz (8 Cores)	Processor
LENOVO 4239CTO	Motherboard
Intel 2nd Generation Core Family DRAM	Chipset
8192MB	Memory
240GB INTEL SSDSC2CW24	Disk
Intel HD 3000 (1300MHz)	Graphics
Intel 6 /C200	Audio
Intel 82579LM Gigabit Connection + Intel Centrino Wireless-N 1000	Network
Fedora 20	OS
3.16.2-200.jtk.fc20.x86_64 (x86_64)	Kernel
GNOME Shell 3.10.4	Desktop
X Server 1.14.4	Display Server
intel 2.99.911	Display Driver
3.1 Mesa 10.2.2	OpenGL
GCC 4.8.3 20140624 + Clang 3.4 + LLVM 3.4 + ICC	Compiler
ext4	File System
1600x900	Screen Resolution

PHORONIX-TEST-SUITE.COM — Phoronix Test Suite 5.2.1

- CFQ / data=ordered,noatime,rw,seclabel
- Scaling Governor: intel_pstate powersave

FIGURE 5.3

Graphic table generated by Phoronix Test Suite displaying system information from Figure 5.1.

If two results from different configurations are merged, the system configuration will highlight differences between the two configurations.

As mentioned in Chapter 4, the ability to clearly communicate performance results is essential for influencing the decisions of others. The advantage of having high quality and professional looking graphs automatically generated, that can be placed on a website or attached to an email, cannot be overstated.

Another useful feature of the Phoronix Test Suite is the ability for automation, including a "batch" mode that runs preconfigured benchmarks without requiring any human interaction. This allows for integration into existing performance frameworks or the ability to utilize only some of the advanced functionality while handling the other aspects with custom implementations.

5.4.1 **RUNNING PHORONIX**

There are two interfaces available for controlling the Phoronix Test Suite, the command-line interface and the GUI, shown in Figure 5.4. This section focuses solely on the command-line interface, as the concepts introduced here also apply to the GUI, so it should be self-explanatory. All commands are multiplexed through the

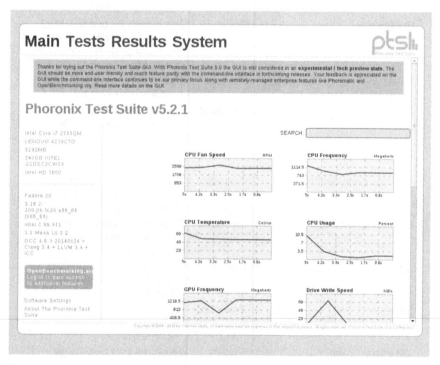

FIGURE 5.4

Phoronix Test Suite experimental GUI.

`phoronix-test-suite` shell script. A complete list of commands can be obtained by running the script without any parameters.

Each benchmark in the Phoronix Test Suite is represented by a corresponding test profile. This profile is responsible for defining how the benchmark will be installed, how the benchmark will be run, how the results will be parsed, and the metadata describing what the results mean. Multiple test profiles can be grouped together to form a test suite.

Included with the framework are a multitude of predefined test profiles and test suites, providing access to popular benchmarks. Table 5.1 samples some of the available benchmarks and their descriptions. Notice that in this list, there are two similar tests, "GZIP Compression" and "System GZIP Compression." The Phoronix tests that lack the "System" designator are designed to hold software constant and test the differences in hardware. To accomplish this, these tests download and compile

Table 5.1 Examples of Available Phoronix Benchmarks

Name	Type	Description
Apache Benchmark	System	Measures how many Apache requests per second a given system can sustain
BlogBench	Disk	Replicates load of a real-world busy file server with multiple threads of random reads, writes, and rewrites
Timed Linux Kernel Compilation	Processor	Measures how long it takes to build the Linux kernel
C-Ray	Processor	Measures floating-point performance via the C-Ray raytracer
Cairo Performance Demos	Graphics	Measures Cairo drawing performance
Gzip Compression	Processor	Measures how long it takes to compress a file using a downloaded `gzip`
System Gzip Compression	Processor	Measures how long it takes to compress a file using the system's `gzip`
Ogg Encoding	Processor	Measures how long it takes to encode a sample WAV file to Ogg format
FFmpeg	Processor	Measures the system's audio/video encoding performance
Idle Power Usage	System	Measures the power usage during system idle

their own versions of software, rather than testing the versions installed by the Linux distribution. When making decisions based on tests, always double-check what is being measured.

The full list of official tests can be retrieved by executing:

```
$ phoronix-test-suite list-available-tests
```

These test profiles, along with test results from the community, are available at http://www.openbenchmarking.org. After the Phoronix Test Suite has finished collecting the desired results, the option is available to upload those results to the OpenBenchmarking website, which publishes the results publicly. Along with the results, some system information, such as distro and software versioning, and hardware information are also published, allowing others to compare results between platforms of interest. Each result is assigned a unique result id, that can be used to reference that test and its results. Aside from hosting public results, the OpenBenchmarking website allows users to publish and share custom test profiles.

When passing tests to the phoronix-test-suite script, there are a number of different methods for referencing tests. Commands can usually perform their actions on one of more of:

Test Profile Command operates on the individual test.
Test Suite Command operates on every test profile contained within the group.
OpenBenchmarking.org ID Command operates on the same test profile or suite associated with the given result ID on OpenBenchmarking.org.
Test Result Command operates on the same test profile or suite associated with the given result name.

Additionally, test profiles and suites can be referenced by their file system path, relative to the appropriate Phoronix directories. This allows for the grouping of related items in subdirectories and for clarification of ambiguous requests.

Test profiles and suites are categorized as either local or official. This categorization serves to indicate where the test came from, and also to reduce ambiguity in the case of two tests with the same name. The directory structure for test profiles and suites also reflects this categorization. Under the directory for available test profiles and suites, two folders exist, `local`, which contains the local tests, and `pts`, which contains the official Phoronix tests. At the time of this writing, the Phoronix Test Suite only checks in those two directories for profiles during installation. Within those directories, and within the test results directory, custom directory hierarchies can be created in order to organize content.

For instance, consider the situation where there are two projects, project 0, and project 1. Each of these projects consists of three test profiles, test0, test1, and test2. In order to accomplish this, two project folders could be created within the `local` test profile directory, and then three test profile directories could be created within each of those folders. Because the names of the test profiles, test0, test1, and test2, are ambiguous, the full path, relative to the test profile directory, would be used to reference the individual tests, that is, `local/project0/test0` and `local/project1/test0`.

By default, Phoronix stores all of the test profiles, test suites, and test results in `${HOME}/.phoronix-test-suite/`. Tests are also typically installed into and execute from this directory. Inside `${HOME}/.phoronix-test-suite/`, the following directories exist:

download-cache Contains local copies of remote files downloaded for testing
installed-tests Contains the installed benchmark executables and any runtime files required for testing
modules Contains available modules
openbenchmarking.org Contains any resources downloaded from the OpenBenchmarking website
test-profiles Contains the test profile definitions which are responsible for describing each test and performing the installation
test-suites Contains the test suite definitions
xsl Contains the eXtensible Stylesheet Language (XSL) files

Configuration

Before installing and running benchmarks, it is necessary to configure the framework. Almost all of the configuration options exposed by the Phoronix framework, as opposed to the individual tests, are controlled by the `${HOME}/.phoronix-test-suite/user-config.xml` file. For reference, Table 5.2 documents all of the options exposed via this XML file.

Changes can be made by directly editing the file, or by executing:

```
$ phoronix-test-suite user-config set key=value
```

If no `user-config.xml` exists, the phoronix-test-suite script will create one with the default values. So at any time, the configuration can be restored to the default values by either deleting the `user-config.xml` file, and letting the phoronix-test-suite script regenerate it, or by executing:

```
$ phoronix-test-suite user-config-reset
```

The basic formatting, colors, and watermarks for the result graphs can be customized by editing the style fields in `${HOME}/.phoronix-test-suite/graph-config.json`.

Aside from these configuration files, there are about twenty environmental variables that can modify the behavior of the tests, result output, and so on.

For convenience, there is also an interactive command for configuring networking:

```
$ phoronix-test-suite network-setup
```

Installing tests

Before any benchmarks can be run, they must first be installed. This operation is performed by executing:

```
$ phoronix-test-suite install <test reference>
```

For example, in order to install the three test profiles that measure boot time with Systemd:

```
$ ./phoronix-test-suite install systemd-boot-kernel \
> pts/systemd-boot-userspace \
> systemd-boot-total

Phoronix Test Suite v5.2.0

    To Install: pts/systemd-boot-kernel-1.0.1
    To Install: pts/systemd-boot-userspace-1.0.1
    To Install: pts/systemd-boot-total-1.0.1

    Determining File Requirements ...................................
    Searching Download Caches .......................................

    3 Tests To Install

    pts/systemd-boot-kernel-1.0.1:
        Test Installation 1 of 3
        Installing Test @ 11:04:51

    pts/systemd-boot-userspace-1.0.1:
        Test Installation 2 of 3
        Installing Test @ 11:04:51

    pts/systemd-boot-total-1.0.1:
        Test Installation 3 of 3
        Installing Test @ 11:04:51
```

First, Phoronix creates a lock file in the client's temporary directory, entitled "phoronix-test-suite.active." This serves to prevent multiple instances of Phoronix processes from interfering with each other.

Second, the test profile's `support_check.sh` script runs to determine whether the benchmark is actually appropriate for the current system. For instance, in the previous example, the systemd boot time test profiles, this script checks whether the system uses systemd as the init program. If not, there is no point in attempting to install the test, since it has no meaning on this system. The exit status from the script is used to communicate whether the features needed by the test are supported.

Third, the list of test dependencies is checked against the currently installed software. For convenience, Phoronix integrates with the package managers of many popular Linux distributions, such as Fedora, Gentoo, and Ubuntu, in order to automate the dependency installation process. To facilitate this, the dependencies of each test profile are expressed with a generic name, which is then translated to the distro-specific package name via a predefined list. For instance, a test profile might require the generic "gtk-development" package, which will translate to "gtk2-devel" on Fedora, "x11-libs/gtk+" on Gentoo, and "libgtk2.0-dev" on Ubuntu. In the case where packages must be installed but the current user does not have the necessary privileges, the user will be prompted for their root password, and then the packages will be installed automatically. The generic package names and their corresponding package names for each package manager can be found in `${PTS_SRC}/pts-core/external-test-dependencies/xml/`.

Fourth, a directory is created for the test installation. This directory will reside within the `${HOME}/.phoronix-test-suite/installed-tests` directory, under either the `pts`, for official tests, or `local`, for custom tests, directories. For example, if the official test profile `unpack-linux-1.0.0` is installed, it will be installed into `${HOME}/.phoronix-test-suite/installed-tests/pts/unpack-linux-1.0.0`.

Fifth, any remote resources required for testing are downloaded. These resources typically include the benchmark's workloads or source code. Phoronix supports checking both the file size and checksum in order to verify each file's download integrity. Before each file is downloaded, the download cache is searched. If the file is found, and meets the integrity requirements, the download will be skipped and the file will be copied from the download cache into the test's installation directory. By manually copying files into the download cache, tests can be installed and run on systems that lack a network connection. If the file is not found within the download cache, Phoronix will attempt to download it into the cache and then copy it into the test's installation directory.

Sixth, the test profile's `install.sh` script is executed. This script is responsible for creating the executable, typically a script, that will set up and perform the actual benchmarking, as well as setting up any prerequisites. For example, a common function of the installation script is to compile any downloaded code and then create the script that runs the benchmark.

Once this script has finished executing, the test is installed and ready to be run. If a test suite is referenced, this process will occur for every test profile contained within the test suite. If a local or OpenBenchmarking.org result is referenced, this process will occur for every test profile referenced within the test result.

Running tests

Once a benchmark has been installed, it is ready to be run and for results to be collected. Running individual benchmarks or test suites can be accomplished by running

```
$ phoronix-test-suite run <test-reference>
```

First, the Phoronix Test Suite will check to ensure that the selected benchmark, or benchmarks, are installed. If not, the user will be prompted whether they wish to install the tests or abort.

Second, the pre-test script, `pre.sh`, will be run, assuming it is present in the test profile. This allows the benchmark to set up the initial system state prior to execution. For example, this might involve starting a daemon or altering the system configuration.

Third, the test executable will be invoked repeatedly. The exact number of benchmark runs will depend on a few factors, such as whether `DynamicRunCount` is enabled in `user-config.xml`, the value of `StandardDeviationThreshold` in `user-config.xml`, and also the value of the TOTAL_LOOP_TIME environmental variable. In between each invocation of the benchmark's executable, the interim test script, `interim.sh`, will run, assuming it exists in the test profile directory. This script allows the benchmark to clean up any state left over after each test, providing a clean slate for each run.

Fourth, the post-test script, `post.sh`, will be run, assuming it is present in the test profile. This allows for the benchmark to clean up any state initialized during the benchmark run. In general, any changes made to the system by the pre-test script should be reversed.

Finally, the results, along with the system logs, will be saved into the `ResultsDirectory`, with the directory named after the test name. Typically this directory will be `${HOME}/.phoronix-test-suite/test-results`.

Inside each test result directory is a number of files that represent the system state during the test run, the results of the test, and the resources generated for summarizing the test results.

The `system-logs` directory contains a copy of various system logs from the time of execution. This includes files such as the full `dmesg`, the compiler version and configuration, the environment variables, the CPU information, and so on. Essentially a snapshot of relevant files in `/proc` and `/var/log`, this information allows for performance disparities in future results to be debugged. Additionally, if leveraging the Phoronix Test Suite as part of a larger performance infrastructure comprised of multiple machines, these files can be parsed to determine what configuration the results correspond to.

The `results-graph` directory contains a copy of each of the generated graphics for the test, each stored in Scalable Vector Graphics (SVG) format. Using a vector-based format, as opposed to a bitmap-based format, allows for the images to be scaled to various sizes, without losing image quality. For each test profile in the result, two images will be generated. A bar graph plot of the test results are seen in Figure 5.1 and a table summary of the results are seen in Figure 5.2. The names of these files correspond with the test numbers. So if the test was the *x*th test run, the plot will be called `x.svg`, and the table will be called `x_table.svg`.

Apart from the two images generated per test profile, two summary images are also created. An overview table, `overview.svg`, contains an entry for each test profile, summarizing the results. Also as shown in Figure 5.3, a table is created, `systems.svg`, that lists the system's hardware information. If different pieces of hardware are compared, the differences in configuration are highlighted.

The raw results for each test profile are stored in an XML file. Similar to the test result image, the name of the file depends on the test number. For test number *x*, the results are stored in `test-x.xml`. Parsing this file allows for the raw results to be retrieved. Note that the file contains the average result and also the raw values for each test run. This is especially useful if using the Phoronix Test Suite along with a custom performance infrastructure, since all of the samples across multiple runs can be aggregated for reporting and analysis. Finally, all of the individual test results are combined into a single XML file, `composite.xml`, that contains all of the results.

Batch mode

Running the Phoronix Test Suite in batch mode allows for operations, such as installing and running tests, to occur in a manner that requires no human interaction. This is especially useful if integrating into an automated performance infrastructure.

Before batch benchmarks can be run, the batch mode options must be configured. As shown in Table 5.2, the batch mode options are part of the `PhoronixTest-Suite.Options.BatchMode` schema. If `PhoronixTestSuite.Options.BatchMode.Configured` is set to false, batch mode operations will fail with an error message stating that batch mode must first be configured. Because batch mode is not interactive, these configuration options dictate how the benchmarks are run.

Once configured, tests can be installed and run with:

```
$ phoronix-test-suite batch-install <test reference>
$ phoronix-test-suite batch-run <test reference>
```

5.4.2 WORKING WITH RESULTS

Typically, when using the Phoronix Test Suite, the interesting data is not one specific test result, but a comparison of multiple test results, highlighting the performance delta between one or more changes. To accommodate this, Phoronix has commands for splicing and extracting test data from one result into another result.

Any of the test results posted to OpenBenchmarking.org can be downloaded locally with:

```
$ phoronix-test-suite clone-result <Test Id>
```

This downloads the full result, including the `system-logs` folder, which allows for researching the exact system configuration, the `composite.xml` file, containing all of the test results, and the graphs. These files are downloaded into the default `test-results` directory, with the directory named after the test id.

Multiple results, such as a local result and a result cloned from OpenBenchmarking.org, can be combined with:

```
$ phoronix-test-suite merge-results <result> <result> ...
```

If there is test overlap, that is, the same test was run in both results, those results will be merged onto the same graph. The test results being merged aren't modified by the merge operation. Instead, a new result is created in the default `test-results` directory, starting with the name `merge-`.

5.4.3 CREATING CUSTOM TESTS

Regardless of whether published or not published, adding custom tests to the default repertoire is very simple. Essentially, a test profile is a collection of XML files and executables, normally shell scripts, for performing installation and benchmarking.

First, create a new directory for the test profile in `$HOME/.phoronix-test-suite/test-profiles/local`. In this directory, all of the files needed for installing the test, except for any external resources, will be created.

The heart of a test profile is the `test-definition.xml` file. This XML file describes not only the test metadata, such as the name and description, but also the required software dependencies, `PhoronixTestSuite.TestProfile.External Dependencies`, the executable for running the actual benchmark, `Phoronix-TestSuite.TestInformation.Executable`, as well as data about the result metrics. The `PhoronixTestSuite.TestInformation.ResultScale` property is the label used for the metric, such as "seconds" or "MB/s." The `PhoronixTest-Suite.TestInformation.Proportion` property sets whether the metric is reported as "HIB" or "LIB".

Due to the complexity of the `test-definition.xml` file, the author recommends simply copying one from any existing test profile, and then updating or adding fields as required. Listing 5.4 demonstrates a simple test definition.

```
1   <?xml version="1.0"?>
2   <!--Phoronix Test Suite v4.4.0m1 (Forsand)-->
3   <PhoronixTestSuite>
4     <TestInformation>
5       <Title>System XZ Decompression</Title>
6       <Description>This test measures the time to decompress a Linux
                      kernel tarball using XZ.</Description>
7       <ResultScale>Seconds</ResultScale>
8       <Proportion>LIB</Proportion>
9       <TimesToRun>3</TimesToRun>
10    </TestInformation>
11    <TestProfile>
12      <Version>1.0.2</Version>
13      <SupportedPlatforms>Linux, BSD</SupportedPlatforms>
14      <SoftwareType>Utility</SoftwareType>
15      <TestType>Processor</TestType>
16      <Maintainer>Jim Kukunas</Maintainer>
17    </TestProfile>
18  </PhoronixTestSuite>
```

LISTING 5.4

`test-definition.xml` for the `system-decompress-xz` test profile.

If the test profile depends on a specific system configuration, create a `support-check.sh` script. This script runs before the test is installed in order to determine whether the test is applicable to the system. A positive return value from this script indicates that the test is not applicable for the current system configuration. Listing 5.5 demonstrates a simple support check script.

```
1  #!/bin/sh
2
3  which xz
4  if [ $? -gt 0 ]; then
5          echo "The system must provide xz for this test profile."\
6               "Some Linux distributions provided xz through the"\
7               xz-utils package." > $TEST_CUSTOM_ERROR
8  fi
```

LISTING 5.5

`support-check.sh` for the `system-decompress-xz` test profile.

Next, if the test requires any external dependencies, a download manifest is created in `downloads.xml`. This XML file lists the URL, filename, filesize, and MD5 checksum for each required file. At install time, these files will be fetched from the URL, validated against the filesize and MD5 checksum, and then copied into the test profile directory under `$HOME/.phoronix-test-suite/installed-tests/`. Listing 5.6 demonstrates a simple download manifest.

```
1   <?xml version="1.0"?>
2   <!--Phoronix Test Suite v4.4.0m1 (Forsand)-->
3   <PhoronixTestSuite>
4     <Downloads>
5       <Package>
6         <URL>http://www.kernel.org/pub/linux/kernel/v3.x/linux-3.7.
                    tar.xz</URL>
7         <MD5>21223369d682bcf44bcdfe1521095983</MD5>
8         <FileSize>69736096</FileSize>
9       </Package>
10    </Downloads>
11  </PhoronixTestSuite>
```

LISTING 5.6

`downloads.xml` for the `system-decompress-xz` test profile.

Next, create an `install.sh` script, which will carry out the actual installation of the test. Typically, this script is responsible for generating the shell script that will run the actual benchmark and redirect the results to the Phoronix result parser. Listing 5.7 demonstrates a simple install script. Notice how the executable benchmarking script, system-decompress-xz, is created on line 6. All of the test output is redirected to the $LOG_FILE environmental variable. This is very important, as only the output sent to $LOG_FILE will be parsed for results. Also, always remember to make the script executable, as seen on line 11.

```
1   #!/bin/bash
2
3   XZ='which xz'
4   echo $? > ~/install-exit-status
5
6   cat > system-decompress-xz << EOT
7   #!/bin/sh
8   ${XZ} -dk --stdout linux-3.7.tar.xz > /dev/null 2>&1
9   EOT
10
11  chmod +x system-decompress-xz
```

LISTING 5.7

install.sh for the system-decompress-xz test profile.

Additionally, if pre.sh, interim.sh, or post.sh scripts are present in the test profile directory, these scripts will be executed before, between runs, and after the benchmark, respectively.

Finally, the last step is to define a results-definition.xml file. This XML file explains how Phoronix should parse the test output. Results can come either from the output of the benchmarking script, or from the Phoronix sensors. Listing 5.8 demonstrates a result definition that utilizes the time sensor to monitor the script's duration.

```
1   <?xml version="1.0"?>
2   <!--Phoronix Test Suite v4.4.0m1 (Forsand)-->
3   <PhoronixTestSuite>
4     <SystemMonitor>
5       <Sensor>sys.time</Sensor>
6     </SystemMonitor>
7   </PhoronixTestSuite>
```

LISTING 5.8

results-definition.xml for the system-decompress-xz test profile.

Alternatively, the results definition can be sample output, or a snippet of sample output, from the benchmarking script, that is, the output that was written to the $LOG_FILE environmental variable. In the sample output, the numbers to be parsed out of the results are replaced with parser variables. Parser variables begin with a "#_" and end with a "_#." Thus for the majority of cases, replace the one important result in the sample output with #_RESULT_#.

5.4.4 PHORONIX RESOURCES

Table 5.2 Schema of user-config.xml (Larabel, 2012)

PhoronixTestSuite
  Options
    OpenBenchmarking		

AnonymousUsageReporting	bool	Enable anonymous reporting of usage, such as test installations and durations
AnonymousSoftwareReporting	bool	Enable anonymous reporting of software configuration
AnonymousHardwareReporting	bool	Enable anonymous reporting of hardware configuration
IndexCacheTTL	int	The number of days to consider cached data from OpenBenchmarking.org valid
AlwaysUploadSystemLogs	bool	Upload system logs without prompting
General		
DefaultBrowser	str	The default web browser used for displaying results
UsePhodeviCache	bool	Enable the Phodevi smart cache for caching hardware and software configurations
DefaultDisplayMode	str	Controls command-line text brevity [DEFAULT, CONCISE]
Modules		
LoadModules	str	Comma-separated list of modules to load
Installation		
RemoveDownloadFiles	bool	Conserve disk space by deleting downloaded files after installation. Will break tests that rely on downloaded files at runtime
SearchMediaForCache	bool	Search for a download cache on removable media (under /media)
SymLinkFilesFromCache	bool	Conserve disk space by using symbolic links into the download-cache to avoid duplicates
PromptForDownloadMirror	bool	If FALSE, a mirror is selected at random

Table 5.2 Schema of user-config.xml (Larabel, 2012)—cont'd

PhoronixTestSuite Options OpenBenchmarking		
EnvironmentDirectory	str	The path to the directory where tests will be installed
CacheDirectory	str	The path to where downloaded files will be cached
Testing		
SaveSystemLogs	bool	Save system logs, such as Xorg.log and dmesg, with test results
SaveInstallationLogs	bool	Save log generated by test profile installation
SaveTestLogs	bool	Save full output generated by test run
RemoveTestInstallOnCompletion	bool	Uninstall test profile after run
ResultsDirectory	str	The path to where results will be saved
AlwaysUploadResultsToOpen Benchmarking	bool	Upload results to OpenBenchmarking without prompting
AutoSortRunQueue	bool	Sort the benchmark queue to run similar tests together
TestResultValidation		
DynamicRunCount	bool	Continue running benchmark until standard deviation falls below StandardDeviationThreshold
LimitDynamicToTestLength	int	Maximum minutes to run benchmark with DynamicRunCount
StandardDeviationThreshold	real	Acceptable percentage of standard deviation for DynamicRunCount
ExportResultsTo	str	Path to a script which verifies colon delimited results
BatchMode		
SaveResults	bool	Automatically save results in Batch Mode
OpenBrowser	bool	Automatically open results in DefaultWebBrowser in Batch Mode

Continued

Table 5.2 Schema of user-config.xml (Larabel, 2012)—cont'd

PhoronixTestSuite Options OpenBenchmarking		
UploadResults	bool	Automatically upload results in Batch Mode
PromptForTestIdentifier	bool	Whether to prompt or randomly generate test identifier in Batch Mode
PromptForTestDescription	bool	Whether to prompt or use default test description in Batch Mode
PromptSaveName	bool	Whether to prompt or automatically generate test name in Batch Mode
RunAllTestCombinations	bool	Whether to run all test combinations in Batch Mode
Configured	bool	Batch Mode will not run unless this is TRUE
Networking		
NoNetworkCommunication	bool	Completely disables uploads and downloads
Timeout	int	Network Timeout
ProxyAddress	str	Proxy Address
ProxyPort	int	Proxy Port
Server		
RemoteAccessPort	int	Port number to access built-in web interface. FALSE disables
Password	str	SHA256 sum of password to authenticate web interface
WebSocketPort	int	Port to use for WebSocket server

REFERENCES

Goldberg, D., 1991, March. What every computer scientist should know about floating-point arithmetic. Comput. Surv. http://docs.oracle.com/cd/E19957-01/806-3568/ncg_goldberg.html.

Larabel, M., 2012, 01. pts_config.php. Phoronix Test Suite PHP Source Code. ${PTS_SRC}/pts-core/objects/client/pts_config.php.

Larabel, M., 2014, 05. Phoronix Test Suite User Manual. http://www.phoronix-test-suite.com/documentation/phoronix-test-suite.pdf. Software Manual.

Miller, I., Miller, M., 1998, 05. John E. Freund's Mathematical Statistics, 6th ed. Prentice Hall, Upper Saddle River, NJ.

mmap(2) - Linux Manual Page. 2014. http://man7.org/linux/man-pages/man2/mmap.2.html.

Renze, J., Weisstein, E.W., 2014. Law of Large Numbers. From MathWorld – A Wolfram Web Resource. http://mathworld.wolfram.com/LawofLargeNumbers.html.

Rohland, C., 2007. TMPFS - Linux Kernel Documentation. ${LINUX_SRC}/Documentation/filesystems/tmpfs.txt.

sched_setaffinity(2) - Linux Manual Page. 2014. http://man7.org/linux/man-pages/man2/sched_setaffinity.2.html.

Weisstein, E.W., 2014. Bessel's Correction. From MathWorld – A Wolfram Web Resource. http://mathworld.wolfram.com/BesselsCorrection.html.

Welford B.P, 1962, 09. Note on a Method for Calculating Corrected Sums of Squares and Products. Technometrics. doi:10.2307/1266577.

Monitors

Introduction to Profiling

CHAPTER CONTENTS

Homines quod volunt credunt (Men believe what they want)
Julius Caesar

The Pareto principle applied to software optimization, as a general rule of thumb, states that 80% of the time is spent in 20% of the code. Donald Knuth echos this sentiment, although his numbers are slightly different, with 90% of the time spent in 10% of the code. Regardless of which principle the reader adheres to, the takeaway point is identical. Software optimization is most beneficial when it focuses on that critical 10% or 20% of code responsible for the majority of the time consumed.

This task is not as straightforward as it may seem, as described in Chapters 1–3. Modern hardware and software platforms are far too complicated for a programmer to reliably estimate where that 10% or 20% resides. In the first chapter, the concept of premature optimization was defined to be an optimization conducted without first performing the necessary analysis to actually locate these areas. In order to isolate these areas, and avoid premature optimization, system data must be collected and interpreted, a process referred to as *profiling*.

An analogy can be drawn between the process of profiling a performance bottleneck and the relationship between a statistical sample and population, as described in the previous chapter. Both the bottleneck and population are constant, yet their form is metaphorically obstructed from the viewer. The actions of collecting samples and performing profiling serve to slowly reveal this form via observation. Just like collecting samples, profiling may require correlating multiple data points in order to obtain an accurate picture.

These data points are collected through *monitors*. A monitor is a tool that measures transitions between system states. Monitors can vary significantly in level of complexity. For instance, a simple monitor might instrument an application with counter variables in order to determine the number of times a function is called. On the other hand, a complex monitor might statistically sample events occurring in multiple processes running on multiple cores. Monitors are frequently referred to as profilers or tracers.

In order to empower monitors with deep visibility into processor behavior, Intel® processors support dedicated hardware for monitoring performance events. This hardware is known as the Performance Monitoring Unit (PMU). The next section focuses on the fundamentals of leveraging the PMU. This provides the necessary basics for using and interpreting the performance monitors that leverage the PMU, such as Intel® VTune™ Amplifier XE, Chapter 7, and perf, Chapter 8. Finally, the last section explains how the PMU can be used for isolating performance problems.

6.1 PMU

As mentioned earlier, modern hardware platforms are far too complex for developers to accurately estimate how their code will execute. Performance counters serve to eliminate that imprecise guesswork, providing engineers with a method for querying low-level processor metrics in order to identify performance issues.

To expose this functionality, each core has its own dedicated PMU, for collecting data local to that core. Additionally, an uncore PMU, for collecting data related to resources shared between the cores, may be available.

The low-level processor metrics exposed through the PMU are referred to as *events*. Events can be categorized as either architectural or nonarchitectural. *Architectural events* maintain consistent behavior between processor generations. On the other hand, *nonarchitectural events* are specific to a microarchitecture, and therefore their behavior can change between processor generations. A full list of events, both architectural and nonarchitectural, can be found in Volume 3, Chapter 19 of the Intel® *Software Developer Manual* (SDM). When looking up nonarchitectural events, make sure to only use events listed in the tables corresponding to the correct processor generation.

Some events are suffixed with .CORE or .THREAD. The distinction between these two suffixes is that events ending with .THREAD count at the hardware thread granularity, that is, per logical core. On the other hand, events ending with .CORE count at the physical core granularity, including one or more hardware threads.

While architectural events are guaranteed to have consistent behavior between microarchitectures, that does not mean that all processors will support all of the predefined events. The architectural events supported by the current processor can be enumerated with CPUID, specifically the Architectural Performance Monitoring

Leaf, *EAX* = 0x0A. In this leaf, each bit in the *EBX* register corresponds to a specific architectural event. If that bit is set, then the respective architectural event is not supported. Bits 24 through 31 of the *EAX* register contains the number of nonreserved bits in *EBX*, that is, bits that are valid to check.

The collection methodology for both event types can be categorized as either counting or sampling. The first method, counting, simply measures how many times the given event occurs. As shown in Section 6.1.2, this is especially useful for calculating the ratios and metrics that help identify what performance issues are responsible for performance degradation. The second method, sampling, only measures some of the total events, that is, a sample, but focuses on correlating those events with other information that helps identify what instructions are responsible for generating that event.

6.1.1 EVENT COUNTERS

In Linux, most users of performance counters will not directly program the event counters. Instead, most will use the kernel's performance event counter interface or the Intel VTune interface. However, as performance counters are unportable by nature, the design of these interfaces must be flexible enough to allow for advanced microarchitecture-specific usages. As a result of this tightly coupled nature between the interface and hardware, an understanding of the formats and techniques for utilizing the PMU will aid in advanced profiling. As an example, the format used for configuring the event counters is the same format expected by the perf counter's interface for handling raw events.

There are two different types of event counters, fixed-function and programmable. Both of these types are controlled via a series of MSRs, although their formats are slightly different.

Each fixed-function counter is reserved for a specific architectural event. The number of these counters per core can be enumerated with CPUID, specifically the Architectural Performance Monitoring Leaf. The bits 0 through 4 of the *EDX* register in this leaf contains the number of fixed-function counters. The bits 5 through 12 contain the bit width of the counter.

At the time of this writing, there are currently three fixed-function counters. The first counter, IA32_FIXED_CTR0, records the number of instructions retired. The second counter, IA32_FIXED_CTR1, records the number of unhalted core cycles. The third counter, IA32_FIXED_CTR2, records the number of unhalted reference cycles.

Unlike the fixed-function counters, which only measure one event each, programmable event counters can select from a large number of different events. Events are identified through an event number and unit mask (umask). The event number chooses the logic unit that performs the actual counting. The unit mask configures the conditions that are counted. For instance, an event number of 0x3C selects the logic unit that counts cycles. Specifying an umask of 0 instructs the logic unit to count unhalted core cycles, whereas specifying an umask of 1 instructs the logic unit to count reference cycles.

Aside from these fields, there are a number of bits that control the behavior of the event. All of these fields are combined according to the format for the IA32_PERFEVTSELx MSR, where *x* represents an integer specifying which counter to modify. Figure 6.1 illustrates this MSR format.

The user mode, USR, and operating system mode, OS, bits control whether collection occurs while the hardware is operating in rings one through three, and ring zero, respectively. In Linux, the kernel runs in ring zero, while user space runs in ring three. Rings one and two aren't currently used. In other words, these bits control whether data collection includes only kernel space, only user space, or both kernel and user space.

The edge detect bit, E, modifies the collection of the logic unit in order to collect data relative to the boundary conditions of the event. Events that support this bit, along with its exact meaning for that event, are documented in the comment section of the relevant SDM documentation. For instance, the Fourth Generation Intel® Core™ processor family supports the event CPL_CYCLES.RING0, which counts the number of unhalted core cycles while the hardware is operating in ring zero. Setting the edge detect bit for this event changes the collection to instead count the number of transitions into ring zero.

The enabled bit, EN, controls whether the current performance counter is enabled or disabled. If set, the counter is enabled. If not set, the counter is disabled.

The APIC interrupt enable bit, INT, controls whether an interrupt is generated through the local APIC to signal counter overflows. This enables sampling, where the counter overflow interrupt handler records the requested information about the execution state that caused the last event. In order to set the sampling frequency, that is, how many events should occur before an interrupt is generated, the counter is initialized so that adding the desired number of events will overflow the counter. One important consideration when selecting the sampling frequency is the tradeoff between generating too few interrupts, leading to an insufficient sampling, and generating too many interrupts, causing excessive overhead.

Because of the overhead for processing an interrupt, the instruction which raised the interrupt may have already finished executing. Thus, the wrong instruction is held responsible for the event generated. This phenomenon is referred to as *skid*. As a general rule of thumb, events that are counted closer to retirement have smaller skids than events that are counted earlier in the CPU pipeline.

To reduce skid, modern Intel Architectures support Precise Event Based Sampling (PEBS). With PEBS enabled, the software provides a memory buffer for storing extra event information. When events are generated, a PEBS record is created with the precise accounting data, reducing skid. Not all performance events support PEBS.

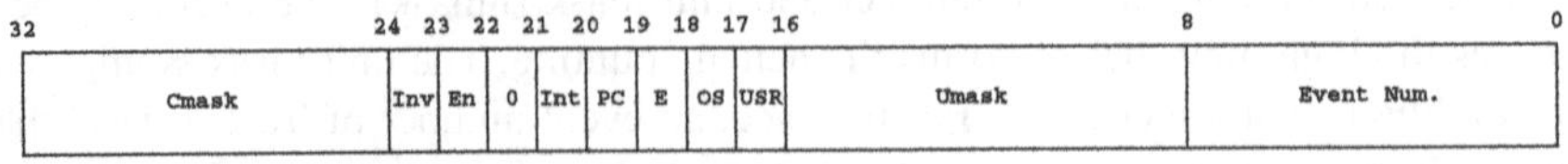

FIGURE 6.1

IA32_PERFEVTSELx MSRS (Intel Corporation, 2013).

Note that on modern Intel platforms, there are three fixed-function event counters and eight programmable event counters; however, these eight programmable counters are per-core, and thus must be shared between hardware threads. In other words, when Intel® Hyper-Threading is disabled, there are eight programmable counters, and when Hyper-Threading is enabled, each hardware thread has access to four of the eight counters. Therefore, most of the time a maximum of seven events can be monitored at any given time, assuming all three fixed-function events are desired. This needs to be accounted for when determining which events to collect. Due to the limited number of event counters, larger numbers of events can only be collected by rotating the enabled counters, and then scaling the results to estimate the total counts.

6.1.2 USING EVENT COUNTERS

As seen in the previous sections, the PMU provides access to a significant number of performance events. However, in order to successfully conduct performance analysis, these events must be wielded correctly. To do so requires focus on two key aspects, collecting the correct data and interpreting that data correctly. Failure to do either will lead to wasted time and effort.

The first step of microarchitectural performance analysis, assuming that the workload is CPU bound, is to determine what inefficiency or stall is impacting performance. In order to accomplish this, the Top-Down Hierarchical approach is used to categorize productive and unproductive clock cycles. This approach supplies metrics to quantify the impact of the various architectural issues. These metrics are derived from the performance counters described above. Since this first step focuses on determining what bottleneck is limiting performance, and is less concerned with what code is responsible for the bottleneck, this is the time for counting events, rather than sampling them.

Note that these metrics are typically ratios of multiple events. Single event counts typically have little meaning in a standalone context. Instead, their usefulness comes from their relation to the other collected metrics. For instance, stating the number of branches executed during a code sequence doesn't provide much insight. On the other hand, stating the number of branches executed in relation to the number of correctly predicted branches, or in relation to the total number of instructions executed, does provide insight. As such, it's important that all of elements used to calculate these metrics are collected together and are not stitched together from multiple profiling sessions.

Once the bottleneck has been discovered, the next step is to correlate that bottleneck to specific code. This code then becomes the target for the optimization efforts, with the exact optimizations attempted dependent upon the type of bottleneck. For this stage, events are sampled rather than counted. Each sample attributes the event to a specific instruction, although this instruction may not be the exact instruction responsible due to skid. As samples are collected, the number of times an instruction is counted estimates how responsible the given instruction is for the total number of events. Logically, the optimizations should then focus on the code that was the most responsible.

6.2 TOP-DOWN HIERARCHICAL ANALYSIS

Top-Down Hierarchical analysis is a technique, developed by Intel, for using PMU events to decompose the flow of μops, in order to identify what pipeline stalls are affecting the overall pipeline efficiency. Each level within this hierarchy partitions the execution pipeline into a group of categories. Each category then has zero or more subcategories, which increase the level of detail for further investigating the parent category. It is important to note that when the level of detail increases, by moving to lower levels within the hierarchy, the level of error also typically increases. Intel provides a series of formulas that use the PMU event counts to calculate the percentage of μops attributed to each category. These formulas can be found in Figures 6.2–6.7.

This approach scales across multiple levels of granularity. For instance, this technique can be used over an entire application, by function, and so on.

Starting at the first level, that is, the very top of the hierarchy, μops are divided into four distinct categories. These categories partition the execution pipeline based on the μop flow through a pipeline slot. A *pipeline slot* is an abstraction of the various resources, which vary according to microarchitecture, required for a μop to pass through the execution pipeline. The number of pipeline slots, also known as the width of the pipeline, controls the number of μops that can allocate and the number of μops that can retire in one clock cycle. At the time of this writing, a width of four is common.

The Front End of the execution pipeline is responsible for fetching and decoding instructions from the instruction cache or memory. The act of delivering a μop from the Front End to the Back End, in order to begin execution, is referred to as *allocation*. Allocation marks the entry of the μop into one of the pipeline slots. As the execution of the μop in the Back End completes, its removal from the pipeline slot is referred to as *retirement*. Since one instruction can be comprised of multiple μops, an instruction isn't retired until all of its μops have retired.

The four categories, at the very top of the Top-Down hierarchy, are organized based on whether a μop was allocated. If a μop was not allocated, there are two possible categories, which determine whether the Front End or Back End was responsible for the stall. The first category, *Front End Bound*, corresponds to stalls during the instruction fetch and decode phases. In other words, the Front End couldn't keep up with the Back End. The second category, *Back End Bound*, corresponds to stalls where the fetch and decode occurred without incident, but the Back End was unable to accept the new μop. In other words, the Back End couldn't keep up with the incoming μops from the Front End.

On the other hand, if a μop was successfully allocated, the next question is whether that μop retired, leading to two additional categories. The first category, *Bad Speculation*, corresponds to the situation where a μop was successfully allocated but was associated with a branch mispredict. As a result, the μop was removed from the pipeline without retiring. The second category, *Retiring*, corresponds to the ideal situation, where the μop is successfully allocated and then successfully retired.

Notice that three of the four categories, Bad Speculation, Front End Bound, and Back End Bound, all sound fairly ominous. Each of these categories represent stalls within the CPU pipeline, that is, unproductive cycles. Therefore, the percentage attributed to these categories are a less-is-better metric. On the other hand, the fourth category, Retiring, represents forward progress in the CPU pipeline, that is productive cycles. Therefore, the percentage attributed to the Retiring category is a higher-is-better metric.

The formulas for calculating the percentages attributed to each category are shown in Figure 6.2. The variables at the top of this figure, excluding W, are the PMU events required for the analysis. The `IDQ_UOPS_NOT_DELIVERED.CORE` event is a nonarchitectural event introduced in the Second Generation Intel® Core™ processor family. As a result, this analysis type requires a processor based on the Second Generation Intel Core microarchitecture or newer.

Since the pipeline width represents the number of μops that can be allocated per cycle, the denominator in each of these equations, the pipeline width times the total number of cycles, represents the theoretical maximum number of μops that could be allocated. Ideally, as shown in Equation 6.2(c), the number of retired μops would equal this theoretical maximum.

Once these metrics have been calculated, the next steps depend on which category dominates the results. Obviously, it is beneficial to first focus on the three categories that represent unproductive cycles. While a high retiring percentage indicates efficient pipeline utilization, it doesn't necessarily mean that further performance can't be obtained.

$$D = \text{IDQ\_UOPS\_NOT\_DELIVERED.CORE}$$
$$M = \text{INT\_MISC.RECOVERY\_CYCLES}$$
$$N = W \times \text{CPU\_CLK\_UNHALTED.THREAD}$$
$$R = \text{UOPS\_RETIRED.RETIRE\_SLOTS}$$
$$U = \text{UOPS\_ISSUED.ANY}$$
$$W = \text{pipeline width}$$

$$\text{P\_FE} = \% \text{ Front End Bound} \qquad\qquad = \frac{D}{N} \times 100 \qquad (6.2a)$$

$$\text{P\_BS} = \% \text{ Bad Speculation} \qquad = \frac{(U - R + (W \times M))}{N} \times 100 \qquad (6.2b)$$

$$\text{P\_R} = \% \text{ Retiring} \qquad\qquad = \frac{R}{N} \times 100 \qquad (6.2c)$$

$$\text{P\_BE} = \% \text{ Back End Bound} \qquad = 100 - (\text{P\_BS} + \text{P\_FE} + \text{P\_R}) \qquad (6.2d)$$

FIGURE 6.2

Equations for decomposing μops (Intel Corporation, 2014).

6.2.1 FRONT END BOUND

As mentioned earlier, the Front End of the CPU pipeline is responsible for fetching instructions, decoding these instructions into one or more μops, and then finally delivering these μops to the Back End for execution. The general rule of thumb is to only focus on the Front End Bound category when the percentage is above 30% (Intel Corporation, 2014).

Instructions are fetched and decoded via the Legacy Decoder Pipeline, often referred to as the MITE. The MITE is responsible for fetching instructions from memory and decoding them into μops. These instruction fetches occur in 16-byte chunks. A dedicated instruction cache, the ICache, and TLB, the ITLB, are used to reduce the overhead of memory accesses. In older processor generations, the L1 cache was used for both instructions and data; however, modern Intel processors now provide separate L1 caches for each.

Once the instructions have been fetched, they must now be decoded. This is handled by a series of decoding units. Each decoding unit is capable of generating a certain number of μops each cycle. In the case where an instruction generates more μops than the selected decoding unit can generate, the instruction will require multiple cycles to decode. Once the instructions have been decoded into the appropriate μops, those μops are output to the μop queue, to await execution. Additionally, starting with the Second Generation Intel Core microarchitecture, the μops will also be added to the Decoded ICache.

The Decoded ICache, often referred to as the DSB, caches the results of the Legacy Decode Pipeline. This caching occurs in 32 byte chunks of instructions, which are indexed by the instruction pointer. There are various architectural restrictions on what instruction sequences can be cached. For example, on the Second Generation Intel Core microarchitecture, only two branches are allowed per entry and a maximum of 19 μops.

Before the MITE is invoked, the DSB is searched for the given instruction chunk, based on the address to fetch. If found within the cache, the fetch and decode phases are skipped, and the μops are delivered into the μop queue directly from the DSB cache. If not found, the MITE performs the fetch and decode, and then attempts to add the results to the cache.

In the formula for Front End Bound, shown in Equation 6.2(a), the IDQ_UOPS_NOT_DELIVERED.CORE event is compared against the theoretical maximum of μops. IDQ stands for the Instruction Decoder Queue, which is from where μops are allocated. In other words, this event measures the number of times where the maximum number of μops was not delivered from the IDQ for allocation. As a result, the P_FE metric is the percentage of pipeline stalls caused by issues during the fetching or decoding of instructions.

Once the Front End Bound category has been identified as having a significant impact on pipeline efficiency, it is time to explore additional metrics, which increase the level of detail with regards to the Front End. There metrics can be found in Figure 6.3.

$$D = \text{IDQ.DSB\_UOPS}$$
$$I = \text{INST\_RETIRED.ANY}$$
$$M = \text{ICACHE.MISSES}$$
$$S = \text{IDQ.MS\_UOPS}$$
$$T = \text{IDQ.MITE\_UOPS}$$
$$U = D + S + T$$

$$\% \ \mu ops \text{ from Decoded ICache} = \frac{D}{U} \times 100 \qquad (6.3a)$$

$$\% \ \mu ops \text{ from Legacy Decoder Pipeline} = \frac{T}{U} \times 100 \qquad (6.3b)$$

$$\% \ \mu ops \text{ from Microcode Sequencer} = \frac{S}{U} \times 100 \qquad (6.3c)$$

$$\% \ \text{ICache Misses} = \frac{M}{I} \times 100 \qquad (6.3d)$$

FIGURE 6.3

Front End Bound μop decomposition (Intel Corporation, 2014).

It may be enlightening to decompose the μop delivery by their source. Use Equations 6.3(a)–6.3(c) to determine the percentage of μops delivered from the DSB, MITE, and Microcode Sequencer, respectively. The Microcode Sequencer is used to handle special instructions and situations, which the MITE is unable to handle, that is, it is a software fallback for functionality that isn't implemented in hardware. As a result, the Microcode Sequencer is capable of generating a large number of μops.

When interpreting these metrics, a low percentage of delivery from the Microcode Sequencer and a high percentage of delivery from the Decoded ICache is desirable. The Microcode Sequencer is required for delivering certain instructions, so determine what instructions or situation is responsible, and try to avoid them. Each microarchitecture has a series of hardware limitations for the Decoded ICache, so a low percentage of DSB delivery may indicate less than optimal code organization that is triggering one or more of these limitations.

Another metric to consider is the percentage of ICache misses, as shown in Equation 6.3(d). Even a small percentage of ICache misses can have serious repercussions for performance. Typically, ICache misses are the result of bloated code size or branch mispredictions. Common culprits for bloated code size include excessive loop unrolling, function inlining, and other optimizations that attempt to trade code size for speed.

Since most of these aspects are controlled via the compiler, it may be possible to alleviate this problem by altering the compiler flags. For example, at optimization level -02 GCC doesn't perform optimizations that can significantly bloat the code size; however, at optimization level -03 it does. Compiler optimizations and flags will be discussed in further detail in Chapter 12.

6.2.2 BACK END BOUND

After allocation of a μop by the Front End, the Back End is responsible for executing the μop until it retires. The Back End Bound metric represents the situations where the Front End was able to allocate the maximum number of μops, but the Back End was unable to accept one or more. This is caused by stalls within the Back End that consume resources that would otherwise be needed for the μop to begin execution.

These types of stalls can be further divided into two categories. The first category, memory stalls, occur when the execution unit is waiting for a memory resource to become available. The second category, execution stalls, occurs due to issues within the execution pipeline.

The equations in Figure 6.4 provide the percentage of Back End stalls caused by each of these categories.

One of the longstanding challenges in quantifying the impact of memory accesses is accounting for out-of-order execution. This is because the execution pipeline may be able to mask some memory latencies by scheduling other μops until those memory resources are available. The `CYCLE_ACTIVITY.STALLS_LDM_PENDING` PMU event is designed to only count memory accesses whose latencies could not be masked. This event was added in the Third Generation Intel® Core™ microarchitecture, so these, and newer, processors are capable of a more accurate memory analysis than the Second Generation Intel Core processor family.

Once these metrics have identified what issues are contributing to the Back End Bound category, another increase in detail is possible.

Memory bound

As the name implies, the Memory Bound category quantifies the percentage of cycles the execution pipeline is stalled awaiting data loads. As a result of this stall, the maximum number of μops was unable to be allocated. When the Back End Bound

$$C = \text{CPU\_CLK\_UNHALTED.THREAD}$$
$$E = \text{CYCLE\_ACTIVITY.CYCLES\_NO\_EXECUTE}$$
$$S = \text{CYCLE\_ACTIVITY.STALLS\_LDM\_PENDING}$$
$$U1 = \text{UOPS\_EXECUTED.THREAD:c1}$$
$$U2 = \text{UOPS\_EXECUTED.THREAD:c2}$$

$$\% \text{ EXE} = \frac{E + U1 - U2}{C} \times 100 \qquad (6.4\text{a})$$

$$\% \text{ Memory Bound} = \frac{S}{C} \times 100 \qquad (6.4\text{b})$$

$$\% \text{ Core Bound} = \% \text{ EXE} - \% \text{ Memory Bound} \qquad (6.4\text{c})$$

FIGURE 6.4

Back End Bound μop decomposition (Intel Corporation, 2014).

category represents a significant share of pipeline stalls, and the Memory Bound category is flagged as the underlying cause for the Back End Bound stalls, there are two optimizations available. The first is to correlate these events to a specific algorithm, or related data structure, and then work to reduce that algorithm or data structure's total memory consumption. The second is to reorganize the relevant data structure to better utilize the processor's cache. Cache misses can also be caused by the processor entering a deep sleep that power-gates the processor's caches. As a result, after exiting this sleep state the cache will be cold. Another cause for cache misses can be the operating system scheduler migrating the process to a different processor. Chapter 14 provides more information on optimizing for cache efficiency.

Increasing the level of detail on the Memory Bound category divides memory stalls by their level in the memory hierarchy. For more information on the memory hierarchy, see Section 14.1. Figure 6.5 provides the equations for calculating the percentage of stalls at each level of the hierarchy.

Notice that in Equations 6.5(c) and 6.5(d), the variables M and N are estimations that utilize the L3 cache latency ratio, variable W. This is required because there is no equivalent STALLS_L3_PENDING PMU event. For the Third Generation Intel Core microarchitecture, the recommended value for W is 7 (Intel Corporation, 2014).

$$C = \text{CPU\_CLK\_UNHALTED.THREAD}$$
$$H = \text{MEM\_LOAD\_UOPS\_RETIRED.LLC\_HIT}$$
$$M = \frac{W \times R}{H + R}$$
$$N = \frac{H}{H + W \times R}$$
$$O = \text{CYCLE\_ACTIVITY.STALLS\_L1D\_PENDING}$$
$$R = \text{MEM\_LOAD\_UOPS\_MISC\_RETIRED.LLC\_MISS}$$
$$S = \text{CYCLE\_ACTIVITY.STALLS\_LDM\_PENDING}$$
$$T = \text{CYCLE\_ACTIVITY.STALLS\_L2\_PENDING}$$
$$W = \text{L3 cache latency ratio}$$

$$\% \text{ L1 Bound} = \frac{S - O}{C} \times 100 \tag{6.5a}$$
$$\% \text{ L2 Bound} = \frac{O - T}{C} \times 100 \tag{6.5b}$$
$$\% \text{ L3 Bound} = \frac{T \times N}{C} \times 100 \tag{6.5c}$$
$$\% \text{ Memory Bound} = \frac{T \times M}{C} \times 100 \tag{6.5d}$$

FIGURE 6.5

Memory Bound cache level decomposition (Intel Corporation, 2014).

A high percentage in the L2, L3, or Memory Bound categories suggests that cache isn't being utilized very effectively. A high percentage in the L1 Bound category suggests that too many memory loads and stores are occurring.

Core bound

The Core Bound category quantifies the percentage of cycles the execution pipeline is stalled. These stalls are often caused by μops within the pipeline taking a long time to retire, and thereby tying up resources.

Figure 6.6 provides the formulas for attempting to determine what resources in the execution pipeline are overutilized.

Equation 6.6(a) calculates the total percentage of cycles where a Back End resource over-utilization prevented a μop from beginning to execute. If this percentage is significant, then Equations 6.6(b)–6.6(f), will further decompose the resource stalls by individual execution resources. If any of these percentages are significant, look at rewriting the code to avoid overutilizing the associated resource.

Equations 6.6(c) and 6.6(b) represent the percentage of cycles where a load or store was ready to be allocated, but all of the pipeline load or store buffers were already being used, that is, the μop could not be allocated until one of the existing loads or stores completes. Equation 6.6(d) represents the percentage of cycles where a new branching μop could not be allocated because the Branch Order Buffer was full.

$$A = \text{RESOURCE\_STALLS.ANY}$$
$$B = \text{RESOURCE\_STALLS2.BOB}$$
$$C = \text{CPU\_CLK\_UNHALTED.THREAD}$$
$$L = \text{RESOURCE\_STALLS.LB}$$
$$O = \text{RESOURCE\_STALLS.ROB}$$
$$R = \text{RESOURCE\_STALLS.RS}$$
$$S = \text{RESOURCE\_STALLS.SB}$$

$$\% \text{ Resource Stalls} = \frac{A}{C} \times 100 \qquad (6.6a)$$

$$\% \text{ Stalled Store } \mu op = \frac{S}{C} \times 100 \qquad (6.6b)$$

$$\% \text{ Stalled Load } \mu op = \frac{L}{C} \times 100 \qquad (6.6c)$$

$$\% \text{ Stalled Branch } \mu op = \frac{B}{C} \times 100 \qquad (6.6d)$$

$$\% \text{ Reservation Station Full} = \frac{R}{C} \times 100 \qquad (6.6e)$$

$$\% \text{ Reorder Buffer Full} = \frac{O}{C} \times 100 \qquad (6.6f)$$

FIGURE 6.6

Core Bound cycle decomposition (Intel Corporation, 2014).

Equations 6.6(e) and 6.6(f) represent the percentage of cycles where a μop could not be allocated because either the Reservation Station or Reorder buffer were full. The Reservation Station is the buffer in which μops are stored until their resources are loaded and one of the appropriate execution units becomes available. The Reorder buffer is used to store a μop until its associated instruction is scheduled to retire. Instruction retirement occurs in the same order as the program requested, and at this point all of the μops effects are made visible external to the execution pipeline. In other words, the Reorder buffer is used to ensure that out-of-order execution occurs transparently to the developer.

6.2.3 BAD SPECULATION

Unlike the case of the Front End and Back End Bound categories, in the Bad Speculation category μops are successfully allocated from the Front End to the Back End; however, these μops never retire. This is because those μops were being speculatively executed from a branch that was predicted incorrectly. As a result, all of the μops associated with instructions from the incorrect branch need to be flushed from the execution pipeline.

It is important to note that this category doesn't quantify the full performance impact of branch misprediction. Branch prediction also impacts the Front End Bound category, since the branch predictor is responsible for deciding which instructions to fetch.

Equation 6.7(a) in Figure 6.7 provides an estimate of the percentage of cycles wasted due to removing mispredicted μops from the execution pipeline. The branch misprediction penalty, variable P, is estimate at around 20 cycles (Intel Corporation, 2014).

Obviously, in the case of bad speculation, the culprit is branch mispredicts. The next step is to use sampling to determine which branches are responsible, and then work on improving their prediction. Chapter 13 goes into more detail on improving branch prediction.

6.2.4 RETIRE

Upon completion of execution, μops exit the pipeline slot, that is, they retire. Since a single instruction might consist of multiple μops, an instruction is retired only if all of

$$C = \text{CPU\_CLK\_UNHALTED.THREAD}$$
$$M = \text{BR\_MISP\_RETIRED.ALL\_BRANCHES\_PS}$$
$$P = \text{branch misprediction penalty}$$

$$\% \text{ Cycles Wasted} = \frac{P \times M}{C} \times 100 \qquad (6.7a)$$

FIGURE 6.7

Bad speculation cost (Intel Corporation, 2014).

its corresponding μops are ready for retirement in the Reorder buffer. Unlike the other three categories, the Retiring category represents forward progress with productive cycles, as opposed to stalls with unproductive cycles; however, just because the pipeline is operating efficiently doesn't mean that there isn't the possibility for further performance gains.

In this situation, improving performance should revolve around reducing the number of cycles required for the algorithm. There are a couple techniques for accomplishing this, such as algorithmic improvement, utilizing special purpose instructions, or through vectorization. Chapter 15 goes into more detail about vectorization and Chapter 16 introduces some helpful instructions designed to accelerate certain operations.

REFERENCES

Intel Corporation, 2013, 10. Intel 64 and IA-32 Architectures Software Developer's Manual. Computer Hardware Manual.

Intel Corporation, 2014, 10. Intel 64 and IA-32 Architectures Optimization Reference Manual. Order Number: 248966-030.

Marusarz, J., Cepeda, S., Yasin, A., 2013, 05. How to Tune Applications Using a Top-Down Characterization of Microarchitectural Issues. https://software.intel.com/en-us/articles/how-to-tune-applications-using-a-top-down-characterization-of-microarchitectural-issues.

Yasin, A., 2014, March, A top-down method for performance analysis and counters architecture. 2014 IEEE International Symposium on Performance Analysis of Systems and Software (ISPASS), pp. 35–44.

Intel® VTune™ Amplifier XE

CHAPTER CONTENTS

Intel® VTune™ Amplifier XE is a powerful cross-platform profiler capable of performing algorithmic analysis, PMU sampling, and power analysis. The tool is comprised of a few different components, including a set of Linux kernel drivers, which are responsible for performing the actual data collection, as well as both command-line and GUI tools for controlling the drivers and generating reports.

By default, VTune installs a significant amount of documentation into `${VTUNE_INSTALL}/documentation`. This includes detailed walkthroughs and guides for collecting data and analyzing the result. Additionally, the documentation also provides a series of reference documents, including a reference of event metrics and their meanings, as well as a copy of the second volume of the Intel® *Software Developer Manual*, listing all of the instructions and their encodings.

Once installed, updates to VTune are conducted through the Intel® Software Manager, which is typically installed to `/opt/intel/ism`. Through this Java application it is possible to download and install updates to all Intel software products as soon as they are released. Typically, VTune releases are grouped into optional and recommended updates. Optional updates occur more frequently and provide earlier access to new features. On the other hand, recommended updates occur less frequently, and combine all of the previous optional updates. As a result, the

119

optional updates are designed for users interested in the latest functionality, while recommended updates are designed for users interested in only updating occasionally.

At the time of this writing, a VTune license for noncommercial use on Linux can be obtained for free. For more information about both the tool and the commercial and noncommercial licensing, visit the VTune website at https://software.intel.com/en-us/intel-vtune-amplifier-xe.

7.1 INSTALLATION AND CONFIGURATION

VTune provides its own out-of-tree Linux kernel drivers for collecting system information and programming the PMU. The source code for these drivers is shipped with VTune and can be found in the `${VTUNE_INSTALL}/sepdk/` directory. This allows for the driver modules to be built for the system's current kernel version.

As part of the default installation process, the installation script will automatically build the driver modules and will install an init script that inserts the modules into the kernel at boot. One or both of these steps can be skipped during the installation by selecting to customize the installation and then deselecting the desired steps. In order to be as portable across as many distributions as possible, the init script generated is designed to be compatible with the legacy sysv init system. Modern init systems, such as `systemd`, provide backward compatibility with these old style scripts, and therefore work as well.

There are three driver modules that must be loaded before collection can begin. The first module, `pax`, handles multiplexing a single PMU between multiple processes. This driver creates a `pax` special device file in `/dev/pax`. Each VTune process that needs to access the PMU will first open this device file and use its `ioctl(2)` interface to reserve and unreserve the PMU for the given process. This locking mechanism prevents one process from interfering with the profiling of another.

The second module, `sep`, handles the actual PMU event programming. It is often referenced as `sepX_Y`, where X and Y represent the major and minor driver version numbers. The `sep` driver provides its own APIC interrupt handler for handling PMU events and also handles all of the architectural-specific aspects of programming events and configuring the system for profiling. This driver creates a directory, `/dev/sepX_Y/`, where a special device file is created per-cpu for sampling. For example:

```
$ ls /dev/sep3_15/
c%  m%  s0% s1% s2% s3% s4% s5% s6% s7%
```

The third module, `vtsspp`, is responsible for monitoring process execution. This driver records the specifics of the process being monitored, such as the stack traces, the registers, and so on. This information is then correlated with the information from the PMU interrupts in order to attribute PMU events to ELF files, functions, and lines of code. This driver exposes a configuration directory within the proc filesystem. For instance:

```
$ ls -alh /proc/vtsspp
total 0
dr-xr-xr-x.   2 root vtune 0 Sep 12 23:08 ./
dr-xr-xr-x. 211 root root  0 Sep 12 21:56 ../
-rw-rw-rw-.   1 root vtune 0 Sep 12 23:17 .control
-rw-rw-rw-.   1 root vtune 0 Sep 12 23:17 .cpu_mask
-rw-rw-rw-.   1 root vtune 0 Sep 12 23:17 .debug
-rw-rw-rw-.   1 root vtune 0 Sep 12 23:17 .def_sav
-rw-rw-rw-.   1 root vtune 0 Sep 12 23:17 .targets
-rw-rw-rw-.   1 root vtune 0 Sep 12 23:17 .time_limit
-rw-rw-rw-.   1 root vtune 0 Sep 12 23:17 .time_source
```

In earlier versions of VTune, there was also a fourth driver, `apwr.ko`, which was part of the powerdk, as opposed to the sepdk, to which the other three drivers belong. This driver was used for measuring some power metrics, but was recently removed due to lack of usage. If the reader depends on this driver, the author recommends contacting Intel support.

7.1.1 BUILDING THE KERNEL MODULES

In order to build the three sepdk drivers manually, there is a script entitled `build-driver` located at `${VTUNE_INSTALL}/sepdk/src`. Before running this script, ensure that the proper development tools, including GCC, GNU make, and the kernel development package, are installed. Additionally, check the VTune release notes to determine whether the kernel version is supported. Typically VTune tracks the latest distros, such as Fedora, Ubuntu, and RHEL.

Running the `build-driver` script will build all three drivers, although there are also `build-driver` scripts within the `vtsspp` and `pax` subdirectories. By default, these scripts are all interactive, prompting the user for which compiler to use, the path to the kernel source tree, and where to install the results. The script can also be run noninteractively with the `--non-interactive` command-line argument. In non-interactive mode, the defaults for each option will be used, unless a different value is specified via command-line arguments. A full list of these arguments, such as `--c-compiler=`, `--kernel-src-dir=`, or `--install-dir`, can be obtained by running `build-driver --help`. In the case where the build fails on a newer kernel, contact Intel support.

Once the driver modules are successfully built, they can be manually inserted into the kernel, or the init system can be configured to automatically insert them at boot. In the same directory as the `build-driver` script, there is also a script named `boot-script`. This script will automatically generate an sysv-style init script and then add it to the default runlevel for the system.

Since the drivers are modules, it's simple to test if the boot script works. Simply reboot and then check whether the modules were automatically loaded. This can be done by checking the list of currently inserted modules and looking for the three belonging to the sepdk. For example:

```
$ lsmod | grep "pax\|sep\|vtsspp"
vtsspp              339319  0
sep3_15             522427  0
pax                  13093  0
```

7.1.2 SYSTEM CONFIGURATION

Due to the visibility into the system provided, access to these drivers is restricted to a specific group. This groups is typically named vtune, although that name can be overridden when creating the boot script. All user accounts that want to use VTune will need to be added to this group. The simplest method for determining the group name is to check the log generated by the kernel drivers as they are inserted. An example of this log is presented in Listing 7.1.

```
1  (aperion:/home/jtk) # systemctl status sep3_15 -l
2  sep3_15.service - LSB: loads/unloads the sep3_15 driver at boot/
                       shutdown time
3     Loaded: loaded (/etc/rc.d/init.d/sep3_15)
4     Active: active (exited) since Fri 2014-09-12 21:20:18 PDT; 23s ago
5    Process: 517 ExecStart=/etc/rc.d/init.d/sep3_15 start
              (code=exited, status=0/SUCCESS)
6
7  sep3_15[517]: Executing: insmod ./sep3_15-x32_64-3.11.10-301.fc20
                 .x86_64smp.ko
8  sep3_15[517]: Creating /dev/sep3_15 base devices with major number
                 244 ... done.
9  sep3_15[517]: Creating /dev/sep3_15 percpu devices with major number
                 243 ... done.
10 sep3_15[517]: Setting group ownership of devices to group "vtune"
                 ... done.
11 sep3_15[517]: Setting file permissions on devices to "666" ... done.
12 sep3_15[517]: The sep3_15 driver has been successfully loaded.
13 sep3_15[517]: Checking for vtsspp driver ... not detected.
14 sep3_15[517]: Executing: insmod ./vtsspp/vtsspp-x32_64-3.11.10-301.
                 fc20.x86_64smp.ko gid=1001 mode=0666
15 sep3_15[517]: The vtsspp driver has been successfully loaded.
16 systemd[1]: Started LSB: loads/unloads the sep3_15 driver at boot/
                 shutdown time.
```

LISTING 7.1

Log of Intel® VTune™ Amplifier XE modules loaded successfully.

Notice, on line 10 of this listing, that the group name is given as "vtune," the default. Therefore, any uses wishing to perform data collection with these drivers will need to be a member of the vtune group. For instance, in order to add a user, jtk, into the vtune group:

```
# groupmems -g vtune -l
# groupmems -g vtune -a jtk
# groupmems -g vtune -l
jtk
```

Remember that a user must completely log out of the system before any group updates take effect.

Additionally, data collection requires that the kernel's NMI watchdog and kernel pointer hiding functionality are disabled. The NMI, nonmaskable interrupt, watchdog timer programs a reoccurring APIC timer in order to detect if the kernel has become unresponsive. From the generation of the interrupt, the kernel has a certain time threshold to handle the interrupt. If this threshold is exceeded, the kernel is considered to be deadlocked, and the system is rebooted. Since the NMI watchdog uses the PMU to measure this threshold, it conflicts with any application that uses the PMU. This feature can be disabled either by adding nmi_watchdog=0 to the kernel boot command-line, by writing a zero character to the file /proc/sys/kernel/nmi_watchdog, or by setting the kernel.nmi_watchdog sysctl property to zero.

The kernel pointer hiding functionality controls how the kernel prints addresses, both in logs and system files. With this feature enabled, unless the user has the necessary privileges, all kernel pointer addresses are printed as NULL. This is designed to improve security by hiding the exact location of some of the kernel's data structures. At the same time, this makes it difficult to correlate the collected instruction pointers to kernel functions. This feature can be disabled either by setting the kernel.kptr_restrict sysctl property to zero, or by writing a zero character to the file /proc/sys/kernel/kptr_restrict. For example:

```
# echo 0 > /proc/sys/kernel/kptr_restrict
# grep  __do_page_fault /proc/kallsyms
ffffffff8164e780 t __do_page_fault
# echo 2 > /proc/sys/kernel/kptr_restrict
# grep  __do_page_fault /proc/kallsyms
0000000000000000 t __do_page_fault
```

The status of both of these features can quickly be queried with the sysctl command:

```
# sysctl -a | grep "nmi_watchdog\|kptr"
kernel.kptr_restrict = 0
kernel.nmi_watchdog = 0
```

The final step of configuration is to modify the system's environment variables to reflect the new binaries, man pages, and so on. This step is automated by the amplxe-vars.sh and amplxe-vars.csh scripts, which should be sourced in the shell's startup file. The amplxe-vars.sh script is designed for shells based on the POSIX sh shell, including the popular bash shell. The amplxe-vars.csh script is designed for shells based on the C shell, such as tcsh.

7.2 DATA COLLECTION AND REPORTING

Once the kernel drivers are installed and the system has been configured accordingly, data collection and reporting are now possible. There are two primary interfaces for interacting with the VTune data collection drivers, a command-line interface, amplxe-cl, and the GTK GUI, amplxe-gui. Both of these interfaces are fully functional, as typically the GUI just invokes the command-line interface for data collection anyway, although data reporting with the command-line interface is more Spartan and lacks the guidance the GUI provides when interpreting results.

For the graphical interface, all configurations are controlled through a XML project file, suffixed with .amplxeproj. When a new project is created, a dialog box prompts the user with the available configuration options. These results are saved into the project XML file and then utilized across each analysis session. Figure 7.1 is a screenshot of this dialog box. These configuration options can be changed at any time by right clicking on the project name within the Project Navigator window and selecting the Properties context menu item. Any change made to the project's configuration will not be reflected within the preexisting analyses until those results are reanalyzed. Within the GUI, this is performed by right-clicking on the analysis name in the Project Navigator window and selecting the Re-resolve action context menu item.

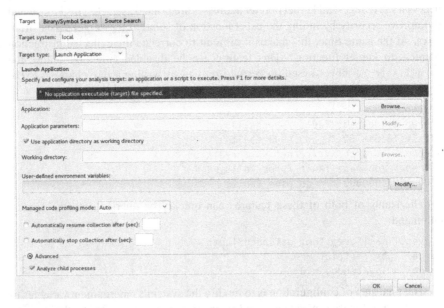

FIGURE 7.1

Intel® VTune™ Amplifier XE Project Configuration Dialog.

On the other hand, the command-line interface does *not* use the project files created by the GUI, nor does it create its own. Instead, each configuration option must be specified as a command-line argument. The author assumes this is because the command-line interface yields itself well to scripting, so any functionality provided by a project file can be replicated, with less effort, through the creation of a shell script.

The comprehensive list of available configuration options and their meanings can be found in either the VTune documentation, the man pages for each command, or through the `help` command built into the command-line tool. For example, executing `amplxe-cl -help` will list the available actions, while executing `amplxe-cl -help collect` will list all of the possible configuration options for that specific action.

At the time of this writing, there are eight actions available in the command line interface. For most profiling situations, knowledge of only two of these actions is necessary. These include the `collect` action, which performs the actual data collection, and the `report` action, which summarizes the data collected during the `collect` action in a human readable format.

7.2.1 COLLECT ACTION

The data collected is determined by the specified analysis type. In order to simplify data collection, VTune combines the basic building blocks of data collection into a high-level structure known as an analysis type. An *analysis type* is comprised of one or more data points, typically PMU events although other metrics are supported, along with "knobs" for controlling the behavior of the data collection. Through the use of analysis types, VTune simplifies the process of creating, running, and sharing complicated performance analyses.

VTune provides a set of predefined analysis types designed by Intel engineers to cover the most common profiling situations. Additionally, the user is free to create their own custom analysis types. Each analysis type is defined in an XML file. The predefined types are located at `${VTUNE_INSTALL}/config/analysis_type`, while the user's custom types are defined in `${HOME}/.intel/amplxe/analysis_type`.

Each analysis is categorized as either an algorithmic analysis or a microarchitectural analysis. In general, the algorithmic analyses are available for most x86 processors, while the microarchitectural analyses depend on features present in only some PMUs. As a result, the microarchitectural analyses are further divided into Intel hardware generations. Not all processor SKUs within a hardware generation support all of the PMU features required for every analysis within that generation's category. When performing microarchitectural analysis, the `general-exploration` analysis type is a good starting point, since it is designed to automatically perform the Top-Down profiling methodology described in Section 6.2.

The analysis type is a required argument for the command-line interface and should immediately follow the `-collect` argument. The last argument provided should be the command to profile. For instance, if the `bandwidth` analysis type was desired to be run on the executable `foo`, the command invocation, without any further configurations, would be `amplxe-cl -collect bandwidth foo`. Additionally, VTune is capable of attaching to an existing process. In lieu of providing the command to execute, the `-target-pid` or `-target-process` arguments specify the pid or name of the existing process to attach to.

Once the collection has completed, a results directory will be created. The name of this directory will be comprised of three separate components. The first component is the lower case letter "r." The second component is a three-digit number, representing the analysis number. Finally, the third component is an abbreviation of the analysis type. Continuing the previous example with the knowledge that the `bandwidth` analysis is abbreviated as `bw`, the first run would produce a directory named `r000bw`, the second run would produce a directory named `r001bw`, and so on.

In the graphical interface, data collection begins by right-clicking on the project name in the Project Navigator window and selecting the New Analysis context menu item, or by clicking on the menubar shortcut that resembles an orange triangle pointing to the right. This will then open a hierarchical list of the available analysis types and their subsequent configuration options. Figure 7.2 illustrates this window.

Notice that in the bottom right side of the window is a button labeled Command Line. Selecting this button will display the exact `amplxe-cl` command that will be executed. This can be used to determine how the GUI is performing some actions.

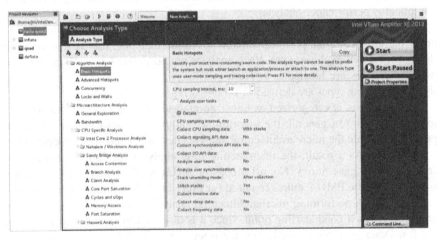

FIGURE 7.2

Intel® VTune™ Amplifier XE GUI analysis type selection.

Configuration

Between the `-collect` argument and the final argument, the application to profile, are the configuration options that control how the analysis occurs and is interpreted. In the graphical interface, all of these configuration items are set within the project properties.

Typically, the user wants to correlate data samples from memory addresses to lines of source code. In order for this to work properly, the user needs to specify where the source and binary files are located. The `-source-search-dir=dir` argument adds `dir` to the source search path. The `-search-dir=dir` argument adds `dir` to the binary search path. Both of these arguments may be duplicated as many times as necessary.

As discussed in Chapter 6, the PMU can only monitor a limited number of events simultaneously. As a result, there are a number of techniques for handling the situation where more events are specified to be collected than can be enabled simultaneously. In this situation, the set of events is partitioned into a series of subsets capable of being programmed together. If the program can execute only once, as is the case with the default VTune data collection, these subsets take turns being enabled on the PMU. The `-allow-multiple-runs` argument allows for the data collection to run multiple times, each time with a different subset of the events active. As a result, this option minimizes the error of multiplexing the events. Obviously for this to work correctly, the executable must be capable of executing repeatedly without user interaction between runs.

When profiling with sampling, it is necessary to determine an appropriate sampling frequency, that is, how frequently the PMU events should be collected. Some analysis types support a configuration option, referred to as a knob, that controls the sampling interval. This knob, `sampling-interval`, specifies the number of milliseconds between collections, ranging from 1 to 1000 ms. The default interval is 10 ms. Not all analysis types support the `sampling-interval` knob. This, along with other knobs supported by the analysis type, can be configured via the `-knob name=value` command-line argument. For example, in order to increase the sampling interval to 100 ms for an `advanced-hotspots` analysis type, the command would look like `amplxe-cl -collect advanced-hotspots -knob sampling-interval=100`.

In order to simplify the configuration of the sampling interval, VTune also exposes a `-target-duration-type=category` command-line argument. This argument is supported for all analysis types, regardless of whether they support the `sampling-interval` knob. Rather than specifying an exact interval, the user categorizes the estimated duration of the application's execution. Based on this category, VTune automatically configures the internal collection intervals. There are four duration categories. The first category, `veryshort`, specifies that the program execution is shorter than 1 min. The second category, `short`, specifies that the program execution is longer than 1 min, but shorter than 15 min. This category is the default. The third category, `medium`, specifies that the program execution is longer than 15 min, but shorter than 3 h. The fourth category, `long`, specifies that the program execution is longer than 3 h. For example, rather than worrying about specifying the exact sampling interval, selecting the proper sampling interval for an advanced-hotspots analysis on an application that takes 5 min to run is as simple as specifying `amplxe-cl -collect advanced-hotspots -target-duration-type=short`.

The default data collection configuration only monitors the process given on the command-line. For some cases, this is acceptable, but for other cases a more global view of the system is required. In this case, the `-analyze-system` argument expands data collection to every process on the system. This argument can be combined with a nop executable, like `sleep(1)`, in order to ascertain which processes on the system are consuming CPU time. Additionally, VTune supports a `-duration=nsec` argument that essentially does the same thing. In other words, `amplxe-cl -collect bandwidth -analyze-system sleep 15` is essentially the same as `amplxe-cl -collect bandwidth -analyze-system -duration 15`.

The `-call-stack-mode=mode` argument filters which functions should appear in the stack traces. There are three valid values for `mode`. The first mode, `user-only`, only records functions present within the profiled executable. As a result, kernel functions won't appear in the trace. This is the default mode. The second mode, `user-plus-one`, records all of the functions that would be recorded in `user-only` mode, but also any kernel functions directly invoked by the application. As a result, this mode shows where the call stack invokes the kernel, but filters out any of the internal kernel function call chains. The third mode, `all`, records all functions, both within the application and the kernel.

Additionally, inlined functions can be included within the call stack via the `-inline-mode=on`, or excluded via `-inline-mode=off`, command line argument.

By default, all data collection is performed on the local system; however, VTune also supports remote data collection over the SSH and ADB (Android Debug Bridge) protocols. At the time of this writing, the ADB protocol is only supported in the version of VTune provided with Intel® System Studio. With remote data collection, the `collect` action will be specified on the host system, the data will be collected on the remote system, and then the results will be copied back to the host system for local analysis.

In order for remote data collection to work, the data collection kernel modules that were described in Section 7.1 must be installed and enabled on the remote system. When profiling a remote embedded device, it's probably easier to build the data collection drivers on the host system, and then add them into the system image that will be provisioned on the device. Additionally, in order to fit within size constraints, it is possible to skip the installation of the graphical interface tools and libraries. Within the VTune install tarball, there is a directory named `CLI_Install`. This directory contains the install scripts and files required for a minimal installation, consisting of only the command-line tools and data collection drivers. These files can either be installed directly into the system image for the remote device before provisioning, or physically copied onto the remote device and installed manually.

Once the remote system is configured for data collection, and for the remote protocol, data collection can begin on the host system by specifying the protocol, username, and hostname or IP address of the remote system via the `-target-system` argument. For SSH, the argument is formatted as `ssh:user@hostname`. For ADB, the argument is formatted as `android:devicename`.

7.2.2 FINALIZE ACTION

Once data collection has finished, there is an intermediate step required before the results can be translated into a human readable report. First, the results must be finalized or, in the parlance of the GUI, resolved.

During this stage, the raw data that was collected is cooked, attributing data samples to specific ELF symbols and calculating the associated metrics for the report phase. Typically, this step is automatically run at the end of the `collect` action, unless the `-no-auto-finalize` argument was provided. Regardless, there are situations where it may be desirable to refinalize the results manually. The most common of these situations is the case where the previous finalization did not have the proper symbol information, leading to a less than optimal report.

Because finalization typically happens automatically after the `collect` action, most of the `collect` arguments relating to correlating or reporting data are also supported by the `finalize` command. These include the `-search-dir` and `-source-search-dir` commands for choosing the source and binary files for analysis. Additionally, arguments like `-inline-mode` and `-call-stack-mode` can be selected in order to further filter the data results.

The `-result-dir` argument specifies the result directory to finalize. If this argument is omitted, the latest result is selected. For example, if the result `r000bw` needed to be refinalized to add the source directory `foo/src`, the command would look like `amplxe-cl -finalize -result-dir r000bw -source-search-dir foo/src`.

7.2.3 REPORT ACTION

Once the results have been collected and finalized, they are ready to be converted into a human readable format. While reporting is an area where the graphical interface really excels with advanced features, both the graphical and command-line interfaces are sufficient for conducting analysis on results.

Command-line interface

With the command-line interface, the various result metrics are viewed with text reports. Each of these reports utilize a predefined set of metrics, and therefore are only useful when applied to the results of an analysis type that collects those metrics. Just like the `finalize` command, a specific result can be specified with the `-result-dir` argument. If multiple `-result-dir` arguments are present, the results are compared, and each report, along with their deltas, are reported. The reports that ship with VTune can be found in `${VTUNE_INSTALL}/config/report`, and custom user reports can be created in `${HOME}/.intel/amplxe/report`. The list of currently available reports can be found with the built-in help command, as seen in Listing 7.2.

```
$ amplxe-cl -help report | tail -n 12
Available Reports:

    callstacks              Display CPU or wait time for callstacks.
    frequency-analysis      Display CPU frequency scaling time.
    gprof-cc                Display CPU or wait time in the
                            gprof-like format.
    gpu-computing-tasks     Display GPU computing tasks.
    hotspots                Display CPU time.
    hw-events               Display hardware events.
    sleep-analysis          Display CPU sleep time and wake-up
                            reasons.
    sleep-extended-analysis
    summary                 Display data about overall performance.
    top-down                Display a call tree for your target
                            application and provide CPU and wait
                            time for each function.
```

LISTING 7.2

Available reports.

Further details about each of these reports can be found either in the VTune documentation or with the built-in help command. For instance, in order to get more information about the callstacks report, and its supported options, execute the command amplxe-cl -help report callstacks.

The summary report type is a good starting point for most analyses. It displays the metrics calculated by the analysis type, and a summary of the event counts. For example, when run on a general-exploration analysis, the summary report will print the percentages for each Top-Down category. This can be seen in Listing 7.5.

For analysis types that perform sampling, there are four useful reports for identifying which functions consumed the most CPU time. The first, the hotspots report type, displays the time accounted to each function, excluding functions called from within that function. This report is sorted so that the functions that consume the most time are toward the top of the list. The second, the top-down report type, displays both the time spent within each function, and the percentage of total time spent within that function, including functions called from within that function. This report is sorted so that the functions responsible for the greatest percentage of total CPU time are toward the top of the list. The third, the callstacks report type, and the fourth, the gprof-cc report type, provide additional information about the stack traces associated with the hotspots.

By default, reports typically group items at a function-level granularity. The grouping can be changed with the -group-by argument. The available groupings supported by each report type will be listed in their respective help page. One of the most useful of these is the source-line grouping, which correlates each hotspot to a specific line of code. When interpreting this information, remember to account for potential PMU skid. Listing 7.3 illustrates the default function grouping for a hotspots report run on data collected with a general-exploration analysis type.

On the other hand, Listing 7.4 illustrates the same data and report, but grouped by source code line.

```
$ amplxe-cl -report hotspots -result-dir r000ge | head -n 15
Function                    Module         CPU Time:Self
-------------------------   ------------   -------------
deflate_quick               minigzip           5.708
compare258                  minigzip           5.442
quick_insert_string         minigzip           5.055
quick_send_bits             minigzip           2.635
quick_send_bits             minigzip           1.548
[vmlinux]                   vmlinux            1.525
crc_fold_copy               minigzip           1.293
static_emit_ptr             minigzip           1.171
quick_send_bits             minigzip           1.075
fill_window_sse             minigzip           0.992
_mm_subs_epu16              minigzip           0.658
static_emit_lit             minigzip           0.494
```

LISTING 7.3

Excerpt of hotspots report of General Exploration analysis.

```
$ amplxe-cl -report hotspots -result-dir r000ge -group-by=source-line
Source File              Source Line  Module         CPU Time:Self
----------------------   -----------  ------------   -------------
deflate_quick.c          31           minigzip           5.399
deflate_quick.c          155          minigzip           4.592
deflate_quick.c          182          minigzip           1.613
[Unknown source file]    [Unknown]    vmlinux            1.525
emmintrin.h              702          minigzip           1.128
deflate_quick.c          95           minigzip           0.986
deflate_quick.c          183          minigzip           0.946
deflate_quick.c          86           minigzip           0.907
deflate_quick.c          104          minigzip           0.866
emmintrin.h              1081         minigzip           0.747
deflate_quick.c          94           minigzip           0.584
deflate_quick.c          189          minigzip           0.554
```

LISTING 7.4

Excerpt of source grouped hotspots report of General Exploration analysis.

Graphical interface

In general, the graphical user interface is very flexible, with reporting formats changing depending on the data collected, the viewpoint, and many other user configurable options. As a result, it is not productive to attempt to document all of these interfaces and their meanings. Instead, this section attempts to highlight some important points and explain the general concepts. If more detail is required, either check the VTune documentation or contact Intel support.

As mentioned earlier, reporting is an area where the graphical interface really excels. VTune is programmed with the normal thresholds for each metric and will use these thresholds to automatically highlight any abnormalities. Additionally, almost every metric and category provides a detailed explanation on mouseover. As a result, the graphical interface provides a lot more guidance, in terms of making suggestions to the analyst about what to investigate.

Consider the example Bottom-Up report displayed in Figure 7.3. The graphical interface is partitioned into two parts, the data table at the top of the screen, and a timeline at the bottom of the screen.

Within the data table, the results of the report are summarized. The data fields displayed vary, depending on what data was collected by the analysis type. How the data is summarized depends on the viewpoint. The current viewpoint, which in Figure 7.3 is the "General Exploration viewpoint," is displayed below the top toolbar, but above the individual report windows. Selecting the "change" button next to the viewpoint will show the list of available viewpoints for the current analysis type. For example, during this General Exploration analysis, the `collect-memory-bandwidth` knob was enabled. As a result, a memory bandwidth view is available, and can be seen in Figure 7.4. This viewpoint is completely different from the previous one, with graphics highlighting the total, read, and write memory bandwidth measured during data collection. Below this graph is a different data table, with fields relevant to the memory analysis.

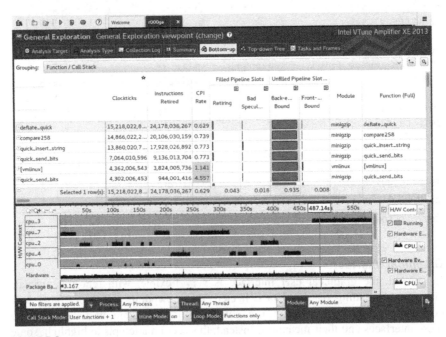

FIGURE 7.3

Example Intel® VTune™ Amplifier XE GUI report.

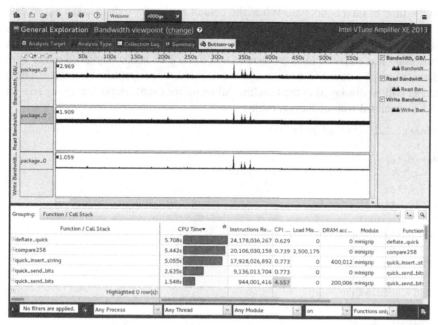

FIGURE 7.4

Example of a different Intel® VTune™ Amplifier XE report viewpoint.

Some data fields have an arrow in the top right corner of their header. An arrow pointing to the right indicates that this field contains subcategories. Clicking the right-pointing arrow will expand the field, thereby exposing the subfields. An already expanded field will have an arrow pointing to the left. Clicking the left-pointing arrow will contract the fields, leaving only the parent field exposed.

Other data fields have a yellow star in the top right corner of their header. This indicates a column of interest, which is utilized by various views to organize the display. The rows in a column of interest have a yellow background. A column can be set as the field of interest by right-clicking on the header, and selecting the "Set Column as Data of Interest" context menu item. Grouping and filtering are controlled through drop down boxes above and below the data table.

Double-clicking on a function will open up an annotated version of the source code, showing the same table fields, but at an instruction or source-line granularity. Remember to account for skid when interpreting these results.

The fields within the tables can either be displayed as a number, as a bar, or both. Fields that are outside the predefined thresholds will be highlighted with a red background. This can be set per-column by right-clicking on the field header or row, and then selecting the "Show Data As" context menu item.

The timeline at the bottom of Figure 7.3 allows for events to be traced as the process migrates between threads. The events displayed can be configured by using the dialog box on the right side of the timeline. Notice that the timeline corresponds to the time of data collection. While the default setting is to display the entire data collection, it is also possible to zoom the timeline in on specific time intervals. This can be used to correlate data between multiple analyses. Additionally, during data collection it is possible to mark instances in time. This is accomplished either with the `amplxe-cl -command mark` command or through the graphical interface. These marks will be displayed in the timeline, allowing for events important to the analyst to be correlated with collection events.

```
 1  General Exploration Metrics
 2  --------------------------
 3  Parameter                                  r000ge
 4  -----------------------------------        ---------------
 5  Clockticks                                 25858038787.000
 6  Instructions Retired                       38206057309
 7  CPI Rate                                   0.677
 8  MUX Reliability                            0.962
 9  Filled Pipeline Slots                      0.0
10   Retiring                                  0.428
11    Assists                                  0.0
12   Bad Speculation                           0.210
13    Branch Mispredict                        0.217
14    Machine Clears                           0.0
15  Unfilled Pipeline Slots (Stalls)           0.0
16   Back-end Bound                            0.258
17    Memory Latency                           0.0
18     LLC Miss                                0.0
19     LLC Hit                                 0.010
20     DTLB Overhead                           0.002
21     Contested Accesses                      0.0
22     Data Sharing                            0.0
23    Memory Replacements                      0.0
24     L1D Replacement Percentage              1.000
25     L2 Replacement Percentage               1.000
26     LLC Replacement Percentage              0
27    Memory Reissues                          0.0
28     Loads Blocked by Store Forwarding       0.000
29     Split Loads                             0.0
30     Split Stores                            0.0
31     4K Aliasing                             0.018
32    DIV Active                               0.0
33    Flags Merge Stalls                       0.021
34    Slow LEA Stalls                          0.003
35   Front-end Bound                           0.160
36    ICache Misses                            0.000
37    ITLB Overhead                            0.0
38    DSB Switches                             0.0
```

LISTING 7.5

Excerpt of `amplxe-cl -report summary` output for a General Exploration analysis.

REFERENCES

Gerber, R., Bik, A.J.C., Smith, K.B., Tian, X., 2006, 03. The Software Optimization Cookbook: High-Performance Recipes for IA-32 Platforms, Intel Press, Intel Corporation, Hillsboro, OR.

Intel Corporation, 2014a. AMPLXE-CL(1) Manual Page.

Intel Corporation, 2014, 05b. lwpmudrv.c. SEPDK C Source File.

Intel Corporation 2014, 05c. module.c. SEPDK C Source File.

Intel Corporation, 2014, 05d. pax.c. SEPDK C Source File.

Perf

8

CHAPTER CONTENTS

The Linux kernel's performance event infrastructure is designed to expose both hardware and software performance counters. In theory, this interface provides an abstraction of performance events to user space. In reality, hardware performance counters are too processor-specific to fully abstract. Instead, the performance event infrastructure focuses on providing a flexible interface to accommodate architecture-specific usages. As a result, an understanding of PMU fundamentals, discussed in Chapter 6, is required.

The most common method for utilizing this infrastructure is the perf tool. This application multiplexes a series of tools designed to complement different profiling situations. Additionally, the kernel infrastructure is also available for direct use. This allows developers to write highly customized monitors and to embed the use of performance counters into their applications.

This chapter begins with an introduction to the kernel's performance event infrastructure API, and also provides the necessary information and examples to utilize it from user space. Then, Section 8.2 explores the `perf` tool and its usage.

8.1 EVENT INFRASTRUCTURE

The first step is to determine whether the kernel supports the event infrastructure and whether the system is configured appropriately for data collection. In order for the events to be available, the kernel must have been compiled with the appropriate Kconfig options: `CONFIG_HAVE_PERF_EVENTS`, `CONFIG_PERF_EVENTS`, `CONFIG_HAVE_PERF_EVENTS_NMI`, `CONFIG_HAVE_PERF_REGS`, and `CONFIG_HAVE_PERF_USER_STACK_DUMP`. At the time of this writing, most Linux distributions enable these options by default.

Similar to Intel® VTune™ Amplifier XE, data collection with the performance events infrastructure requires that the kernel's NMI watchdog and kernel pointer hiding functionality are disabled. A discussion on these features, why they interfere with data collection, and instructions on how to disable them can be found in Section 7.1.2.

Additionally, the visibility of the data collection can be controlled with the `/proc/sys/kernel/perf_event_paranoid` file. If this file does not exist, either the kernel was compiled without support for performance events or procfs isn't mounted. If the file does exist, it contains a string of an integer. This integer specifies the access restrictions enforced by the kernel for measurements. Table 8.1 lists the possible values and their subsequent meanings.

8.1.1 perf_event_open(2)

The actual functionality of the performance infrastructure is exposed by the kernel through one system call, `perf_event_open(2)`. Prior to invoking this system call,

Table 8.1 Values for `perf_event_paranoid` (Molnar et al., 2014)

Value	Measurements Allowed
2	User-Space
1	User-Space and Kernel-Space
0	CPU Events But Not Kernel Tracepoints
−1	No Restrictions

a struct, `perf_event_attr`, is populated. This struct describes the event to be collected, how the measurements should occur, and how the results should be reported. The system call then returns a file descriptor that is utilized for accessing the data collected. In other words, this system call is invoked once for each event to be monitored.

At the time of this writing, no wrapper exists for this system call in glibc, and thus the call must be invoked either with `syscall(2)`, or manually, for instance, with the `SYSENTER` instruction. The function prototype can be found in Listing 8.1.

```
1  int perf_event_open(struct perf_event_attr *attr, pid_t pid,
2                      int cpu, int group_fd, unsigned long flags);
```

LISTING 8.1

perf_event_open(2) function prototype.

As mentioned above, the `attr` argument is responsible for communicating the event configuration.

The `pid` argument specifies the process to monitor. A `pid` of 0 measures the current process, a `pid` of −1 measures all processes on the system, and a positive `pid` measures the process with the given pid.

The `cpu` argument specifies the logical processor to monitor. A `cpu` value of −1 monitors all logical processors, while a positive or zero value limits collection to the specified logical processor.

The `group_fd` argument is the file descriptor of the group leader. This allows for multiple events to be grouped together. An event group is only scheduled to be collected when all members are available to be measured. Thus, all events that will be calculated or compared together should be members of the same group, ensuring that each event metric is computed based on similar code execution. The first event, the leader, is created with a `group_fd` of −1. The file descriptor returned for the leader is then passed as the value for `group_fd` during the creation of all other events in the group.

Finally, the `flags` argument allows for specifying any behavioral modifiers. Currently, the only flag the author sees of any value is `PERF_FLAG_PID_CGROUP`, which allows for system-wide monitoring limited to a cgroup.

The `perf_event_open(2)` function follows the standard conventions for a function that opens a file descriptor, that is, returning the new file descriptor or −1 and setting `errno`.

8.1.2 SELECTING AN EVENT

Events are selected by populating the `perf_event_attr` structure and then passing it to the kernel. This data structure, as expected by the kernel ABI, is defined in `/usr/include/linux/perf_event.h`. This header file also includes the enumerations for the various events, as well as any other ABI definitions.

Due to the flexibility of the interface, the event attribute structure is fairly complex. Determining which fields to populate in this structure depends on the desired information.

The first step is to select the event and event type, corresponding to the `perf_event_attr.config` and `perf_event_attr.type` fields, respectively. At the time of this writing, the following predefined event types are listed in the `perf_event.h` header file:

PERF_TYPE_HARDWARE Hardware Event
PERF_TYPE_SOFTWARE Software Event
PERF_TYPE_TRACEPOINT Tracing Event
PERF_TYPE_HW_CACHE Hardware Cache Event
PERF_TYPE_RAW Raw Hardware Event
PERF_TYPE_BREAKPOINT Hardware Breakpoint

Additionally, the supported events and event types can be enumerated via sysfs.

The event types can be iterated via the `event_source` bus in sysfs. Each directory in `/sys/bus/event_source/devices/` represents an event type. To select that event type, set the `perf_event_attr.type` field to the value in that corresponding directory's `type` file. Notice that the values exported via sysfs should correspond with the predefined values. For instance:

```
$ ls /sys/bus/event_source/devices/
breakpoint@  cpu@  power@  software@  tracepoint@
$ cat /sys/bus/event_source/devices/software/type
1
$ grep PERF_TYPE_SOFTWARE /usr/include/linux/perf_event.h

        PERF_TYPE_SOFTWARE                      = 1,
$ cat /sys/bus/event_source/devices/power/type
6
```

Each of these event types has a corresponding directory in `/sys/devices`. Within some of these directories is an `events` subdirectory. Within this `events` directory is a file for each predefined event. These predefined event files contain the necessary information to program the event. For example:

```
$ ls /sys/devices/cpu/events
Branch-instructions   cache-misses            instructions
Ref-cycles            branch-misses           cache-references
Mem-loads             stalled-cycles-backend  bus-cycles
cpu-cycles            mem-stores              stalled-cycles-frontend
$ cat /sys/devices/cpu/events/cpu-cycles
event=0x3c
$ cat /sys/devices/cpu/events/ref-cycles
event=0x00,umask=0x03
$ ls /sys/devices/power/events
```

```
energy-cores         energy-gpu         energy-pkg
energy-cores.scale   energy-gpu.scale   energy-pkg.scale
energy-cores.unit    energy-gpu.unit    energy-pkg.unit
```

Notice that in the above sysfs example, an event type named "power" was available; however, this event type was not present in the prior list of ABI event types. This is because, at the time of this writing, the ABI header doesn't have a corresponding entry in the `perf_type_id` enum for this type. The "power" event type, introduced less than a year ago, adds events that utilize the RAPL interface, described in Section 3.2.4, to provide power consumption information. This illustrates how quickly the infrastructure is evolving. Andi Kleen has written a library, libjevents, to parse the events listed in sysfs. It is available at https://github.com/andikleen/pmu-tools/tree/master/jevents.

PERF_TYPE_HARDWARE

When `perf_type_attr.type` is set to `PERF_TYPE_HARDWARE`, the contents of `perf_event_attr.config` are interpreted as one of the predefined processor events. Some of these events and their meanings are listed in Table 8.2. The exact PMU counter corresponding to each of these events can be determined by searching for the event name in the `${LINUX_SRC}/arch/x86/kernel/cpu/` directory. This information can then be cross-referenced with Volume 3, Chapter 19 of the Intel® *Software Developer Manual* to determine the precise meaning.

As mentioned in the introduction, abstracting PMU events is challenging. The vast majority of events are nonarchitectural, that is, their behavior can vary from one processor architecture to the next. As a result, defining predefined events for every available event would clutter the API with thousands of events that are only useful on a specific platform. Thus, most PMU events are only accessible with the `PERF_TYPE_RAW` event type.

Another challenge with the predefined events is that there is no guarantee that these events will continue measuring the same counters in future kernel versions.

In summary, the predefined events of type `PERF_TYPE_HARDWARE` are convenient for basic PMU usage. For more serious performance work, it is better to use the `PERF_TYPE_RAW` events and specify the desired counters directly.

PERF_TYPE_RAW

The interpretation of `perf_event_attr.config` when `perf_event_attr.type` is set to `PERF_TYPE_RAW` depends on the architecture. For Intel® platforms, the expected format is that of the programmable PMU MSR, shown in Figure 6.1. Of these bits, only the ones that identify the event are required. The kernel automatically sets the other bits based on the other attributes in the `perf_event_attr` struct. For example, whether the `OS` and `USR` fields are set depends on the values of `perf_event_attr.exclude_kernel` and `perf_event_attr.exclude_user`. In other words, only the umask and event number fields need to be set for most events. Some events may also require setting the cmask, inverse, or edge detect fields. The encoding information for each event is listed in Volume 3, Chapter 19 of the Intel *Software Developer Manual*.

Table 8.2 Architectural Events of Type `PERF_TYPE_HARDWARE`
(Kleen et al., 2014)

Event	Meaning
PERF_COUNT_HW_CPU_CYCLES	Unhalted Core Cycles. This counter only increments when the core is in C0 and is not halted. Affected by changes in clock frequency.
PERF_COUNT_HW_INSTRUCTIONS	Instructions Retired. This counter increments once when the last μop of an instruction is retired. Only incremented once for an instruction with a REP prefix.
PERF_COUNT_HW_CACHE_REFERENCES	LLC Reference.
PERF_COUNT_HW_CACHE_MISSES	LLC Miss.
PERF_COUNT_HW_BRANCH_INSTRUCTIONS	Branch Instruction At Retirement. Due to PMU skid, the flagged instruction during sampling is typically the first instruction of the taken branch.
PERF_COUNT_HW_BRANCH_MISSES	Mispredicted Branch Instruction at Retirement. Due to PMU skid, the flagged instruction during sampling is typically the first instruction of the taken branch.
PERF_COUNT_HW_BUS_CYCLES	Unhalted Reference Cycles. Unlike Unhalted Core Cycles, this counter increments at a fixed frequency.
PERF_COUNT_HW_REF_CPU_CYCLES	This event currently uses the Fixed-Function events rather than the programmable events. Similar to BUS_CYCLES, this counter increments at a fixed rate, irrespective of frequency. Since the event code in the kernel source assumes programmable events, the event code and umask hard coded in the config are bogus.

Additionally, some PMU events also require configuring other MSRs. Within the kernel are lists, partitioned by processor generation, of these events and the MSRs they utilize. When one of these events is selected, the contents of `perf_event_attr.config1` and `perf_event_attr.config2` are loaded into the extra MSRs. Since these extra registers vary depending on the event, the format will be specific to the event. Obviously for this to work, the event must be properly configured within the kernel's PMU lists. These lists, arrays of type `struct extra_reg`, can be found in `${LINUX_SRC}/arch/x86/kernel/cpu/perf_event_intel.c`.

PERF_TYPE_SOFTWARE

When `perf_type_attr.type` is set to `PERF_TYPE_SOFTWARE`, the contents of `perf_event_attr.config` are interpreted as one of the predefined software events. Some of these events can be found in Table 8.3. As the name implies, software events are provided and updated by the kernel. Therefore, these events focus on aspects of the software's interaction with the operating system. Unlike the hardware events, these events should be available and consistent across all platforms.

PERF_EVENT_TRACEPOINT

In order to count kernel tracepoints, set `perf_event_attr.type` to `PERF_TYPE_TRACEPOINT` and set `perf_event_attr.config` to the tracepoint id. This value can be retrieved from debugfs by looking at the respective `id` file under the appropriate subdirectory in `/sys/kernel/debug/tracing/events/`. For more information about kernel tracepoints, see Chapter 9.

PERF_EVENT_HW_CACHE

In order to utilize hardware counters to measure cache events, the value of `perf_event_attr.type` is set to `PERF_TYPE_HW_CACHE`, and the value of `perf_event_attr.config` is based on Figure 8.1.

The `Cache_ID` field in Figure 8.1 can be one of the following:

PERF_COUNT_HW_CACHE_L1D L1 Data Cache
PERF_COUNT_HW_CACHE_L1I L1 Instruction Cache

Table 8.3 `PERF_TYPE_SOFTWARE` Events (Molnar et al., 2014; Torvalds and et al., 2014)

Event	Meaning
PERF_COUNT_SW_CPU_CLOCK	The wall time, as measured by a monotonic high-resolution timer.
PERF_COUNT_SW_TASK_CLOCK	The process time, as measured by a monotonic high-resolution timer.
PERF_COUNT_SW_PAGE_FAULTS	The number of page faults.
PERF_COUNT_SW_CONTEXT_SWITCHES	The number of context switches.
PERF_COUNT_SW_CPU_MIGRATIONS	The number of migrations, that is, where the process moved from one logical processor to another.
PERF_COUNT_SW_PAGE_FAULTS_MIN	The number of minor page faults, that is, where the page was present in the page cache, and therefore the fault avoided loading it from storage.
PERF_COUNT_SW_PAGE_FAULTS_MAJ	The number of major page faults, that is, where the page was not present in the page cache, and had to be fetched from storage.

31	24	15	7	0
0	Cache Result	Cache Op	Cache ID	

FIGURE 8.1

perf_event_attr.config format for PERF_TYPE_HW_CACHE.

> **PERF_COUNT_HW_CACHE_LL** LLC
> **PERF_COUNT_HW_CACHE_DTLB** Data TLB
> **PERF_COUNT_HW_CACHE_ITLB** Instruction TLB
> **PERF_COUNT_HW_CACHE_BPU** Branch Prediction Unit
> **PERF_COUNT_HW_CACHE_NODE** Local memory

The Cache_Op field in Figure 8.1 can be one of the following:

> **PERF_COUNT_HW_CACHE_OP_READ** Read Access
> **PERF_COUNT_HW_CACHE_OP_WRITE** Write Access
> **PERF_COUNT_HW_CACHE_OP_PREFETCH** Prefetch Access

Finally, the Cache_Result field in Figure 8.1 can be one of the following:

> **PERF_COUNT_HW_CACHE_RESULT_ACCESS** Cache Reference
> **PERF_COUNT_HW_CACHE_RESULT_MISS** Cache Miss

PERF_TYPE_BREAKPOINT

Unlike the other event types, PERF_TYPE_BREAKPOINT doesn't use the value in perf_event_attr.config. Instead, it should be set to zero. The breakpoint is set by setting perf_event_attr.bp_type to one or more of the memory access types described in Table 8.4. Then, set perf_event_attr.bp_addr and perf_event_attr.bp_len, to set the address, as well as the length of bytes after perf_event_attr.bp_addr to break upon.

8.1.3 MEASUREMENT PARAMETERS

Now that the event is configured, it's time to configure how the event will be measured and how the results will be reported.

Table 8.4 Values for perf_event_attr.bp_type (Howells, 2012)

Value	Meaning
HW_BREAKPOINT_EMPTY	Don't Break
HW_BREAKPOINT_R	Break on Read
HW_BREAKPOINT_W	Break on Write
HW_BREAKPOINT_RW	Break on Reads or Write
HW_BREAKPOINT_X	Break on Code Fetch

In order to determine which API revision the system call should conform to, the perf_event_attr.size field is set to the size of the perf_event_attr structure. If a specific revision is desired, the field can be set to the corresponding size for that revision. These values are defined in the perf_event.h header file, taking the form of PERF_ATTR_SIZE_VER. For instance:

```
1  $ grep PERF_ATTR_SIZE_VER /usr/include/linux/perf_event.h
2  #define PERF_ATTR_SIZE_VER0    64     /* sizeof first published
                                            struct */
3  #define PERF_ATTR_SIZE_VER1    72     /* add: config2 */
4  #define PERF_ATTR_SIZE_VER2    80     /* add: branch_sample_type */
5  #define PERF_ATTR_SIZE_VER3    96     /* add: sample_regs_user */
```

Besides the size, the other common configuration options are bitfields within the structure. There are four bitfields that allow for the exclusion of contexts: (0) perf_event_attr.exclude_user (1) perf_event_attr.exclude_kernel (2) perf_event_attr.exclude_hv, for hypervisor, (3) perf_event_attr.exclude_idle. There are three bitfields that control the monitoring of child processes, (0) perf_event_attr.inherit, which determines whether child processes should be included in the measurements, (1) perf_event_attr.inherit_stat, which determines whether the counters are preserved between context switches to an inherited process, and (2) perf_event_attr.enable_on_exec, which automatically enables the counters after an exec(2), thus simplifying the task of monitoring another process.

The perf_event_attr.pinned field specifies that the event should always be enabled on the core. The perf_event_attr.exclusive field specifies that the event, including its group, should be the only events enabled on the processor. This is designed for handling events that may interfere with other counters. The perf_event_attr.disabled field specifies that the event should be started disabled, leaving the event to be selectively enabled when measurement is desired.

The perf_event_attr.precise_ip allows for PEBS, as described in Chapter 6, to be enabled.

As mentioned previously, events can be counted and sampled. While counted events are accessed through read(2), samples are accessed via pages obtained with mmap(2). The process of parsing the results will be covered in more detail in Sections 8.1.5 and 8.1.6.

Counted event configuration

Configuring counting events is fairly straightforward. Unlike sampled events, there is really only one counting-specific configuration option, perf_event_attr.read_format. This option controls what information is present in the buffer filled by the read(2) call.

There is no predefined struct in perf_event.h for the result's format. This is because the result's format is customizable. The fields whose associated flags aren't specified in perf_event_attr.read_format will be excluded. As a result, updating the perf_event_attr.read_format field without updating the associated code that

Table 8.5 Values for `perf_event_attr.read_format`
(Gleixner and Molnar, 2014)

Value	Meaning
PERF_FORMAT_TOTAL_TIME_ENABLED	Report the time in nanoseconds that the event was enabled and the task was running.
PERF_FORMAT_TOTAL_TIME_RUNNING	Report the time in nanoseconds that the task was running.
PERF_FORMAT_ID	Report a unique id for this event.
PERF_FORMAT_GROUP	Report values for all counters within a group in one `read(2)`.

parses the result buffer will lead to erroneous data values. Table 8.5 lists the valid options for `perf_event_attr.read_format`.

In the case where `PERF_FORMAT_GROUP` is specified, the reporting format is as follows:

```
1  struct {
2         uint64_t nr;    /* number of reported events
3         uint64_t time_enabled;
4         uint64_t time_running;
5         struct {
6                 uint64_t value;
7                 uint64_t id;
8         } values[nr];   /* array of values for each event */
9  }
```

On the other hand, when `PERF_FORMAT_GROUP` is *not* specified, the reporting format is as follows:

```
1  struct {
2         uint64_t value;
3         uint64_t time_enabled;
4         uint64_t time_running;
5         uint64_t id;
6  }
```

In both cases, the `time_enabled` and `time_running` fields are only enabled if `PERF_FORMAT_TOTAL_TIME_ENABLED` and `PERF_FORMAT_TOTAL_TIME_RUNNING` flags are set.

Sampled event configuration

Similar to the counted event configuration, the result format is customizable. Instead of using the `perf_event_attr.read_format` field, the `perf_event_attr.sample_type` field is used. Table 8.6 contains the supported flags.

Table 8.6 Values for `perf_event_attr.sample_type`
(Gleixner and Molnar, 2014)

Value	Records
PERF_SAMPLE_IP	Instruction pointer
PERF_SAMPLE_TID	Thread id
PERF_SAMPLE_TIME	Timestamp
PERF_SAMPLE_ADDR	Address
PERF_SAMPLE_READ	Counter values
PERF_SAMPLE_CALLCHAIN	Stack backtrace
PERF_SAMPLE_ID	Unique id for group leader
PERF_SAMPLE_CPU	CPU number
PERF_SAMPLE_PERIOD	Sampling period.
PERF_SAMPLE_STREAM_ID	Unique id for opened event
PERF_SAMPLE_RAW	Additional data (depends on event)
PERF_SAMPLE_BRANCH_STACK	Record of recent branches
PERF_SAMPLE_REGS_USER	Userspace CPU registers
PERF_SAMPLE_STACK_USER	Userspace stack
PERF_SAMPLE_WEIGHT	Hardware weight for cost of event
PERF_SAMPLE_DATA_SRC	Data source in hierarchy

Another important configuration is the frequency of events collected. This is controlled with *either* the `perf_event_attr.sample_period` or `perf_event_attr.sample_freq` fields. The `perf_event_attr.sample_period` is the same interface described in Chapter 6, where the counter is set to `(unsigned)-1 - perf_event_attr.sample_period`, generating an interrupt after every `sample_period` events.

On the other hand with `perf_event_attr.sample_freq`, the kernel will adjust the sampling period to receive the requested rate.

8.1.4 ENABLING, DISABLING, AND RESETTING COUNTERS

Event counts can be controlled by performing an `ioctl(2)` on the associated file descriptor. Modifications can be per event or per event group. To modify an individual event, the `ioctl(2)` is invoked on the event's associated file descriptor and uses 0 as the last argument. On the other hand, the full event group can be modified by invoking the `ioctl(2)` on the group leader's file descriptor and using `PERF_IOC_FLAG_GROUP` as the last argument.

The `PERF_EVENT_IOC_ENABLE` and `PERF_EVENT_IOC_DISABLE` ioctls enable and disable the counters, respectively. This does not change the counter values.

The `PERF_EVENT_IOC_RESET` ioctl resets the counter to zero. However, any other data associated with the event counter, such as the `time_enabled` or `time_running` values, are not reset.

8.1.5 READING COUNTING EVENTS

As mentioned earlier, event counts can be accessed by invoking `read(2)` on the event file descriptor. Additionally, all event counts within a group can be obtained together, via a `read(2)` on the group leader's file descriptor, if the `PERF_FORMAT_GROUP` flag was specified as part of `perf_event_attr.read_format`.

Consider the simple example in Listing 8.2. In this example, two branch hardware events, retired and misses, are measured for a trivial workload that alternates back and forth between two branches. Notice that in order to prevent the compiler from optimizing the workload out of the executable, the termination condition is dependent on user input and the results are printed.

On lines 61 and 65, the two event descriptors are created, with the `PERF_COUNT_HW_BRANCH_INSTRUCTIONS` event as the group leader. In this example, the predefined events of type `PERF_TYPE_HARDWARE` are used. This is okay because both counters, branch instructions retired and branch misses retired, are architectural events. If desired, these events could also be encoded using the `PERF_TYPE_RAW` event type. This would require changing the value of `perf_attr.type` on line 22, and then setting `perf_attr.config` to $0x00C4$ and $0x00C5$ instead of `PERF_COUNT_HW_BRANCH_INSTRUCTIONS` and `PERF_COUNT_HW_BRANCH_MISSES` respectively.

On line 25, the `perf_event_attr.read_format` field is set to report both event counts together in the same `read(2)` call, which occurs on line 99. Additionally, it is also set to report the time the counters were enabled and run, in order to monitor counter multiplexing.

Then, the counters are prepared to begin measurement. First, the counters are reset, line 69, to ensure the starting values are known. Secondly, the counters are enabled, line 75, since they were disabled at creation, line 28. Notice that each `ioctl(2)` affects both counters in the group, because of the `PERF_IOC_FLAG_GROUP` flag.

The trivial microbenchmark, lines 81 to 91, is designed to determine whether the branch predictor will correctly identify this pattern. The advantage of such a simple workload for this example is the ease of validating the results. For each loop iteration, two branches occur. The first branch checks whether the loop index, i, has exceeded the limit, max. The second branch checks whether the loop index is even or odd. Therefore, the total number of branches is $(2 * \frac{max}{2}) + 1$ or simply $max + 1$.

Once the workload has finished, the counters are disabled, line 93, and the results are read into the results structure. Remember that the format of this buffer depends on the values set in `perf_event_attr.read_format`. Changing one of those values may require rearranging the structure. Due to the usage of `PERF_FORMAT_GROUP`, only one `read(2)` call is required to return both counter values. Otherwise, a separate read would be necessary on each file descriptor.

```
1   #include <stdio.h>
2   #include <stdlib.h>
3   #include <string.h>
```

```
 4   #include <inttypes.h>
 5
 6   #include <unistd.h>
 7   #include <sys/syscall.h>
 8   #include <linux/perf_event.h>
 9
10   int _perf_event_open(struct perf_event_attr *attr, pid_t pid, int cpu,
11                   int group_fd, unsigned long flags)
12   {
13           return syscall(__NR_perf_event_open, attr, pid, cpu, group_fd,
14                   flags);
15   }
16
17   static int setup_cntr(int *const fd, uint64_t event, int leader)
18   {
19           struct perf_event_attr perf_attr;
20
21           memset(&perf_attr, 0, sizeof(struct perf_event_attr));
22           perf_attr.type = PERF_TYPE_HARDWARE;
23           perf_attr.config = event;
24           perf_attr.size = sizeof(struct perf_event_attr);
25           perf_attr.read_format = PERF_FORMAT_GROUP |
26                                   PERF_FORMAT_TOTAL_TIME_ENABLED |
27                                   PERF_FORMAT_TOTAL_TIME_RUNNING;
28           perf_attr.disabled = 1;
29           perf_attr.exclude_kernel = 1;
30
31           *fd = _perf_event_open(&perf_attr, 0, -1, leader, 0);
32           if (*fd < 0) {
33                   perror("perf_event_open");
34           }
35           return (*fd < 0);
36   }
37
38   #define NUM_EVENTS      2
39   enum { TOTAL = 0, MISS = 1 };
40
41   struct read_format {
42           uint64_t nr;
43           uint64_t time_enabled;
44           uint64_t time_running;
45           uint64_t value[NUM_EVENTS];
46   };
47
48   int main(int argc, char **argv)
49   {
50           int brh_fd[NUM_EVENTS], ret, iter, max;
```

```
51          struct read_format result;
52
53          ret = EXIT_FAILURE;
54
55          if (argc != 2) {
56                  fprintf(stderr, "Usage: %s <num>\n", argv[0]);
57                  goto done;
58          }
59          max = atoi(argv[1]);
60
61          if (setup_cntr(&brh_fd[TOTAL], PERF_COUNT_HW_BRANCH_INSTRUCTIONS
62          ,-1))
63                  goto done;
64
65          if (setup_cntr(&brh_fd[MISS], PERF_COUNT_HW_BRANCH_MISSES,
66          brh_fd[TOTAL]))
67                  goto done_0;
68
69          if (ioctl(brh_fd[TOTAL], PERF_EVENT_IOC_RESET,
70          PERF_IOC_FLAG_GROUP)) {
71                  perror("ioctl(PERF_EVENT_IOC_RESET");
72                  goto done_1;
73          }
74
75          if (ioctl(brh_fd[TOTAL], PERF_EVENT_IOC_ENABLE,
76          PERF_IOC_FLAG_GROUP)) {
77                  perror("ioctl(PERF_EVENT_IOC_ENABLE");
78                  goto done_1;
79          }
80
81          iter = 0;
82          {       /* simple branch test: alternating even or odd */
83                  int i = 0;
84                  while (i < max) {
85                          if (i & 1)
86                                  i++;
87                          else
88                                  i += 3;
89                          iter++;
90                  }
91          }
92
93          if (ioctl(brh_fd[TOTAL], PERF_EVENT_IOC_DISABLE,
94          PERF_IOC_FLAG_GROUP)) {
95                  perror("ioctl(PERF_EVENT_IOC_ENABLE");
96                  goto done_1;
97          }
```

```
98
99              read(brh_fd[TOTAL], &result, sizeof(struct read_format));
100             printf("%d / %d branches mispredicted\n",
101                    result.value[MISS], result.value[TOTAL]);
102             printf("%d\n", iter);
103
104             ret = EXIT_SUCCESS;
105     done_1:
106             close(brh_fd[MISS]);
107     done_0:
108             close(brh_fd[TOTAL]);
109     done:
110             return ret;
111     }
```

LISTING 8.2

Example using read(2) to access hardware counters.

When the author ran the application in Listing 8.2, the following results were produced:

```
$ ./read 100
6 / 133 branches mispredicted
50
$ ./read 100
7 / 133 branches mispredicted
50
$ ./read 100
7 / 133 branches mispredicted
50
$ ./read 100
5 / 133 branches mispredicted
50
```

Earlier, the number of branches during the workload had been calculated as $max + 1$, and thus we would expect 101 branches for our workload, as opposed to the 133 branches recorded. Looking at the example code, another branch can be accounted as checking for the return value for the ioctl(2) to enable the performance counters. Perhaps others can be accounted to the glibc wrapper for ioctl(2), that is, the validation code to check that the various arguments are correct, or perhaps to the return path from the ioctl(2) call that enables the counters. Additionally, this discrepancy could be caused by a nuance of the specific event counter.

When using performance counters, these sorts of discrepancies are common. Remember that PMU events measure the behavior of the processor's internals. In other words, what is counted toward an event and when it is counted, depends on the specific hardware implementation. This is especially problematic when using lower level events, because these events rely more upon internal core state than higher level events. In this example, the counter values remain consistent across multiple runs, which indicates the data is stable enough to be useful.

The important element here is not the individual counter values, but their relationship to one another. For the 133 branch instructions retired, only about 6 branches were mispredicted. That's a branch hit ratio of about 95%, which suggests that the branch predictor is very adept at predicting the trivial branching pattern in this microbenchmark.

8.1.6 READING SAMPLING EVENTS

While counting events provides an estimate of how well a given code snippet is performing, sampling events provides the ability to estimate which instructions are responsible for the generated events. Continuing the trivial microbenchmarking example shown in Listing 8.2, consider if the measuring code were rewritten to determine which branches were being mispredicted. Listing 8.3 is written to leverage the Intel® Last Branch Record (LBR), which stores information about the sampled branch events.

Starting within the `main()` function at line 88, notice that only one event is configured, branch mispredictions. The `perf_attr.sample_period` attribute, set to 1 on line 92, controls how many events occur before an interrupt occurs. By setting this to one, an interrupt is generated after every event. In general, this is a bad idea for frequent events, but for this trivial microbenchmark it is acceptable.

On line 93, the `perf_attr.sample_type` field specifies what information should be recorded for each event. In this situation, there are two items specified. The first, the instruction pointer, identifies which branch was mispredicted. The second, the LBR branch stack, lists the recently encountered branches and whether they were correctly predicted. Notice that in the function signature on line 29, the result structure corresponds to this field.

On line 105, the resulting event file descriptor is mapped into the virtual address space of the process. As events occur, the kernel writes the collected samples into these pages. Starting on line 45, the actual memory mapped data is parsed. The first memory mapped page contains a header, which specifies information about the following event buffer data. This data header is defined by the `perf_event_header` structure. The following buffer data, starting at the second memory mapped page, is a ring buffer. There are two fields in the header that correspond with the read and write offsets into the buffer. The valid unread buffer starts at the offset described by the `data_tail` field and the end of the valid buffer is defined by the `data_head` field. If the pages were mapped as writable, the new entries are marked as read, by the user space process, by writing the new value to the `data_tail` field.

After accessing the `data_tail`, a memory barrier is utilized to ensure that the data written by the kernel to the memory mapped pages is visible to the user space process. This memory barrier is implemented on line 19, and utilizes the `LFENCE` instruction, that is, a load fence.

Each entry into the ring buffer has a header, which describes the record's type and size. The while loop on line 54 handles parsing this header and dispatching the appropriate function to handle that record type.

```
1   #include <stdio.h>
2   #include <stdlib.h>
3   #include <string.h>
4   #include <inttypes.h>
5   #include <assert.h>
6
7   #include <unistd.h>
8   #include <sys/mman.h>
9   #include <sys/syscall.h>
10  #include <linux/perf_event.h>
11
12  int _perf_event_open(struct perf_event_attr *attr, pid_t pid, int cpu,
13                  int group_fd, unsigned long flags)
14  {
15          return syscall(__NR_perf_event_open, attr, pid, cpu, group_fd,
16          flags);
17  }
18
19  static inline void rmb(void)
20  {
21          __asm__ __volatile__ (
22                  "lfence"
23          :
24          :
25          : "memory"
26          );
27  }
28
29  static void process_sample(struct {
30                                  struct perf_event_header hdr;
31                                  uint64_t ip, bnr;
32                                  struct perf_branch_entry lbr[];} *data)
33  {
34          size_t i;
35          printf("SAMPLE %p\n", data->ip);
36          printf("\t%" PRIu64 " Branches in Stack\n", data->bnr);
37          for (i = 0; i < data->bnr; i++) {
38                  printf("\t\tFrom: %" PRIx64 " :", data->lbr[i].from);
39                  if (data->lbr[i].mispred) printf(" mispredicted");
40                  if (data->lbr[i].predicted) printf(" predicted");
41                  printf("\n");
42          }
43  }
44
```

```
45   static void parse_samples(struct perf_event_mmap_page *data)
46   {
47           struct perf_event_header *hdr;
48           void *end;
49
50           hdr = (uintptr_t)data + 4096 +data->data_tail;
51           rmb();
52           end = (uintptr_t)data + 4096 + data->data_head;
53
54           while (hdr != end) {
55                   switch(hdr->type) {
56                   case PERF_RECORD_MMAP:
57                   case PERF_RECORD_LOST:
58                   case PERF_RECORD_COMM:
59                   case PERF_RECORD_EXIT:
60                   case PERF_RECORD_THROTTLE:
61                   case PERF_RECORD_UNTHROTTLE:
62                   case PERF_RECORD_FORK:
63                   case PERF_RECORD_READ:
64                           break;
65                   case PERF_RECORD_SAMPLE:
66                           process_sample(hdr);
67                           break;
68                   default:        assert(!"unknow record");
69                   };
70                   hdr = (uintptr_t)hdr + hdr->size;
71           }
72   }
73
74   int main(int argc, char **argv)
75   {
76           int miss_fd,ret,iter,max;
77           struct perf_event_attr perf_attr;
78           struct perf_event_mmap_page *pages;
79
80           ret = EXIT_FAILURE;
81
82           if (argc != 2) {
83                   fprintf(stderr, "Usage: %s <num>\n", argv[0]);
84                   goto done;
85           }
86           max = atoi(argv[1]);
87
88           memset(&perf_attr, 0, sizeof(struct perf_event_attr));
89           perf_attr.type = PERF_TYPE_HARDWARE;
90           perf_attr.size = sizeof(struct perf_event_attr);
91           perf_attr.config = PERF_COUNT_HW_BRANCH_MISSES;
```

```
92              perf_attr.sample_period = 1;
93              perf_attr.sample_type = PERF_SAMPLE_IP | PERF_SAMPLE_BRANCH_STACK;
94              perf_attr.branch_sample_type = PERF_SAMPLE_BRANCH_ANY;
95              perf_attr.disabled = 1;
96              perf_attr.precise_ip = 2;
97              perf_attr.exclude_kernel = 1;
98
99              miss_fd = _perf_event_open(&perf_attr, 0, -1, -1, 0);
100             if (miss_fd < 0) {
101                     perror("perf_event_open");
102                     goto done;
103             }
104
105             pages = mmap(NULL, 4096 * 9, PROT_READ | PROT_WRITE, MAP_SHARED,
106                     miss_fd, 0);
107             if (pages == MAP_FAILED) {
108                     perror("mmap");
109                     goto done_0;
110             }
111
112             if (ioctl(miss_fd, PERF_EVENT_IOC_RESET, 0)) {
113                     perror("ioctl(PERF_EVENT_IOC_RESET");
114                     goto done_1;
115             }
116
117             if (ioctl(miss_fd, PERF_EVENT_IOC_ENABLE, 0)) {
118                     perror("ioctl(PERF_EVENT_IOC_ENABLE");
119                     goto done_1;
120             }
121
122             iter = 0;
123             {
124                     int i = 0;
125                     while (i < max) {
126                             if (i & 1)
127                                     i++;
128                             else
129                                     i += 3;
130                             iter++;
131                     }
132             }
133
134             if (ioctl(miss_fd, PERF_EVENT_IOC_DISABLE, 0)) {
135                     perror("ioctl(PERF_EVENT_IOC_DISABLE");
136                     goto done_1;
137             }
138
```

```
139          parse_samples(pages);
140
141          ret = EXIT_SUCCESS;
142   done_1:
143          munmap(pages, 4096 * 9);
144   done_0:
145          close(miss_fd);
146   done:
147          return ret;
148   }
```

LISTING 8.3

Example using mmap(2) to sample hardware counters.

One run of this code sample is replicated below:

```
$ ./mmap 100
SAMPLE 0x400c4c
        10 Branches in Stack
                From: 400c4c : mispredicted
                From: 400c62 : predicted
                From: 400c52 : predicted
                From: 400c62 : predicted
                From: 400c4c : mispredicted
                From: 400c62 : predicted
                From: 400c42 : predicted
                From: 400c26 : predicted
                From: 3aac2ebdcf : mispredicted
                From: ffffffff8172e8be : predicted
SAMPLE 0x400c4c
        16 Branches in Stack
                From: 400c4c : mispredicted
                From: 400c62 : predicted
                From: 400c52 : predicted
                From: 400c62 : predicted
                From: 400c4c : mispredicted
                From: 400c62 : predicted
                From: 400c52 : predicted
                From: 400c62 : predicted
                From: 400c4c : mispredicted
                From: 400c62 : predicted
                From: 400c52 : predicted
                From: 400c62 : predicted
                From: ffffffff8172f407 : predicted
                From: 400c4c : mispredicted
                From: 400c62 : predicted
                From: 400c52 : predicted
```

```
SAMPLE 0x400c4c
        16 Branches in Stack
                From: 400c4c : mispredicted
                From: 400c62 : predicted
                From: 400c52 : predicted
                From: 400c62 : predicted
                From: 400c4c : predicted
                From: 400c62 : predicted
                From: 400c52 : predicted
                From: 400c62 : predicted
                From: 400c4c : mispredicted
                From: 400c62 : predicted
                From: 400c52 : predicted
                From: 400c62 : predicted
                From: 400c4c : mispredicted
                From: 400c62 : predicted
                From: 400c52 : predicted
                From: 400c62 : predicted
SAMPLE 0x400710
        16 Branches in Stack
                From: 400710 : mispredicted
                From: 400c78 : predicted
                From: 400c52 : predicted
                From: 400c62 : predicted
                From: 400c4c : predicted
                From: 400c62 : predicted
                From: 400c52 : predicted
                From: 400c62 : predicted
                From: 400c4c : predicted
                From: 400c62 : predicted
                From: 400c52 : predicted
                From: 400c62 : predicted
                From: 400c4c : predicted
                From: 400c62 : predicted
                From: 400c52 : predicted
                From: 400c62 : predicted
```

Looking at these results, a couple of different branches are highlighted. These results seem to corroborate the earlier hypothesis that the branch predictor was very adept at predicting the microbenchmark workload. The branches with an instruction pointer around $0x400000$ are clearly the user space application's branches, while addresses such as $0xffffffff8172e8be$ are clearly branches in kernel code. Notice that on line 97 of Listing 8.3, `perf_attr.exclude_kernel` is set. As a result, even if one of the kernel branches was mispredicted, it would not appear in the sample data. At the same time, the LBR records all branches, which is why both user and kernel space addresses appear in the branch stack.

While this example prints the raw results, a more sophisticated application could perform some automatic analysis on the results. For instance, as branches show up in the profile, a running tally, associated by the instruction pointer, could be kept. After the workload finishes, this tally could be used to summarize the results, listing the hottest branches.

Additionally, the application could look up the source code lines associated with these instruction pointers for its report. This would involve examining the virtual address space of the process, by parsing the associated `maps` file in procfs, such as `/proc/self/maps`. This will correlate virtual memory addresses with specific memory mapped files, including executables and shared libraries. Then, using debug information, the offset from the base address of the file can be translated into a source code file and line. For simplicity's sake, this information can also be obtained on the sample application:

```
$ addr2line -e mmap 0x400c4c
/home/jtk/mmap.c:126
$ addr2line -e mmap 400c62
/home/jtk/mmap.c:125
$ addr2line -e mmap 400c52
/home/jtk/mmap.c:127
```

8.2 PERF TOOL

The `perf` tool leverages the functionality of the kernel's performance event infrastructure for profiling. In other words, `perf` provides access to counting and sampling events, handles the parsing of the results and relevant debug information, and produces reports that highlight the corresponding hotspots in the code.

Data collection can occur either for specific processes, either by `perf` forking a new process or attaching to an existing process, or for every process on the system. To monitor a new process, simply pass the command and related arguments to perf as the last arguments. For instance, `perf stat ls` would cause `perf` to create a new process running the `ls` executable, and then perform the requested monitoring on that process. To attach to an existing process, the `-p` argument is used. For instance, `perf record -p 12345` would cause `perf` record to attach to an existing process with a process id of 12345, and then perform measurements. Finally, every process can be monitored by instead passing `perf` the `-a` option.

8.2.1 EXPRESSING EVENTS

Events are selected by using the `-e` command argument. Multiple events can be specified by either repeating the argument per event, or by providing the argument with a comma-separated list of events. Event groups are created by enclosing the comma-separated list of events in brackets, e.g., `perf stat -e "{cycles, instructions}."` For most perf tools, if no events are specified, CPU cycles are used.

The events described in Section 8.2.1, excluding `PERF_TYPE_RAW`, fall into the category of "cooked" events. A full list of these events, and how they should be expressed on the command line, can be obtained with `perf list`.

Events not contained in that list, that is, "raw" events, can be used with the format "r<config number>." Where the config number is the hexadecimal representation of the MSR format described in Section 6.1. For most cases, this will simply be "r<umask value><event value>." For instance, given that the architectural event for Unhalted Core Cycles, that is, the "cooked" cycles event, has an Event Number of 0x3C and a Umask Value of 0x00:

```
$ perf stat -e cycles -e r003C ls > /dev/null

Performance counter stats for 'ls':

        3,165,711 cycles                    #    0.000 GHz
        3,165,705 r003c


     0.002415953 seconds time elapsed
```

Those are the only two required fields most of the time because event modifiers have a special syntax. These are expressed by appending a colon to the end of the event they modify, and then a list of modifiers. Table 8.7 lists the available modifiers. Modifiers can be applied to either "cooked" or "raw" events. Consider:

```
$  perf stat -e cycles:u -e cycles:k -e r003c:uk ls > /dev/null

Performance counter stats for 'ls':

          553,892 cycles:u                  #    0.000 GHz
        2,611,126 cycles:k                  #    0.000 GHz
        3,165,403 r003c:uk


     0.002384599 seconds time elapsed
```

When sampling, the "p" and "pp" modifiers attempt to leverage PEBS to reduce skid.

Table 8.7 Perf Event Modifiers
(Zijlstra et al., 2014)

Value	Meaning
u	Restrict events to userspace
k	Restrict events to kernelspace
h	Restrict events to the hypervisor
G	Restrict events to Guest
H	Restrict events to Host
p	Constant skid for SAMPLE_IP
pp	Request 0 skid for SAMPLE_IP
D	Events pinned to PMU

8.2.2 PERF STAT

The `perf stat` tool counts the specified performance counters for the given process or processes. This provides the ability to calculate the necessary metrics in order to determine where further analysis should focus, and allows for the comparison of multiple implementations.

As mentioned in Section 5.2.2, each counter value represents one member of a sample that estimates the infinite population. As the number of samples increases, the more accurate the sample becomes. To accommodate this, `perf stat` supports a `--repeat N` command line argument, which causes the measurement to be performed N times, with the average and standard deviation reported.

If no events are specified, the default events, including the "task-clock," "wall-clock," and the number of "context-switches," "migrations," "page-faults," "cycles," "stalled-cycles-frontend," "stalled-cycles-backend," "instructions," "branches," and "branch-misses," are chosen.

For instance, to calculate the CPI, $\frac{cycles}{instructions}$, for compressing a Linux kernel tarball with `gzip`, at the default deflate compression ratio:

```
$ perf stat --repeat 20 -e "{cycles:u,instructions:u}" gzip -c \
        /dev/shm/linux-3.15.tar > /dev/null

Performance counter stats for 'gzip -c /dev/shm/linux-3.15.tar'
(20 runs):

58,559,095,434 cycles:u         # 0.000 GHz           ( +-  0.09% )
86,967,639,500 instructions:u   # 1.49  insns per cycle ( +-  0.00% )

17.984938993 seconds time elapsed                     ( +-  0.08% )
```

Therefore, $\text{CPI} = \frac{58,559,095,434}{86,967,639,500} = 0.67$. Notice that the standard deviation is reported at the end of the line for each event. As mentioned in Chapter 6, it's important to only correlate events collected together. Notice that the events calculated together are included within the same event group. It would be incorrect to calculate the CPI with the cycles from one run of `perf stat`, and the instructions from a different run.

8.2.3 PERF RECORD, PERF REPORT, AND PERF TOP

Once analysis of the counting values isolates the bottleneck, sampling can be used to determine what instructions are responsible. This can be performed with either `perf record` or `perf top`. The main difference between the two is that `perf top` dynamically displays the results of the samples collected, updating as new samples are collected. The delay between data updates is controlled with the `-d` command line argument, taking as an argument the number of seconds between refreshes.

On the other hand, `perf record` saves the sampling data into a file, which can then be manipulated once all of the data collection has completed. By default, the data file created will be called `perf.data`. If that file already exists, the existing file will be moved to `perf.data.old`, and then `perf.data` will be created. However, a backup will not be made of `perf.data.old` if it already exists, resulting in that data being lost. The output file name can be changed via the `-o` command-line argument. If using an output file name other than the default, then all subsequent perf commands that manipulate that file will need the `-i` command line argument, specifying the correct file name to use. For instance, continuing the example from the previous section, to determine which instructions are consuming the most CPU time while compressing a Linux kernel tarball using `gzip`:

```
$ perf record -e cycles -g ./gzip -c /dev/shm/linux-3.15.tar > \
       /dev/null
[ perf record: Woken up 14 times to write data ]
[ perf record: Captured and wrote 3.298 MB perf.data (~144096 samples) ]
```

Using the `-g` command-line argument instructs perf to record not only the instruction pointer of the sample, but also the function callchain. Now that the data has been collected, the `perf report` and `perf annotate` commands will allow for accessing the collected data.

If the terminal supports it, the `perf report` command will open an interactive text user interface (TUI) for reviewing the results. This view consists of a list of functions, sorted by the functions with the highest event counts, along with their percentage of sampled events, the file, executable or shared library they reside in, and their callchain. Otherwise, `perf report` will print a similar noninteractive view. When navigating the TUI, the arrow keys move the cursor to the next or previous lines. Pressing Enter when the cursor highlights a line beginning with "+" will expand that line, to show the callchain. Functions from executables or libraries that lack debug information will be displayed as hexadecimal numbers. This can be remedied by compiling with or installing the appropriate debug flags or packages, and this does not require rerunning the data collection.

Figure 8.2 shows the interactive TUI for the data collection from above. Looking at the results, out of approximately sixty billion cycle events recorded, 60.34% resided in one function, `longest_match`. From these results, it follows that optimizing this function, or its callers to invoke it less, has the potential to improve performance much more significantly than, say optimizing `build_tree`, which only accounts for about 0.05%.

While knowing which functions to focus on is incredibly helpful, the profiler can help even more. By highlighting an entry in the TUI and pressing the "a" key, the disassembly for the function will be shown, annotated with the event samples. This is the same as invoking `perf annotate [function name]`. Just like `perf report`, depending on the terminal capabilities, `perf annotate` will either launch an interactive TUI or print the results to stdout. If the source code is available, perf will interleave the instructions with their associated lines of code.

Figure 8.3 shows a snippet of the annotation for the `longest_match` function highlighted in Figure 8.2. On the far left side is the percentage of samples accounted to that instruction. By default, the cursor will start on the instruction with the

```
Samples: 72K of event 'cycles:ppu', Event count (approx.): 61722942901
+  60.34%  gzip  gzip                  [.] longest_match
+  14.51%  gzip  gzip                  [.] deflate
+   8.37%  gzip  gzip                  [.] updcrc
+   5.74%  gzip  gzip                  [.] fill_window
+   3.47%  gzip  gzip                  [.] compress_block
+   3.47%  gzip  gzip                  [.] send_bits
+   3.00%  gzip  gzip                  [.] ct_tally
+   0.61%  gzip  [kernel.kallsyms]     [k] sysret_check
+   0.16%  gzip  gzip                  [.] pqdownheap
+   0.16%  gzip  libc-2.18.so          [.] __memcpy_sse2_unaligned
+   0.05%  gzip  gzip                  [.] build_tree
+   0.04%  gzip  [kernel.kallsyms]     [k] irq_return
+   0.02%  gzip  gzip                  [.] scan_tree
+   0.02%  gzip  gzip                  [.] bi_reverse
+   0.02%  gzip  gzip                  [.] send_tree
+   0.01%  gzip  gzip                  [.] gen_codes
+   0.01%  gzip  gzip                  [.] init_block
+   0.00%  gzip  gzip                  [.] copy_block
+   0.00%  gzip  gzip                  [.] read@plt
+   0.00%  gzip  libc-2.18.so          [.] __GI___libc_read
+   0.00%  gzip  gzip                  [.] read_buffer
+   0.00%  gzip  gzip                  [.] file_read
Press '?' for help on key bindings
```

FIGURE 8.2

Perf report TUI.

```
longest_match   /home/jtk/rpmbuild/BUILD/gzip-1.6/gzip
                      do {
                            Assert(cur_match < strstart, "no future");
                            match = window + cur_match;
   0.74  4028a0:   mov    %edi,%ecx
                            len = (MAX_MATCH - 1) - (int)(strend-scan);
                            scan = strend - (MAX_MATCH-1);

                #else /* UNALIGNED_OK */

                            if (match[best_len]   != scan_end  ||
   5.53  4028a2:   movslq %eax,%rsi
  31.73  4028a5:   movzbl 0x650020(%rsi,%rcx,1),%r8d
                      }
                            Assert(strstart <= window_size-MIN_LOOKAHEAD, "insufficient

                      do {
                            Assert(cur_match < strstart, "no future");
                            match = window + cur_match;
   0.21  4028ae:   lea    0x650020(%rcx),%r15
                            len = (MAX_MATCH - 1) - (int)(strend-scan);
                            scan = strend - (MAX_MATCH-1);
Press 'h' for help on key bindings
```

FIGURE 8.3

Perf annotate TUI.

highest percentage. Pressing the Tab key will cycle through the other instructions in decreasing order of samples.

Remember when interpreting annotations to account for skid. For example, a constant skid of 1 would mean that the samples reported are for the instruction prior to the one labeled.

8.2.4 PERF TIMECHART

Perf timechart is a tool to graphically describe the interactions on the system. These interactions include those between the processes, cores, and sleep states.

Timechart commands are multiplexed through the `perf timechart` command. First, events are collected using the `record` command, which takes a command to run, similar to `perf record`. Next, `perf timechart` is run without any arguments. This generates a SVG timeline, named `output.svg`, of system events. That is,

```
$ perf timechart record <command>
$ perf timechart
```

For example, running perf timechart on a gzip compression workload:

```
$ perf timechart record gzip -c -6 /dev/shm/linux-3.15.tar > \
        /dev/null
[ perf record: Woken up 3 times to write data ]
[ perf record: Captured and wrote 0.883 MB perf.data (~38600 samples) ]
$ perf timechart
Written 16.2 seconds of trace to output.svg
```

The output for this example can be seen in Figure 8.4.

The advantage of using a vector image format is the ability to provide scalable detail. Viewing the graph at different sizes, that is, zooming in and out, shows different levels of detail. For instance, zooming in on the CPU bars shows different color bars representing the transitions in CPU state, such as the idle state. In order to properly utilize the zoomable levels of detail, make sure to view the SVG in an SVG editor or viewer, such as `inkscape`, and not one that converts the vector image to a bitmap image for viewing.

The downside to the zoomable detail is the size of both the file and the timeline. In order to keep the results manageable, the author recommends avoiding the use of timechart on long running processes.

The timeline itself highlights the interactions between various processes. At the top of the graph is a series of bars representing CPU state. At a high level of detail, these bars show what the CPU is doing at that moment in time. These categories include Running, Idle, Deeper Idle, Deepest Idle, Sleeping, Waiting for CPU, and Blocked on IO. Increasing the level of detail, that is, zooming into the image, reveals more information about the state. This is shown in Figure 8.5.

Below the CPU state are bars representing processes active on the system at the given time. Similar to the CPU bars, these bars also show the individual process state with the same color-coded categories.

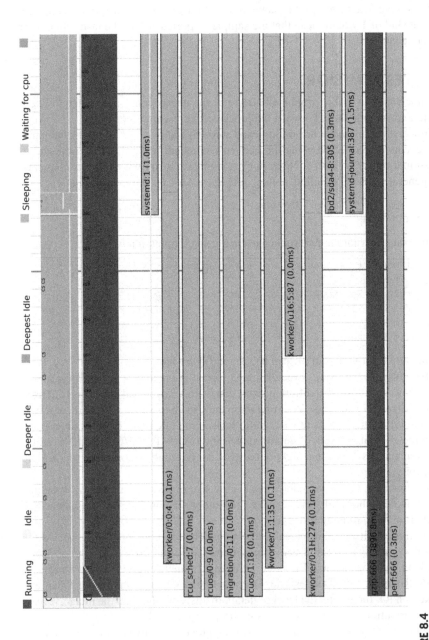

FIGURE 8.4

Perf timechart output sample.

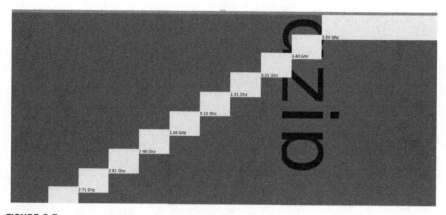

FIGURE 8.5

Perf timechart CPU zoomed.

REFERENCES

Gleixner, T., Molnar, I., 2014, 05. perf_event.h. ${LINUX_SRC}/include/uapi/linux/perf_event.h.

Howells, D., 2012, 11. hw_breakpoint.h. ${LINUX_SRC}/include/uapi/linux/hw_breakpoint.h.

Intel Corporation, 2013. Intel 64 and IA-32 Architectures Software Developer's Manual.

Kleen, A., Eranian, S., Molnar, I., Zijlstra, P., 2014, 02. perf_event_intel.c. ${LINUX_SRC}/arch/86/kernel/cpu/perf_event_intel.c.

Molnar, I., Zijlstra, P., Gleixner, T., et al., 2014, 06. Performance events core code. ${LINUX_SRC}/kernel/events/core.c. Linux Kernel Source.

Torvalds, L., et al., 2014, 06. fault.c. ${LINUX_SRC}/arch/x86/mm/fault.c. Linux Kernel Source.

Weaver, V., 2013, 07. perf_event_open manual page.

Zijlstra, P., Molnar, I., Howells, D., et al., 2014, 01. parse_events.c. ${LINUX_SRC}/tools/perf/util/parse-events.c. Linux Kernel Source.

Ftrace

CHAPTER CONTENTS

Ftrace is a debugging infrastructure within the Linux kernel that exposes the kernel's internal behavior. This data allows for the analyst to gain insights into what code paths are being executed, as well as helping to isolate which kernel conditions are contributing to performance issues. Ftrace is an abbreviation of "function tracer," yet ftrace is capable of monitoring much more than just function calls. Ftrace can also monitor the static and dynamic *tracepoints* within the kernel, referred to as *events*. *Static tracepoints* are predefined events, created by the various subsystem authors, marking the occurrence of interesting events. By tracing these events, application developers can better understand how their code interacts with the kernel, and subsequently the hardware.

For example, at the time of this writing, the Intel® i915 graphics driver exposes almost thirty static tracepoints. Most focus on recording the operations on the i915 GEM memory objects, such as `i915_gem_object_create`, `i915_gem_object_evict`, and `i915_gem_object_destroy`. The other couple i915 tracepoints focus on recording when the driver updates device registers, `i915_reg_rw`, or important rendering events, such as `i915_flip_request` and `i915_flip_complete`.

Aside from these predefined static tracepoints, ftrace also supports monitoring dynamic tracepoints. *Dynamic* tracepoints allow for custom tracepoints to be inserted almost anywhere at runtime. In order to accomplish this, tracepoints are not defined as high level events, but instead as memory offsets from exported kernel symbols. Additionally, the state at each dynamic tracepoint can be recorded by specifying a list of register names, memory addresses, memory labels, and stack offsets for the relevant data at the tracepoint location. Because of this, utilizing dynamic tracepoints requires at least some basic knowledge about the code path which is being traced.

Whereas the performance tools discussed in Chapters 7 and 8, Intel® VTune™ Amplifier XE and perf, utilize statistical sampling in order to attribute events to their relevant hotspots, ftrace instruments the kernel to log the pertinent information each time an event occurs. The Linux kernel tracepoint infrastructure is optimized such that tracepoints, even though compiled into the kernel, have very low overhead, typically just a branch, in the case where they are disabled at runtime. This contributes greatly to the usefulness of ftrace, because this low overhead encourages Linux distributions to enable tracepoints within their default kernel configurations. Otherwise, significant tracepoint overhead, with the tracepoint disabled, would relegate their use to only debug kernels.

At the time of this writing, most common Linux distributions, such as Android, Fedora, and Red Hat Enterprise Linux, enable the tracing infrastructure in their default kernel configurations. The main kernel configuration option required for ftrace is CONFIG_FTRACE. Other configuration options provide fine-grain control over what tracing functionality is available. These options include CONFIG_FUNCTION_TRACER, CONFIG_FUNCTION_GRAPH_TRACER, CONFIG_IRQSOFF_TRACER, CONFIG_FTRACE_SYSCALLS, and so on. For example, checking the default kernel configuration for x86_64 on Fedora 20:

```
$ grep CONFIG_FTRACE /boot/config-'uname -r'
CONFIG_FTRACE=y
CONFIG_FTRACE_SYSCALLS=y
CONFIG_FTRACE_MCOUNT_RECORD=y
# CONFIG_FTRACE_STARTUP_TEST is not set
$ grep CONFIG_FUNCTION /boot/config-'uname -r'
CONFIG_FUNCTION_TRACER=y
CONFIG_FUNCTION_GRAPH_TRACER=y
CONFIG_FUNCTION_PROFILER=y
```

9.1 DEBUGFS

The ftrace API is exposed through the debugfs memory-backed file system. As a result, unlike the other performance tools discussed within this book, all of the functionality of ftrace can be accessed without any dedicated tools. Instead, all operations, such as selecting which data to report, starting and stopping data collection, and viewing results, can be accomplished with the basic utilities, such as cat(1) and echo(1).

This, combined with the fact that many distributions enable ftrace in their default kernel configurations, means that ftrace is a tool that can be used almost anywhere. This scales up from tiny embedded systems, where busybox has all the tools needed, mobile platforms, such as Android, to large enterprise distributions.

The first step in utilizing the API is to mount the debugfs file system. Traditionally, Linux distributions automatically mount debugfs under sysfs, at /sys/kernel/debug. Checking whether debugfs is already mounted is as simple as querying the list of mounted file systems, either with the mount(1) command, or by looking at /proc/mounts or /etc/mtab. For example:

```
$ mount | grep debugfs
debugfs on /sys/kernel/debug type debugfs (rw,relatime)
$ grep debugfs /proc/mounts
debugfs /sys/kernel/debug debugfs rw,relatime 0 0
$ grep debugfs /etc/mtab
debugfs /sys/kernel/debug debugfs rw,relatime 0 0
```

Additionally, the file system can be manually mounted anywhere with:

```
# mount -t debugfs nodev /mnt/location
```

Once the file system is mounted, a tracing/ subdirectory will be available. This directory holds all of the files for controlling ftrace. Some files are read-only, designed for extracting information from the API about the current configuration or results. Other files allow both reading and writing, where a read queries an option's current value, whereas a write modifies that value. Note that, because ftrace provides such visibility into the kernel, accessing this directory, and thereby utilizing the tool, requires root privileges.

```
# pwd
/sys/kernel/debug/tracing
# ls
available_events              max_graph_depth        stack_trace
available_filter_functions    options/               stack_trace_filter
available_tracers             per_cpu/               trace
buffer_size_kb                printk_formats         trace_clock
buffer_total_size_kb          README                 trace_marker
current_tracer                saved_cmdlines         trace_options
dyn_ftrace_total_info         set_event              trace_pipe
enabled_functions             set_ftrace_filter      trace_stat/
events/                       set_ftrace_notrace     tracing_cpumask
free_buffer                   set_ftrace_pid         tracing_max_latency
function_profile_enabled      set_graph_function     tracing_on
instances/                    set_graph_notrace      tracing_thresh
kprobe_events                 snapshot               uprobe_events
kprobe_profile                stack_max_size         uprobe_profile
```

9.1.1 TRACERS

A *tracer* determines what information is collected while tracing is enabled. The list of tracers enabled in the current kernel configuration can be obtained by reading the contents of the available_tracers file, a read-only file. If the desired tracer is missing from this list, then it wasn't compiled into the kernel. In this case, rebuild the kernel after adding the relevant configuration option.

A tracer is selected by writing its name into the `current_tracer` file, This file is both writable, to set the current tracer, and readable, to get the currently selected tracer. For example:

```
# cat available_tracers
blk function_graph wakeup_dl wakeup_rt wakeup function nop
# cat current_tracer
nop
# echo function > current_tracer
# cat current_tracer
function
```

One a tracer has been selected, data collection can now begin. The file `tracing_on` controls whether the results of the tracer are being recorded. Take note that this is not the same thing as disabling or enabling the tracers, and their overhead, but merely whether the results are recorded.

The results of data collection are available in the `trace` and `trace_pipe` files. The `trace` file is used for processing all of the data at once, whereas the `trace_pipe` file is used for processing the data piecemeal. As a result, the end of the trace file is marked with an `EOF` marker, whereas the `trace_pipe` is not. More importantly, data read from the `trace_pipe` file is consumed, that is, removed from the tracing ring buffer. On the other hand, `read(2)`'s to the `trace` file are not destructive. In order to clear the contents of the `trace` file, perform a `write(2)` operation, such as using `echo(1)`, on the file. The contents of the write don't matter.

Available tracers

The tracing subsystem has been receiving a significant amount of attention recently. As a result, it tends to advance quickly, adding new features and new tracepoints. As such, rather than trying to provide a comprehensive list of the available tracers and their usage, this section introduces a couple of the most commonly useful.

Despite this rapid change to the infrastructure, the files exported through debugfs by ftrace fall under the kernel ABI. Therefore, in order to avoid breaking user space applications that depend on their formatting and behavior, this content should not change.

function and function_graph

The `function` and `function_graph` tracers record every function call that occurs in kernel space. Function calls from user space are omitted. In order for these function tracers to be available, the kernel must be configured with `CONFIG_FUNCTION_TRACER` and `CONFIG_FUNCTION_GRAPH_TRACER`, respectively.

Listing 9.1 illustrates the default output of the `function` tracer. Note that the author has removed extra whitespace from lines 5 through 25 in order to better fit the output within the page margin. Additionally, the output has been shortened, as the unadulterated output was well over three hundred thousand lines.

The first 11 lines of this trace consist of a header, providing an explanation of the meaning of the fields. It also reports the number of entries written and the number of entries present in the buffer. The difference between these two numbers corresponds to the number of entries lost during data collection. Finally, the "#P:8" field specifies that it monitored eight logical cores.

Moving beyond the header, starting at line 12, begins the actual data. On the right hand side, each table entry is described by the function caller and function callee. So for instance, on line 12, cpuidle_enter_state() invoked ktime_get().

By default for this tracer, the absolute timestamp, at which time the function call occurred, is recorded. Additionally, the last of the single-digit fields, to the left of the timestamp field, represents the delay column. The delay column is set based on the duration of the function call. For entries with a duration less than or equal to 1 µs, the delay field is encoded as a "." character. For entries with a duration greater than 1 µs but less than 100 µs, the delay field is encoded as a "+" character. Finally, for entries with a duration greater than 100 µs, the delay field is encoded as a "!" character. An example of this can be seen in lines 38, 39, and 41 in Listing 9.2.

```
1   # tracer: function
2   #
3   # entries-in-buffer/entries-written: 333553/1138593   #P:8
4   #
5   #                     _-----=> irqs-off
6   #                    / _----=> need-resched
7   #                   | / _---=> hardirq/softirq
8   #                   || / _--=> preempt-depth
9   #                   ||| /     delay
10  #    TASK-PID   CPU# ||||    TIMESTAMP  FUNCTION
11  #       | |      |   ||||       |          |
12  <idle>-0     [001] dN..  9852.950859: ktime_get <-cpuidle_enter_state
13  <idle>-0     [001] .N..  9852.950862: ns_to_timeval <-cpuidle_enter_state
14  <idle>-0     [001] .N..  9852.950863: cpuidle_reflect <-cpu_startup_entry
15  <idle>-0     [001] .N..  9852.950863: menu_reflect <-cpuidle_reflect
16  <idle>-0     [001] .N..  9852.950864: rcu_idle_exit <-cpu_startup_entry
17  <idle>-0     [001] dN..  9852.950864: rcu_eqs_exit_common.isra.49
                                            <-rcu_idle_exit
18  <idle>-0     [001] .N..  9852.950865: arch_cpu_idle_exit
                                            <-cpu_startup_entry
19  <idle>-0     [001] .N..  9852.950865: atomic_notifier_call_chain
                                            <-arch_cpu_idle_exit
20  <idle>-0     [001] .N..  9852.950866: notifier_call_chain
                                            <-atomic_notifier_call_chain
21  <idle>-0     [001] .N..  9852.950866: tick_nohz_idle_exit
                                            <-cpu_startup_entry
22  <idle>-0     [001] dN..  9852.950866: ktime_get <-tick_nohz_idle_exit
23  <idle>-0     [001] dN..  9852.950867: update_ts_time_stats
                                            <-tick_nohz_idle_exit
```

```
24  <idle>-0      [001] dN..  9852.950867: nr_iowait_cpu <-update_ts_time_stats
25  <idle>-0      [001] dN..  9852.950868: touch_softlockup_watchdog
                                          <-sched_clock_idle_wakeup_event
```

LISTING 9.1

Modified output snippet of the `function` tracer in the `trace` file.

Whereas the `function` tracer only instruments function calls and reports each function caller and callee pair, the `function_graph` tracer instruments both function calls and function exits, allowing for more detailed reporting of the function call hierarchy. This difference is striking when comparing the function call fields between the two different function tracers. Notice that these function calls are structured in an almost C-like format, with a function's direct and indirect calls nested within its braces.

Once again, the first few lines constitute a header, although the `function_graph` header is much more abbreviated due to the simplicity of its fields.

Notice that instead of absolute timestamps, time is expressed as a duration of each function call. The total duration spent in a function, including all subcalls, can be seen on the line corresponding with the function's closing brace. The delay field is not explicitly listed in the header, but is still prepended to the duration field. On lines 38, 39, and 41, the delay field can be seen flagging the location of a long function call. In this case the trace, since it was recorded on an idle system, is calling attention to `tick_irq_enter()`, `tick_do_update_jiffies64()`, and `update_wall_time()`.

```
1   # tracer: function_graph
2   #
3   # CPU  DURATION                  FUNCTION CALLS
4   # |     |   |                      |   |   |   |
5    3)   1.424 us    |  ktime_get();
6    3)   ==========> |
7    3)               |  smp_apic_timer_interrupt() {
8    3)               |    irq_enter() {
9    3)               |      rcu_irq_enter() {
10   3)   0.276 us    |        rcu_eqs_exit_common.isra.49();
11   3)   1.670 us    |      }
12   3)               |      tick_irq_enter() {
13   3)   0.421 us    |        tick_check_oneshot_broadcast_this_cpu();
14   3)   0.191 us    |        ktime_get();
15   3)               |        update_ts_time_stats() {
16   3)   0.251 us    |          nr_iowait_cpu();
17   3)   1.545 us    |        }
18   3)   0.151 us    |        touch_softlockup_watchdog();
19   3)               |        tick_do_update_jiffies64() {
20   3)   0.462 us    |          _raw_spin_lock();
21   3)               |          do_timer() {
22   3)   0.402 us    |            calc_global_load();
23   3)   1.595 us    |          }
```

```
24    3)                  |              update_wall_time() {
25    3)    0.211 us       |                _raw_spin_lock_irqsave();
26    3)    0.190 us       |                ntp_tick_length();
27    3)    0.131 us       |                ntp_tick_length();
28    3)    0.125 us       |                ntp_tick_length();
29    3)                  |                timekeeping_update.constprop.9() {
30    3)    0.697 us       |                  update_vsyscall();
31    3)                  |                  raw_notifier_call_chain() {
32    3)                  |                    notifier_call_chain() {
33    3)    0.361 us       |                      pvclock_gtod_notify [kvm]();
34    3)    2.347 us       |                    }
35    3)    3.426 us       |                  }
36    3)    6.415 us       |                }
37    3)    0.140 us       |                _raw_spin_unlock_irqrestore();
38    3) + 14.340 us       |              }
39    3) + 19.742 us       |            }
40    3)    0.115 us       |            touch_softlockup_watchdog();
41    3) + 28.784 us       |          }
```

LISTING 9.2

Output snippet of the `function_graph` tracer in the `trace` file.

blk

The `blk` tracer records I/O requests at the block level.

In order to utilize this tracer, it is first necessary to select which block devices to monitor. Every block device has a corresponding directory entry in sysfs at `/sys/block`. Within each of these directories is a `trace` directory, containing files that control if and how the device operations are traced. In order to enable tracing for a device, write "1" to the `enable` file in that directory. For example, in order to enable tracing for block device `sda`:

```
# echo 1 > /sys/block/sda/trace/enable
```

Once the device, or devices, have been selected for tracing, the tracer can be used just like the other tracers. Unlike the function tracer, the `blk` trace doesn't print a header, so a little investigation is required into the format used. Starting at the far left, the first column contains the process name and pid. The second column contains the logical processor number that initiated the request. The third column consists of four distinct characters, which, starting from the left, indicates whether interrupts were enabled, whether the task needed to be rescheduled, whether the request occurred due to a software interrupt, hardware interrupt, or neither, and the preemption depth. The fourth column contains the absolute timestamp of the entry. Notice that up to this point, these first four columns mirror the first four fields of the `function` tracer.

The similarities end at the fifth column, which includes the major and minor device numbers for the block device. The sixth column summarizes what action in the block layer the entry represents. These values translate a trace action, `blk-trace_act` as defined in the `${LINUX_SRC}/include/uapi/linux/blktrace_api.h` ABI header, into an ASCII character. Table 9.1 lists the values and their meanings. In the case where this field contains an additional value, not listed in Table 9.1, follow the citations, which point to the source code that define and explain each possible value.

Whereas the sixth column describes the action performed at the block layer, the seventh column describes the actual I/O operation. These values are much more straight forward, with "W" standing for a write, with "R" standing for a read, with "S" standing for a sync, and so on. Finally, the eighth column provides the details of the operation, which depends on the action being taken.

Table 9.1 Encodings of `blk` Trace Entry Actions (Howells, 2012; Rostedt et al., 2009a, b)

Encoding	Action	Meaning
Q	__BLK_TA_QUEUE	I/O request added to queue
M	__BLK_TA_BACKMERGE	I/O request merged into an existing operation (at the end)
F	__BLK_TA_FRONTMERGE	I/O request merged into an existing operation (at the front)
G	__BLK_TA_GETRQ	Allocate a request entry in the queue
S	__BLK_TA_SLEEPRQ	Process blocked awaiting request entry allocation
R	__BLK_TA_REQUEUE	Request was not completed and is being placed back onto the queue
D	__BLK_TA_ISSUE	Request entry issued to device driver
C	__BLK_TA_COMPLETE	I/O request complete
P	__BLK_TA_PLUG	Request entry kept in queue awaiting more requests in order to improve throughput of block device
U	__BLK_TA_UNPLUG_IO	Plugged request has been released to be issued to device driver
I	__BLK_TA_INSERT	Request inserted into run queue
X	__BLK_TA_SPLIT	Request needed to be split into two separate requests due to a hardware limitation
B	__BLK_TA_BOUNCE	A hardware limitation prevented data from being transferred from the block device to memory, so a bounce buffer was used (which requires extra data copying)
A	__BLK_TA_REMAP	Request mapped to the raw block device

For example, Listing 9.3 contains a fragment of a blk trace. This trace records the block I/O operations caused by vi, saving the LaTeX file containing this very sentence to the disk.

Starting at line 3, the "WS" entry in column seven indicates that a write and sync operation are beginning. The value of "A" in column six shows that this operation begins by mapping, __BLK_TA_REMAP, the partition and file offset to a physical sector on the hard drive. The author's home folder, which stores the file of interest, is in the third partition on the device, as shown by the "(8,3)" major and minor numbers in the last column. The mapping operation of this entry completes, providing a physical disk sector of 78752176, and block offset 32.

Moving to line 4, the write and sync operation continues, by enqueuing the I/O request, hence the "Q" in sixth column. On line 5, the enqueuing operation requests that space be allocated to hold the request entry in the queue, hence the "G" in the sixth column. On line 6, the "P" in the sixth column indicates that the request queue will be holding the request, waiting for additional block requests to the same device.

Starting on line 7, the request is finally inserted into the run queue, but the queue is still awaiting more requests. On lines 8 through 9, and 11 through 16, the request is being managed by the I/O scheduler, in this case the Completely Fair Queuing (CFQ) scheduler, whose job is to manage the request queue. On line 10, the request is unplugged, meaning that it will no longer be held to await more operations. On line 17, the request is issued to the device driver and finally on line 18, the I/O request is marked as complete.

```
1   # tracer: blk
2   #
3   nvi-5859  [001] d...   610.322017:   8,0    A  WS 78752176 + 32
                                                      <- (8,3) 77316528
4   nvi-5859  [001] d...   610.322023:   8,0    Q  WS 78752176 + 32 [nvi]
5   nvi-5859  [001] d...   610.322032:   8,0    G  WS 78752176 + 32 [nvi]
6   nvi-5859  [001] d...   610.322035:   8,0    P   N [nvi]
7   nvi-5859  [001] d...   610.322042:   8,0    I  WS 78752176 + 32 [nvi]
8   nvi-5859  [001] d...   610.322050:   8,0    m   N cfq5859SN /
                                                        insert_request
9   nvi-5859  [001] d...   610.322053:   8,0    m   N cfq5859SN / add_to_rr
10  nvi-5859  [001] d...   610.322057:   8,0    U   N [nvi] 1
11  nvi-5859  [001] d...   610.322060:   8,0    m   N cfq workload slice:100
12  nvi-5859  [001] d...   610.322062:   8,0    m   N cfq5859SN /
                                                        set_active wl_class:0
                                                        wl_type:1
13  nvi-5859  [001] d...   610.322066:   8,0    m   N cfq5859SN / fifo=(null)
14  nvi-5859  [001] d...   610.322067:   8,0    m   N cfq5859SN /
                                                        dispatch_insert
15  nvi-5859  [001] d...   610.322070:   8,0    m   N cfq5859SN /
                                                        dispatched a request
16  nvi-5859  [001] d...   610.322072:   8,0    m   N cfq5859SN /
                                                        activate rq, drv=1
```

```
17   nvi-5859    [001] d...   610.322073:   8,0    D  WS 78752176 + 32 [nvi]
18   <idle>-0    [006] d.s.   610.322628:   8,0    C  WS 78752176 + 32 [0]
```

LISTING 9.3

Modified output snippet of the blk tracer in the trace file.

Nop

The nop tracer is the default. As the name implies, this tracer doesn't trace anything; however, it can be used to collect tracepoint events.

Each static event can be searched, enabled, or disabled via the tracing/events directory. Within this directory are additional directories representing each kernel subsystem that exposes events. Within each of these subdirectories are additional directories, each representing a specific event. At each of these directory levels, there are files entitled enable, which are available to enable or disable all events contained within the subdirectories.

Additionally, the enabled events can be selected with the set_event file. Reading this file will provide the list of currently enabled events, while writing to this file will either enable or disable events. Events are enabled by writing the event name, in the form <subsystem>:<event>, to this file. Events are disabled by writing their name, with the "!" prefix. As an aside, care must be taken in using the "!" character, since most shells give it a special meaning. Both of these forms can use wildcards, with the "*" character. For example, to enable all events exposed by the Intel i915 graphics driver, and then disable them:

```
# pwd
/sys/kernel/debug/tracing
# cat set_event
# echo "i915:*" > set_event
# cat set_event | head -n 5
i915:i915_pipe_update_start
i915:i915_pipe_update_vblank_evaded
i915:i915_pipe_update_end
i915:i915_gem_object_create
i915:i915_vma_bind
# echo "\!i915:*" > set_event
# cat set_event
```

By monitoring these events, it is possible to correlate the behavior of user space applications to kernel behavior.

9.2 KERNEL SHARK

While the DebugFS interface to Ftrace is very flexible, requires no special tools, and can be easily integrated into an application, there are two other interfaces available. The first, trace-cmd, is a command-line tool that wraps the DebugFS interface. The second, kernelshark, is a graphical interface that wraps the trace-cmd tool.

The kernelshark tool provides a very intuitive interface for configuring trace recording. Data collection is configured by selecting the Capture item in the menubar, and then selecting the Record menubar item. This will open a dialog that lists all of the events in a hierarchical tree, that is, in the same format as the file system exposes them. In this dialog, the tracer is referred to as the execute plugin, and there is a combo box widget for choosing one of the available tracers. Actual data collection begins and ends by selecting the Run and Stop buttons on this dialog box. After clicking the close button, the data report will be displayed.

The advantage of using a graphical interface like kernelshark is the reporting. Figure 9.1 illustrates an example report. Once the trace has been collected, a timeline shows the events, partitioned between logical CPUs, using the trace's timestamps. The bottom half of the screen is dedicated to displaying the raw trace data. It is possible to zoom in an out of the timeline, by left-clicking and then dragging. Dragging to the right causes the timeline to zoom in on the selected region in between the start and end points. On the other hand, dragging to the left causes the timeline to zoom out.

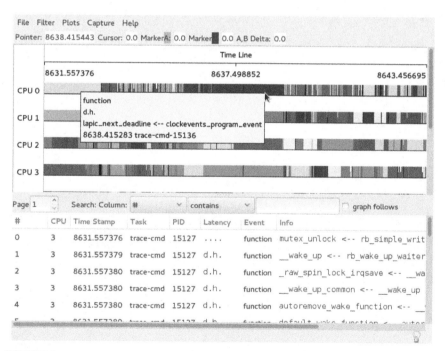

FIGURE 9.1

The graphical interface for kernelshark.

Aside from per-CPU, it is also possible to show events partitioned by process. Each process is selected by clicking the Plots item in the menubar, and then selecting the Task menubar item. This will open a dialog box that lists all of the processes present within the trace. Selecting the check box control next to each process name will add a new plot for that process to the timeline. Additionally, it is possible to further filter data by tasks, events, or processors via the Filter menubar item.

REFERENCES

Howells, D., 2012, 10. enum `blktrace_act` in `${LINUX_SRC}/include/uapi/linux/blktrace_api.h`:37-55. Source Code Header File.

Rostedt, S., 2010, 04. Kernelshark. https://kernel.googlesource.com/pub/scm/linux/kernel/git/rostedt/trace-cmd/+/master/Documentation/HTML/index.html. HTML Documentation File.

Rostedt, S., Zefan, L., Melo, A.-C., Axboe, J., 2009, 03a. `${LINUX_SRC}/kernel/trace/blktrace.c`:1340-1359. Source Code.

Rostedt, S., Zefan, L., Namgyung, K., Heo, T., et al., 2009, 07b. `${LINUX_SRC}/include/trace/events/block.h`. Source Code Header File.

GPU Profiling Tools

10

CHAPTER CONTENTS

While the author personally believes that command-line interfaces are more flexible and efficient than graphical user interfaces, he is in the minority. The majority of users depend on responsive user interfaces for interacting with their systems. As a result of this direct interaction between the user and graphical interface, performance problems within the graphics stack tend to be painfully noticeable, even to the most casual of users. In fact, a significant portion of users evaluate the performance of devices based almost solely on the responsiveness of its user interfaces. For example, if a user notices the graphical interface struggling to render fluidly, he is likely to judge the entire device to be of low quality.

Consider an analogy of a car's performance. The only contact that a car makes with the road is through its tires. Regardless of how much brake horsepower a car's engine is capable of producing, the car's actual performance will be evaluated based on the amount of horsepower that makes it to the wheels, and therefore to the road. In other words, a highly optimized algorithm is naught if the user interface is sluggish and unresponsive.

The first section of this chapter explores the traditional Linux graphics software stack. Architecting a graphics stack is incredibly challenging. This is because computer graphics is an area where technology, and therefore user demands, are constantly evolving. This challenge is further compounded because any discrepancies between the hardware and software architectures lead to inefficiencies. These inefficiencies, abstractions designed to bridge the gap between the two conflicting architectures, typically manifest as highly visible performance problems. For example, whereas older graphics hardware consisted of a rigid fixed-function rendering pipeline, modern graphics hardware is designed for programmability. As a result, the OpenGL specification had to be revamped, leading to a duality in the API between the old paradigm, of a fixed rendering pipeline, and the new paradigm, of programmable shaders. The last few sections of this chapter explore some useful monitors for pinpointing the cause of graphical issues.

Intel publishes a significant amount of documentation for its graphics hardware. This documentation is enlightening, especially with regards to how the graphic APIs actually work, and why they are structured in the way they are. Additionally, the Intel® Linux graphics drivers are completely open source, so their code can also be studied. More information on the documentation and drivers can be found at: https://01.org/linuxgraphics/.

10.1 TRADITIONAL GRAPHICS STACK

Technically, the term "traditional," in reference to the Linux graphics stack, is somewhat of a misnomer, since the stack has been rapidly evolving to meet the needs of modern graphics applications. Additionally, due to the decentralized nature of open source software and the fragmentation of hundreds of different active Linux distributions, each with their own software selection and configuration nuances, it's hard to judge one piece of software as more "traditional" than another. Instead, this section focuses on the most common configuration at the time of this writing, which revolves around X11. The term "traditional" is used to differentiate this stack from the completely different software stack found on Android.

Android completely eschews the X server and almost all of the user space libraries used in the Linux graphics stack. Instead, Android reimplements the stack to accommodate its Java API.

10.1.1 X11

Historically, the Linux graphics stack has revolved around the X Window System protocol. The X protocol defines the interface for interacting between a client and the rendering server, which can be either local to the client system or remote. This interaction allows for graphics hardware to be divided, by the server, between multiple, local and remote, clients, and provides methods for handling user input, such as from a mouse, font management, and drawing routines.

In order to utilize this protocol to interact with the X server, clients leverage the Xlib or XCB libraries. Note that here the term *clients* refers to each individual application, not complete systems, although those applications can be distributed across multiple systems. Xlib is the original library implementation for the client side of the X protocol; however, it abstracts the X protocol from the programmer.

As a result, Xlib function calls are blocking, meaning that they don't return until the associated request's reply has returned from the server. Obviously, this can be less than desirable if the request's reply isn't needed immediately. The XCB library addresses this problem by exposing more of the protocol, and allowing the application to decide whether to block. Most modern applications don't utilize these libraries directly, but instead leverage toolkits like GTK or QT, which in turn use Xlib or XCB.

While the X protocol provides the functionality for window management, this is only applicable to the concept of a window as a canvas for drawing. These drawable canvases are known as *pixmaps*. Other common window elements, such as the window's placement, decorations, including the title bar and minimize, maximize, and close buttons, or behaviors such as resizing a window when the border is dragged, are not controlled by the X protocol. These elements fall into the purview of the window manager, which is a X server client just like the windows it manages. The window manager is responsible for rendering each of the windows, both their content and decorations, together into one image for display on the screen, that is, *compositing* the various windows. As the reader might expect, rendering each window to an internal buffer and then compositing them adds additional overhead that can be detrimental to performance-sensitive tasks. Due to this, most high-quality window managers disable compositing when an application runs in fullscreen mode, thus mitigating the performance overhead.

While many users prefer to only utilize a window manager on top of X, such as OpenBox, Fluxbox, Ratpoint, or dwm, other users choose to utilize a full desktop environment, such as GNOME or KDE. Each desktop environment includes a window manager, such as Metacity and Kwin for GNOME and KDE respectively, but also provides additional software for greater functionality. Most desktop environments can be configured to use a different window manager, if so desired.

10.1.2 HARDWARE AND LOW-LEVEL INFRASTRUCTURE: DRI

Designed in 1984, most of the functionality within the X protocol has outlived its usefulness. This is why the Wayland protocol, which is architected for the needs of modern graphics applications, is the heir presumptive to the future Linux graphics stack. While at the time of this writing the X protocol is still in use, in order to obtain acceptable rendering performance, the stack essentially bypasses the X server at all costs. This occurs through the Direct Rendering Infrastructure (DRI), which enables graphics applications to skip the X server and interface directly with the graphics hardware. This infrastructure is divided into three different kernel components: DRM, GEM, and KMS.

The Direct Rendering Manager (DRM), allows for user applications to submit code directly to the GPU, without involving the X server (Barnes et al., 2012). The interface for the DRM infrastructure is exposed to user space through an API of `ioctl(2)` calls, performed on the GPU's DRI file descriptor. These special DRI device files can be found under `/dev/dri`. In order to simplify this process, the `ioctl(2)` calls in user space are typically handled by a helper library, libdrm.

In many ways, programming the GPU is very similar to programming the CPU, although the instruction set and data state are different. The graphics hardware executes instructions stored in a ring buffer. Since there is only one ring buffer for the GPU, accessing elements within this buffer requires locking, thus making direct access from user space too expensive. Aside from entries that directly contain instructions, the ring buffer also supports pointer entries. These pointer entries reference a chunk of memory, known as a `batchbuffer`, that is comprised of GPU instructions. Upon encountering one of these pointer entries in the ring buffer, the GPU loads and executes all of the instructions contained within the batchbuffer, and then continues with the next entry in the ring buffer. In many ways, this flow control mimics a function call, where the execution flow temporarily changes, and then returns to its original context after execution is completed. Unlike directly updating the ring buffer, a batchbuffer can be generated by the CPU without interrupting the GPU. As a result, batchbuffers are generated by user space applications and then are passed to the kernel's DRM infrastructure, which then handles inserting them into the GPU ring buffer.

In order to facilitate this interaction between the graphics memory and processor memory, a new API for managing memory objects was created. This API, known as the Graphics Execution Manager (GEM), provides an interface for creating, synchronizing, and destroying graphics resources, including batchbuffers, as well as texture and vertex data. Similar to the DRM interface, the GEM API is exposed through a series of `ioctl(2)` calls performed on the relevant DRI device file (Packard, 2008).

Originally, the X server was also required to set the display mode, that is the screen's resolution, color depth, and so on. As a result, the resolution at boot time and for virtual terminals was typically not the native screen resolution. This was remedied with Kernel Mode Setting (KMS) support, which moves the functionality for setting the display mode from the X server to the kernel. This is accomplished by reading the EDID information from the attached monitors and setting the display's resolution accordingly.

10.1.3 HIGHER LEVEL SOFTWARE INFRASTRUCTURE

The higher level graphics stack is partitioned into a series of libraries and applications, such as the actual X server. Each of these provide a different set of functionalities, such as pixel management or the OpenGL implementation.

3D: Mesa

The OpenGL and EGL implementations are provided by the Mesa library. This library exposes the OpenGL API to user applications, and then translates those OpenGL function calls into the appropriate GPU batchbuffers. Using libdrm, Mesa then submits these instructions into the kernel for execution by the GPU. As a result, each supported graphics hardware architecture must provide a driver within Mesa. This driver is responsible for implementing a compiler that targets the GPU instruction set. Additionally, the GPU-specific kernel DRM driver must implement validation, to ensure that the instructions passed from user space to kernel space are valid.

Mesa also provides the GLX interface, which allows for interaction between OpenGL and the X server. For example, this allows for OpenGL to render into a X window pixmap, which can then be composited onto the screen. Using DRI to avoid the X server for routine drawing calls is referred to as *direct rendering*. On the other hand, GLX is able to route OpenGL functions through the X server, which is referred to as *indirect rendering*, and is painfully slow. Indirect rendering is almost always a sign of a missing or misconfigured driver. This can be checked with the `glxinfo` command:

```
$ glxinfo | grep direct
direct rendering: Yes
```

Mesa provides a series of debugging options, which are enabled via environmental variables. Some of these environmental variables are part of Mesa, and some are part of the Intel® GPU driver in Mesa. For example, every time a frame is rendered, Mesa will print the FPS to `stdout` if the `LIBGL_SHOW_FPS` environment variable is set.

The Intel driver checks for the `INTEL_DEBUG` environmental variable. The contents of this variable contains one or more comma-separated flags. Each flag corresponds to debug information, which will be printed to `stdout`. These flags allow for functionality like printing debug messages, disassembling shaders during compilation, printing statistics and so on (Boll et al., 2014). Other flags, such as `perf`, `perfmon`, and `stats`, focus on detecting performance issues. The full list of environmental variables, and their meanings, can be found at http://www.mesa3d.org/envvars.html.

2D: cairo and pixman

While the X server provides two-dimensional drawing commands, like `XDrawLine(3)`, these too are avoided for performance reasons. Instead, the cairo library is used, which aside from X11 pixmaps via XLib and XCB, is also capable of drawing to surfaces like PDF, PNG, PS, and SVG.

One of the great features of the cairo library is that any application that uses it can automatically produce a trace of cairo commands. This trace, consisting only of the cairo workload, can be shared and replayed, without the application. Additionally, the trace can be benchmarked over different backends, such as rendering to an in-memory image or X pixmap. This allows developers to determine how their applications are using cairo, the cost of various operations and backends, and also easily reproduce and measure performance improvements. These traces are collected by using the `cairo-trace` command. In order to collect enough information for benchmarking, use the `--profile` argument. For instance, running `cairo-trace foo` will execute application `foo` and then store the cairo trace in a file named `foo.<pid>.trace`. On the other hand, adding the `--profile` argument will also enable LZMA compression, so the resulting trace will be named `foo.<pid>.lzma`. This trace file can then be replayed by using the `cairo-perf-trace` command. Whereas the `cairo-trace` command is typically available in the software repositories of the major Linux distributions, the cairo-perf-trace command is found within the cairo source tree, under the perf directory.

The Pixman library provides software implementations for various image and pixel operations, such as compositing images. Pixman is used by cairo and the X server as a software fallback when no hardware-accelerated implementation of the operation is available. When a Pixman function appears as a hotspot in performance profiling, the first step is to determine why hardware-acceleration isn't being used. Graphics hardware often has limitations on the image formats, image sizes, and operations that can be accelerated. As a result, detecting software fallback and correcting the code to avoid these limitations, and therefore software fallback routines, will improve performance.

10.2 buGLe

The buGLe library is an instrumented OpenGL shim, designed for collecting OpenGL traces and statistics. Using the LD_PRELOAD mechanism, the buGLe library is loaded before the dynamic linker begins resolving external symbols for the application. Because buGLe provides all of the symbols that are typically provided by libGL.so or libEGL.so, the OpenGL function calls, for a dynamically linked application, are resolved by the dynamic linker to the buGLe instrumented functions. These instrumented functions invoke the traditional libGL.so or libEGL.so functions, but additionally keep track of any desired OpenGL state, such as the function calls made, their durations, and their result.

As a result of this implementation, buGLe allows for data collection to be performed on unmodified, dynamically linked, binaries. At the same time, this implementation also has the downside of requiring buGLe to remain synchronized with the current OpenGL and OpenGL ES implementations.

The recording and reporting capabilities of buGLe are grouped together into *filtersets*. Each filterset, such as stats_basic, trace, and showerror, corresponds to what aspects of OpenGL are traced, and therefore subsequently reported. Additionally, filtersets can export counters, which can be combined and operated on in order to generate custom statistics that can also be displayed.

The definition of one or more enabled filtersets, along with any custom reporting and statistics, is referred to as a *chain*. The chain utilized for tracing is selected at runtime via the BUGLE_CHAIN environmental variable. Custom chains are defined in the ${HOME}/.bugle/filters file, while custom statistics are defined in the ${HOME}/.bugle/statistics file.

Some of the more common filtersets are:

checks Records warnings, and skips the erroneous function call, on programming errors resulting in an invalid use of the API

showerror Records OpenGL errors, that is, glGetError()

trace Records every GL function executed, along with the function parameters

stats_calltimes Records the duration of each OpenGL function call per frame

stats_calls Records the number of times each OpenGL function was executed per frame

stats_basic Records general information, such as frame rate or frame time

showextensions Records the extensions that are used

Each of these filtersets record counters and some, those that begin with the word show, automatically output some of their data to the logfile. The rest make the counters available for reporting and for custom statistics. The location of the log is controlled via the log filterset, and the contents of the log is controlled via the logstats filterset. For example, considering the following chain:

```
1   $ cat ~/.bugle/filters
2   chain examplechain
3   {
4           filterset stats_calls
5           filterset stats_calltimes
6           filterset stats_basic
7
8           filterset logstats
9           {
10                  show "average time per call"  # provided by
                                                     stats_calltimes
11                  show "time in GL"             # provided by
                                                     stats_calltimes
12                  show "frames per second"      # provided by stats_basic
13                  show "ms per frame"           # provided by stats_basic
14          }
15          filterset log
16          {
17                  filename "/tmp/bugle.log"
18          }
19  }
```

Line 1 begins the definition of a new chain, very creatively named examplechain, and thus will be invoked by defining BUGLE_CHAIN=examplechain. Lines 4 through 6 enable three filtersets, stats_calls, stats_calltimes, and stats_basic, for reporting data. Enabling these three filtersets does not automatically output any data, but instead merely enables the counters to be available. The actual reporting definition begins at line 8, with the configuration of the logstats filterset. Each of the text strings on lines 10 through 13 represent a predefined statistic that is calculated using the counters exported through the filtersets on lines 4 through 6. The definition of each of these statistics, in relation to the filterset counters, can be found in the ${HOME}/.bugle/statistics file. Finally, lines 15 through 18 define the log filterset output.

All of the statistics used in this example are part of the defaults provided with the library. The only requirement was copying the provided statistics file into

${HOME}/.bugle/statistics. Included below are some excerpts from that file, defining the formulas for calculating the logstats utilized above.

```
1   $ cat ~/.bugle/statistics
2   #
3   # Core statistics
4   #
5
6   "frames per second" = d("frames") / d("seconds")
7   {
8       precision 1
9       label "fps"
10  }
11
12  "ms per frame" = 1000 * d("seconds") / d("frames")
13  {
14      precision 2
15      label "ms/frame"
16  }
17
18  #
19  # Call time statistics
20  #
21
22  "average time per call" = d("calltimes:*") / d("calls:*") * 1000
23  {
24      precision 3
25      label "* (ms)"
26  }
27
28  "time in GL" = d("calltimes:total") / d("seconds") * 100
29  {
30      precision 1
31      label "%"
32  }
```

Once the desired filtersets and statistics have been configured, data collection can begin by utilizing the LD_PRELOAD mechanism described above. For example, in order to collect the data described in the examplechain chain for the glxspheres64 program:

```
1   $ env LD_PRELOAD=/usr/local/lib/libbugle.so.10.0.1 \
2   > LD_LIBRARY_PATH=/usr/local/lib/ \
3   > BUGLE_CHAIN=examplechain \
4   > glxspheres64
5   Polygons in scene: 62464
6   ATTENTION: default value of option force_s3tc_enable overridden by
              environment.
```

```
7   Visual ID of window: 0x20
8   Context is Direct
9   OpenGL Renderer: Mesa DRI Intel(R) Sandybridge Mobile
```

As defined in the `log` filterset in the `examplechain` chain, the log is written to `/tmp/bugle.log`. Below is an excerpt from that log for one frame:

```
1   [INFO] logstats.average time per call: 0.000 glListBase (ms)
2   [INFO] logstats.average time per call: 0.001 glDrawBuffer (ms)
3   [INFO] logstats.average time per call: 0.001 glViewport (ms)
4   [INFO] logstats.average time per call: 0.000 glTranslatef (ms)
5   [INFO] logstats.average time per call: 0.000 glPopMatrix (ms)
6   [INFO] logstats.average time per call: 4.961 glCallLists (ms)
7   [INFO] logstats.average time per call: 0.001 glLoadIdentity (ms)
8   [INFO] logstats.average time per call: 0.001 glDisable (ms)
9   [INFO] logstats.average time per call: 0.001 glFrustum (ms)
10  [INFO] logstats.average time per call: 0.001 glPopAttrib (ms)
11  [INFO] logstats.average time per call: 0.000 glMaterialfv (ms)
12  [INFO] logstats.average time per call: 8.355 glClear (ms)
13  [INFO] logstats.average time per call: 0.001 glClearDepth (ms)
14  [INFO] logstats.average time per call: 0.004 glRasterPos3f (ms)
15  [INFO] logstats.average time per call: 0.002 glRotatef (ms)
16  [INFO] logstats.average time per call: 0.874 glXSwapBuffers (ms)
17  [INFO] logstats.average time per call: 0.001 glMatrixMode (ms)
18  [INFO] logstats.average time per call: 0.025 glCallList (ms)
19  [INFO] logstats.average time per call: 0.001 glClearColor (ms)
20  [INFO] logstats.average time per call: 0.000 glPushMatrix (ms)
21  [INFO] logstats.average time per call: 0.000 glColor3f (ms)
22  [INFO] logstats.average time per call: 0.001 glPushAttrib (ms)
23  [INFO] logstats.time in GL: 97.9 %
24  [INFO] logstats.frames per second: 61.8\,fps
25  [INFO] logstats.ms per frame: 16.17 ms/frame
```

10.3 APITRACE

Apitrace is a tool for tracing and profiling OpenGL and EGL function calls. The tool consists of both a command-line interface, `apitrace`, and a QT-based graphical interface, `qapitrace`. As with buGLe, this is achieved by preloading an instrumented OpenGL implementation before the dynamic linker loads the real OpenGL code.

One of the great features of Apitrace is its ability to reconstruct the OpenGL state machine per function call. This includes being able to view a screenshot of each frame, a screenshot of each texture, and a list of the changed OpenGL state variables. Additionally, the profiling view shows the per-call durations for both the CPU and GPU.

Collection begins either with the `apitrace trace <application>` command, or through the graphical interface by selecting the File menubar item, and choosing the

New menu item. In both cases, this will produce a trace file, named in the format
`<application>.trace`. For example:

```
$ apitrace trace glxspheres64
error: failed to determine elf class for glxspheres64,
        assuming ELFCLASS64
Polygons in scene: 62464
apitrace: tracing to /home/jtk/glxspheres64.1.trace
apitrace: redirecting dlopen("libGL.so.1", 0x102)
ATTENTION: default value of option force_s3tc_enable overridden
          by environment.
Visual ID of window: 0x20
Context is Direct
OpenGL Renderer: Mesa DRI Intel(R) Sandybridge Mobile
```

At this point, the binary trace file is ready for analysis. At any time, the trace can
be replayed with the `glretrace` command. This command will rerun each OpenGL
command within the trace, allowing for more information to be collected, or for the
trace to be run on another system or configuration.

Figure 10.1 illustrates the trace for `glxspheres64` in the graphical interface.
By default, only the per-frame OpenGL calls, and their parameters are listed. The

FIGURE 10.1

QT interface for Apitrace.

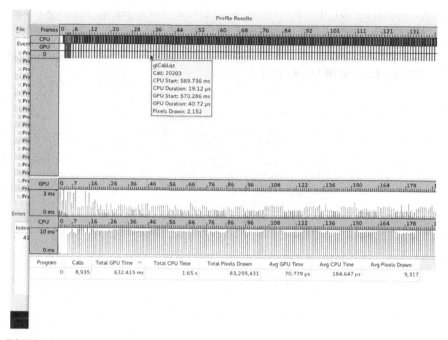

FIGURE 10.2

QT interface for Apitrace profiling.

OpenGL state and surfaces at each call can be obtained by opening the Trace menubar item and then selecting the Lookup State entry. This will cause the trace to be retraced, either for the whole trace or up until the highlighted frame or call. Once this has completed, a sidebar will appear on the right-hand side of the screen containing the data.

Apart from reconstructing the OpenGL state, the trace can also be profiled by opening the Trace menubar item and then selecting the Profile entry. This will again cause the trace to be retraced, and then a window containing a timeline of CPU and GPU times and utilization will open. By highlighting over the entries, the relevant OpenGL information will be displayed. An example of this can be seen in Figure 10.2. Since retracing actually reruns all of the OpenGL commands, this profiling information for a trace can be collected on multiple systems or configurations, in order to determine changes in performance.

REFERENCES

Barnes, J., Pinchart, L., Vetter, D., 2012, 07. Linux DRM Developer's Guide. ${LINUX_SRC}/
    Documentation/DocBook/drm.
Boll, A., Paul, B., Forbes, C., et al., 2014, 01. Mesa 3D Environment Variables. http://www.
    mesa3d.org/envvars.html.

Intel Corporation, 2011, 05. Intel® OpenSource HD Graphics Programmer's Reference Manual (PRM): Volume 1. Part 1: Graphics Core (SandyBridge). https://01.org/linuxgraphics/sites/default/files/documentation/snb_ihd_os_vol1_part1.pdf.

Packard, K., 2008, 05. GEM – The Graphics Execution Manager. http://lwn.net/Articles/283798/. Email to DRI mailing list.

Other Helpful Tools

11

11.1 GNU PROFILER

The GNU profiler, gprof, provides basic algorithmic analysis capabilities. Unlike most of the other monitors in this book, gprof depends on the compiler to instrument the executable to be profiled. This extra code, added automatically by the compiler, performs the actual data collection and outputs it to a file. The gprof(1) tool is then used to translate the collected data in this file into a text-based report.

Since gprof depends on the compiler to insert the necessary profiling code, this profiling method relies on compiler support. At the time of this writing, all three major toolchains support this feature. To use gprof with GCC or LLVM, the code must be compiled and linked with the -pg compiler flag. To use gprof with ICC, the code must be compiled and linked with the -p compiler flag.

Once the instrumented executable has been built, run the test workload. When its execution completes, the profiling data will be saved into a binary file named gmon.out. Multiple runs of the instrumented binary will overwrite this file, each time resulting in the loss of data from the previous run. In order to combine the results of multiple runs without data loss, the data from each run must be summarized into a master file, gmon.sum. This is accomplished by using the --sum flag with gprof(1) and providing the existing gmon.sum, if it exists, as an input file, along with the current test run.

Finally, once all the desired data has been collected, the binary data file, either gmon.out, the default if no specific file is specified, or gmon.sum, is converted into a text report by the gprof(1) tool. For example, to profile an executable test over two runs:

```
$ gcc test.c -o test -pg
$ ./test
$ gprof --sum test
$ ./test
$ gprof --sum test gmon.out gmon.sum
$ gprof test gmon.sum
```

The generated report, printed to stdout by default, is divided into two parts, a flat profile and a call graph. The flat profile lists functions where the most time was accounted. As one would expect, the list is sorted such that the functions at the top are where the most time was spent. Listing 11.1 presents a snippet of the flat profile generated by minigzip compression.

```
1   Flat profile:
2
3   Each sample counts as 0.01 seconds.
4     %   cumulative   self              self     total
5    time   seconds   seconds    calls  s/call   s/call  name
6   58.10     6.75      6.75  50859203   0.00     0.00  std2_longest_match
7   26.77     9.86      3.11     38967   0.00     0.00  deflate_medium
8    9.98    11.02      1.16      4068   0.00     0.00  compress_block
9    2.58    11.32      0.30  66902009   0.00     0.00  _tr_tally
10   1.20    11.46      0.14     34883   0.00     0.00  crc_fold_copy
11   0.69    11.54      0.08     12252   0.00     0.00  build_tree
12   0.52    11.60      0.06     69769   0.00     0.00  fill_window_sse
13   0.09    11.61      0.01      4084   0.00     0.00  _tr_flush_block
14   0.09    11.62      0.01         1   0.01     0.01  gzclose_w
15   0.00    11.62      0.00     53922   0.00     0.00  deflate
16   0.00    11.62      0.00     34883   0.00     0.00  copy_with_crc
17   0.00    11.62      0.00     34883   0.00     0.00  gz_comp
18   0.00    11.62      0.00     34883   0.00     0.00  gzwrite
19   0.00    11.62      0.00     34883   0.00     0.00  read_buf
20   0.00    11.62      0.00     19039   0.00     0.00  _tr_flush_bits
21   0.00    11.62      0.00      8136   0.00     0.00  send_tree
22   0.00    11.62      0.00        16   0.00     0.00  _tr_stored_block
```

LISTING 11.1

Excerpt of gprof flat profile for minigzip compression.

On the other hand, the call graph lists the callers and callees for each function. This output is sorted such that the call chains at the top of the list are responsible for the majority of time spent. Notice that on the left column, the function names are replaced with indexes. The key for these indices are provided at the very end of the report. Listing 11.2 contains a snippet of the flat profile, with the function index key beginning on line 28.

```
 1
 2                       Call graph (explanation follows)
 3
 4
 5   granularity: each sample hit covers 2 byte(s) for 0.09% of 11.62
                 seconds
 6
 7   index % time    self  children    called     name
 8                   0.00    11.62       1/1           file_compress [2]
 9   [1]    100.0    0.00    11.62       1         gz_compress [1]
10                   0.00    11.61   34883/34883        gzwrite [6]
11                   0.01    0.00        1/1           gzclose_w [15]
12                   0.00    0.00        1/1           gzclose [31]
13   ------------------------------------------------------
14                                                     <spontaneous>
15   [2]    100.0    0.00    11.62               file_compress [2]
16                   0.00    11.62       1/1           gz_compress [1]
17                   0.00    0.00        1/1           gz_open [30]
18                   0.00    0.00        1/1           gzopen [32]
19   ------------------------------------------------------
20                   0.00    0.00        5/53922        gzclose_w [15]
21                   0.00    11.61   53917/53922        gz_comp [5]
22   [3]     99.9    0.00    11.61   53922         deflate [3]
23                   3.11    8.50    38967/38967        deflate_medium [4]
24                   0.00    0.00    14955/19039        _tr_flush_bits [120]
25                   0.00    0.00        1/1           crc_fold_init [23]
26                   0.00    0.00        1/1           crc_reset [24]
27                   0.00    0.00        1/1           crc_finalize [21]
28   Index by function name
29
30   [120] _tr_flush_bits       [23] crc_fold_init      [30] gz_open
31    [8] _tr_flush_block       [24] crc_reset          [31] gzclose
32   [122] _tr_init             [3] deflate             [15] gzclose_w
33   [121] _tr_stored_block     [25] deflateEnd         [32] gzopen
34    [10] _tr_tally            [26] deflateInit2_       [6] gzwrite
35    [14] build_tree           [27] deflateReset       [13] read_buf
36    [9] compress_block        [4] deflate_medium      [17] send_tree
37    [16] copy_with_crc        [11] fill_window_sse     [7] std2_longest_
                                                              match
38    [20] crc32                [5] gz_comp             [33] x86_check_
                                                              features
39    [21] crc_finalize         [1] gz_compress         [18] zcalloc
40    [22] crc_fold_512to32     [28] gz_error           [19] zcfree
41    [12] crc_fold_copy        [29] gz_init
```

LISTING 11.2

Excerpts of gprof call graph profile for minigzip compression.

One of the major limitations of gprof is its lack of the ability to profile code located in dynamically linked libraries. A simple workaround is to statically link the executable to be profiled when compiling with the gprof instrumentations.

11.2 GCOV

The GNU code coverage tool, gcov, isn't much of a profiling tool. Instead, its primary use is to measure the code coverage achieved by unit tests; however, the tool is worth mentioning since it provides one important piece of information: the percentage of times each conditional branch was taken. This is especially useful since, outside of routine error handling branches, programmers tend to be poor judges of which branches are frequently taken and which are skipped.

Similar to gprof, gcov also relies on the compiler to instrument the application's executable, but the compiler flag used is different. At the time of this writing, gcov is only well supported by GCC. Both ICC and LLVM provide their own coverage tools, which are incompatible; however, it may be possible to obtain similar information from them.

In order to enable coverage instrumentation with GCC, the application executable must be compiled and linked with the `--coverage` compiler flag. The instrumented executable is then run. The code inserted into the instrumented executable will generate two binary files for each source file, a `.gcno` and `.gcda` file. For instance, `foo.c` will have a corresponding `foo.gcno` and `foo.gcda` file.

These files are converted into a text report by running `gcov(1)` with the desired source file as an argument. Rather than printing the results to `stdout`, a new text file will be created containing the report, corresponding to the coverage for the source file passed as an argument. The name of this file will be the source file name, with a `.gcov` suffix appended. So continuing the previous example, `gcov foo.c` will generate a text report in the file `foo.c.gcov`.

The report will include a full source listing of the file specified, along with annotations about the number of times each line was executed. In order to add the branching information, the `-b` option must be added to the `gcov(1)` command. For example:

```
$ gcc test.c -o test --coverage
$ ./test
$ gcov -b test.c
```

Listing 11.3 provides a sample excerpt from one of these annotated source code reports. In this example, there are two branches of interest, one starting on line 1 and one starting on line 5. The annotations on the left side provide the number of times each statement was executed, along with the percentage of times that branch was taken, the fallthrough case, and the percentage of times where the branch was not taken, the second percentage shown. For example, looking at the branch statistics on lines 2 and 3, it is obvious that this branch is frequently taken. On the other hand, the second branch for this workload was never taken. Additionally, note that the number of statements each line was executed corresponds to the percentage, for example, $\frac{3244}{4209} \times 100 = 77\%$.

```
1        4209:  204:                    if (zlikely((*(unsigned short *)(match
                                        + best_len - 1) != scan_end)))
2    branch  0 taken 77% (fallthrough)
3    branch  1 taken 23%
4        3244:  205:                            continue;
5         965:  206:                    if (*(unsigned short *)match
                                        != scan_start)
6    branch  0 taken 0% (fallthrough)
7    branch  1 taken 100%
8       #####:  207:                            continue;
9          -:  208:
```

LISTING 11.3

Excerpt from `gcov(1)` output.

11.3 PowerTOP

PowerTOP is a monitor, written by Arjan van de Ven, for measuring the system's behavior with regards to power consumption. This includes monitoring the number of processor wakeups, the P and C state residencies, GPU RC state, and system settings. Additionally, PowerTOP is also capable of monitoring device power consumption, either through an external power meter, RAPL, or software modeling. For its software modeling, PowerTOP records power consumption and utilization information over time, providing more accurate estimations as more results are collected. These collections are stored in `/var/cache/powertop`. By monitoring device power consumption for the system, PowerTOP can also estimate the power cost of individual applications.

PowerTOP provides both an interactive ncurses-based interface, as well as the ability to collect data and generate a report noninteractively. The noninteractive reports collect data for a predefined period of time, and then generate a report in either a HTML or CSV format. By default measurements in the noninteractive mode occur for 20 seconds and then produce a HTML report, in the file `powertop.html`. A custom period of time can be specified with the `--time=` parameter, which expects an integer representing the number of seconds for collection. A CSV report can be generated with the `--csv=filename` parameter, where `filename` represents the file for storing the report. Additionally, the default HTML report file, `powertop.html`, can be similarly modified with the `--html=filename` parameter.

The ncurses interface is divided into five separate windows, each displaying a different metric. These windows are traversed with the Tab and Shift-Tab keys combinations. The contents of the current window can be shifted by using the arrow keys. The data can be refreshed manually by pressing the "r" key. Finally, PowerTOP can be quit by pressing the Escape key.

Regardless of whether the interactive or noninteractive is used, the reported information is identical. Due to the nature of the hardware and system data PowerTOP must collect, the tool requires root privileges. The following sections describe the information reported and how it should be interpreted.

11.3.1 OVERVIEW

In "Performance Is Power Efficiency" section of Introduction, the concept of "race to idle" was introduced as a technique for improving power consumption. This concept, of bursting to complete work quickly, is only applicable if the work *can* be completed quickly. Longer running tasks, such as daemons, should be written to allow the processor to take advantage of these deep sleep states.

As described in the "C states" section of Chapter 3, in order for the processor to enter deep sleep, it must be halted, and therefore not executing instructions. Since each C state has an entry and exit latency, it is the job of the intel_idle driver in the Linux kernel to request the deepest C state that meets the latency requirements for when the kernel needs the processor to start executing instructions again. Since the kernel is tickless, only waking up when needed, it is crucial that user space applications are incredibly careful about how often they wake the system from its slumber. PowerTOP reports these occurrences in order to allow the user to identify any misbehaving applications which are impacting power consumption.

Figure 11.1 shows the default window in PowerTOP, running on an idle system. As expected, the backlight, which was on maximum brightness, was consuming the most power. Additionally, the network devices, the wireless card and Ethernet card, are consuming a lot of power. Notice that the wireless interrupts and interrupt handler are also causing a significant number of wakeups.

```
PowerTOP 2.5      Overview    Idle stats   Frequency stats   Device stats   Tunables

The battery reports a discharge rate of 10.6 W
The estimated remaining time is 7 hours, 21 minutes

Summary: 124.0 wakeups/second,   0.1 GPU ops/seconds, 0.0 VFS ops/sec and 0.9% CPU use

Power est.                Usage       Events/s    Category      Description
   10.9 W      86.7%                   Device        Display backlight
   3.54 W       1.1 pkts/s             Device        Network interface: wlp3s0 (iwlwifi)
   241 mW       0.0 pkts/s             Device        Network interface: em1 (e1000e)
   37.3 mW      3.2 ms/s     80.0      Process       [irq/46-iwlwifi]
   4.87 mW    327.7 us/s     14.0      Timer         tick_sched_timer
   4.30 mW    529.0 us/s      2.2      Interrupt     [46] iwlwifi
   3.09 mW    194.1 us/s      9.4      kWork         ieee80211_iface_work
   2.49 mW    336.8 us/s      0.05     Process       /usr/lib/systemd/systemd --switched
   2.46 mW    124.8 us/s      0.4      Process       /usr/libexec/gnome-terminal-server
   1.97 mW    158.5 us/s      0.3      Process       /usr/bin/Xorg :0 -background none -
   1.95 mW    264.5 us/s      0.00     Process       [kworker/u16:5]
   1.92 mW    260.6 us/s      0.00     Process       [kworker/u16:4]
   1.86 mW    231.4 us/s      0.8      Process       /usr/libexec/deja-dup/deja-dup-moni
   1.85 mW    250.6 us/s      0.00     Interrupt     [1] timer(softirq)

<ESC> Exit
```

FIGURE 11.1

PowerTOP ncurses interface overview.

Aside from hardware devices and their interrupts, there are also some user space processes keeping the CPU awake. On this list is gnome-shell, the X server, and the terminal emulator. At the very least, PowerTOP refreshing the ncurses UI can account for the terminal emulator wakeups, and at least some of the X server and gnome-shell usage as the terminal window is composited and displayed.

11.3.2 IDLE STATS

Maintaining residency in deep idle, that is, C, states is necessary for reducing power consumption. The Idle Stats window of PowerTOP dissects the system's idle state residency by processor topology, showing the percentage of time spent in each idle state for the processor packages, cores, and hardware threads. This natural hierarchy allows for an analysis of why certain states were or were not entered, with each level in the topology requiring the underlying levels enter their idle states first. For instance, a processor core can only enter an idle state if both its hardware threads are idle and a processor package can only enter an idle state if all its underlying core and uncore resources are idle.

By monitoring the core and package residencies in the various idle states, it's possible to quantify how power-efficient the software is allowing the hardware to be. Additionally, it can help identify problems within the system's configuration. The lack of the ability to enter a deeper idle state, that is, a residency of zero, can be indicative of a misconfigured or misbehaving driver. Consider that the integrated graphics hardware is present within the processor package, that is, it is an uncore resource. Since all core and uncore resources within a package must be idle as a prerequisite for entering the associated package idle state, which provides the largest power reductions, a misbehaving graphics driver or incorrect graphics configuration that doesn't allow the GPU to enter a RC6 state can drastically affect power and additionally affect the ability of the processor to utilize turbo modes. Unfortunately, this is a very real problem over the last couple of years, as some distributions have disabled RC6 support in the graphics driver in order to improve stability on systems that typically have broken BIOS tables. *Make sure RC6 is enabled and working correctly.*

It is also important to note that *just because PowerTOP displays an idle state does not mean that the underlying hardware necessarily supports that state.* So a zero residency in the deepest sleep state does not necessarily indicate an issue.

Figure 11.2 shows an example of the idle state residencies for a Second Generation Intel® Core™ processor laptop. Notice the processor topology, starting from the left: one processor package, which depends on four cores, which in turn depend on eight hardware threads. Additionally, the GPU residencies can be found at the bottom of the window, which may require scrolling with the arrow keys. Notice that the deepest package idle state has a nonzero residency, and each of the cores and the GPU have high residency percentages in the deepest available states. Additionally, take notice of the zero percent residency in the RC6p and RC6pp states. These residencies are not an error in the configuration, since RC6p support was introduced with the Third Generation Intel® Core™ processors and RC6pp was introduced after that.

```
PowerTOP 2.5      Overview   Idle stats   Frequency stats   Device stats   Tunables

           Package      |          Core     |            CPU 0        CPU 1
                        |                   |  C0 active   0.7%        2.8%
                        |                   |  POLL        0.0%   0.0 ms  0.0%    0.0 ms
                        |                   |  C1E-SNB     0.0%   0.0 ms  0.0%    0.1 ms
  C2 (pc2)   13.1%      |                   |
  C3 (pc3)    0.0%      | C3 (cc3)   0.1%   |  C3-SNB      0.1%   0.3 ms  0.3%    1.0 ms
  C6 (pc6)    0.0%      | C6 (cc6)   0.0%   |  C6-SNB      0.0%   0.0 ms  0.0%    0.0 ms
  C7 (pc7)   71.4%      | C7 (cc7)  88.7%   |  C7-SNB     98.4%  11.8 ms 91.9%    3.4 ms

                        |          Core     |            CPU 2        CPU 3
                        |                   |  C0 active   0.3%        0.1%
                        |                   |  POLL        0.0%   0.0 ms  0.0%    0.0 ms
                        |                   |  C1E-SNB     0.2%   0.3 ms  0.0%    0.0 ms
                        |                   |
                        | C3 (cc3)   0.7%   |  C3-SNB      0.0%   0.0 ms  0.0%    0.0 ms
                        | C6 (cc6)   0.0%   |  C6-SNB      0.0%   0.0 ms  0.0%    0.0 ms
                        | C7 (cc7)  97.4%   |  C7-SNB     98.2%  43.2 ms 99.9%   48.2 ms

                        |          Core     |            CPU 4        CPU 5
                        |                   |  C0 active   0.1%        0.1%
                        |                   |  POLL        0.0%   0.0 ms  0.0%    0.0 ms
                        |                   |  C1E-SNB     0.1%   0.4 ms  0.2%    0.9 ms
                        |                   |
                        | C3 (cc3)   1.5%   |  C3-SNB      0.0%   0.1 ms  0.0%    0.2 ms
                        | C6 (cc6)   0.0%   |  C6-SNB      0.0%   0.0 ms  0.0%    0.0 ms
                        | C7 (cc7)  97.7%   |  C7-SNB     99.6%  34.8 ms 99.7%   30.6 ms

                        |          Core     |            CPU 6        CPU 7
                        |                   |  C0 active   0.3%        0.3%
                        |                   |  POLL        0.0%   0.0 ms  0.0%    0.2 ms
                        |                   |  C1E-SNB     0.0%   0.0 ms  0.0%    0.0 ms
                        |                   |
                        | C3 (cc3)   0.0%   |  C3-SNB      0.0%   0.0 ms  0.0%    0.0 ms
                        | C6 (cc6)   0.0%   |  C6-SNB      0.0%   0.0 ms  0.0%    0.0 ms
                        | C7 (cc7)  96.3%   |  C7-SNB     96.4%  40.7 ms 99.1%   55.8 ms

                        |          GPU      |
                        |  Powered On  0.4% |
                        |  RC6        99.6% |
                        |  RC6p        0.0% |
                        |  RC6pp       0.0% |

<ESC> Exit
```

FIGURE 11.2

PowerTOP ncurses interface displaying C state residencies.

11.3.3 FREQUENCY STATS

The Frequency Stats window displays the percentage of time each package, core, and hardware thread spends running in the various supported frequencies, including both P states and Intel® Turbo Boost frequencies.

Unlike the idle stats window, the various frequencies are only added to the list after they have been observed. Since P states only make sense when the processor is executing instructions, that is, in C0, an idle system often won't display much in terms of frequency information.

Figure 11.3 shows an example Frequency Stats window. Notice that, similar to the idle stats window, the processor topology is sorted with the larger resources and power savings to the left of the screen and then dependencies moving further to the right.

```
PowerTOP 2.5      Overview  Idle stats  Frequency stats  Device stats  Tunables

            Package |              Core |           CPU 0      CPU 1
                    |                   | Actual   1.5 GHz       871 MHz
  Idle      92.7%   | Idle       93.2%  | Idle      99.2%     93.9%
  3.31 GHz   0.1%   | 3.31 GHz    0.0%  | 3.31 GHz   0.0%      0.0%
  1.80 GHz   0.0%   |  900 MHz    1.7%  |  900 MHz   0.0%      1.7%
   900 MHz   1.7%   | 2.21 GHz    0.0%  | 2.21 GHz   0.0%      0.0%
  2.40 GHz   0.1%   |  800 MHz    3.7%  |  800 MHz   0.5%      3.1%
  2.21 GHz   0.2%   | 1400 MHz    0.1%  | 1400 MHz   0.1%      0.0%
   800 MHz   3.8%   | 1500 MHz    0.0%  | 1500 MHz   0.0%      0.0%
  1500 MHz   0.1%   | 1000 MHz    1.2%  |                      1.2%
  1400 MHz   0.1%   |                   |

                    |              Core |           CPU 2      CPU 3
                    |                   | Actual   1.9 GHz      1040 MHz
                    | Idle       99.7%  | Idle      99.7%    100.0%
                    | 3.31 GHz    0.0%  | 3.31 GHz   0.0%      0.0%
                    | 1.80 GHz    0.0%  | 1.80 GHz   0.0%      0.0%
                    | 2.40 GHz    0.1%  | 2.40 GHz   0.1%      0.0%
                    | 2.21 GHz    0.2%  | 2.21 GHz   0.2%      0.0%

<ESC> Exit |
```

FIGURE 11.3

PowerTOP ncurses interface displaying P state residencies.

11.3.4 DEVICE STATS

As mentioned earlier, PowerTOP can aggregate power consumption data from a variety of sources, including actual power meters, the RAPL interface introduced in the Second Generation Intel® Core™ processor family, and software modeling.

The software models provided with PowerTOP are based on actual data collected with a power meter. This power meter information shows how different devices' power consumption scales with utilization, which is another aspect of the system monitored by PowerTOP. By combining these two aspects, PowerTOP is able to estimate the actual power drain per device. It is important to recognize that these are estimates, and that measuring power consumption precisely requires a hardware power meter.

Figure 11.4 illustrates an example Device Stats window.

11.3.5 TUNABLES

PowerTOP automatically checks the system configuration in order to detect any misconfigurations that might hurt power efficiency. By using the Up and Down Arrow keys, it is possible to scroll through each item. With an item marked Bad highlighted, pressing the Enter key will cause PowerTOP to attempt to modify the misconfigured item to a more appropriate value. This is accomplished by writing to various files in sysfs and is not a persistent modification. This functionality is for testing the impact of various configurations, since PowerTOP is not designed for configuring system settings each boot. Instead, a daemon like `tuned` can be used to automatically set the desired configuration at boot. The `tuned` daemon is packaged with a tool `powertop2tuned` that runs PowerTOP and then translates its suggestions into a custom `tuned` profile.

```
PowerTOP 2.5      Overview   Idle stats   Frequency stats   Device stats   Tunables

The battery reports a discharge rate of 13.5 W
System baseline power is estimated at 14.3 W

Power est.    Usage      Device name
  6.31 W      86.7%        Display backlight
  4.67 W      62.7%        Display backlight
              0.0 pkts/s   Network interface: em1 (e1000e)
  477 mW      1.2%         CPU core
  455 mW      1.2%         CPU misc
  295 mW      0.3 ops/s    GPU core
  127 mW      0.0 pkts/s   nic:virbr0
 3.36 mW      0.3 ops/s    GPU misc
  246 uW      0.2 pkts/s   Network interface: wlp3s0 (iwlwifi)
    0 mW      2439 rpm     Laptop fan
    0 mW      100.0%       Radio device: iwlwifi
    0 mW      0.0%         USB device: usb-device-8087-0024
    0 mW      0.0%         USB device: EHCI Host Controller
    0 mW      0.0%         USB device: Integrated Camera (Ricoh Company Ltd.)
    0 mW      0.0%         USB device: usb-device-8087-0024

<ESC> Exit
```

FIGURE 11.4

PowerTOP ncurses interface displaying device power estimates.

```
PowerTOP 2.5      Overview   Idle stats   Frequency stats   Device stats   Tunables

>> Bad            Enable Audio codec power management
   Bad            Enable SATA link power Management for host4
   Bad            Enable SATA link power Management for host5
   Bad            Enable SATA link power Management for host2
   Bad            Enable SATA link power Management for host3
   Bad            Enable SATA link power Management for host0
   Bad            Enable SATA link power Management for host1
   Bad            VM writeback timeout
   Bad            Runtime PM for PCI Device Intel Corporation 6 Series/C200 Series Chipset
   Bad            Runtime PM for PCI Device Intel Corporation QM67 Express Chipset Family L
   Bad            Runtime PM for PCI Device Intel Corporation 6 Series/C200 Series Chipset
   Bad            Runtime PM for PCI Device Intel Corporation 6 Series/C200 Series Chipset
   Bad            Runtime PM for PCI Device Intel Corporation 6 Series/C200 Series Chipset
   Bad            Runtime PM for PCI Device Intel Corporation 6 Series/C200 Series Chipset
   Bad            Runtime PM for PCI Device Intel Corporation 6 Series/C200 Series Chipset
   Bad            Runtime PM for PCI Device Intel Corporation 6 Series/C200 Series Chipset
   Bad            Runtime PM for PCI Device Intel Corporation 82579LM Gigabit Network Conne
   Bad            Runtime PM for PCI Device Intel Corporation 6 Series/C200 Series Chipset
   Bad            Runtime PM for PCI Device Intel Corporation 2nd Generation Core Processor
   Bad            Runtime PM for PCI Device Intel Corporation 2nd Generation Core Processor
   Bad            Runtime PM for PCI Device Intel Corporation 6 Series/C200 Series Chipset
   Bad            Runtime PM for PCI Device Intel Corporation Centrino Wireless-N 1000 [Con
   Bad            Runtime PM for PCI Device Ricoh Co Ltd PCIe SDXC/MMC Host Controller
   Bad            Runtime PM for PCI Device Ricoh Co Ltd R5C832 PCIe IEEE 1394 Controller
   Bad            Wake-on-lan status for device em1
   Good           NMI watchdog should be turned off
   Good           Autosuspend for USB device Integrated Camera [Ricoh Company Ltd.]
   Good           Autosuspend for USB device EHCI Host Controller [usb1]
   Good           Autosuspend for USB device EHCI Host Controller [usb2]
   Good           Autosuspend for unknown USB device 1-1 (8087:0024)
   Good           Autosuspend for unknown USB device 2-1 (8087:0024)
   Good           Wake-on-lan status for device virbr0-nic
   Good           Wake-on-lan status for device virbr0
   Good           Wake-on-lan status for device wlp3s0
   Good           Using 'ondemand' cpufreq governor

<ESC> Exit  | <Enter> Toggle tunable  | <r> Window refresh
```

FIGURE 11.5

PowerTOP ncurses interface displaying system tunables.

The status of runtime power management is typically listed for each device. This controls whether the device is able to enter low power states, such as whether a PCI device can enter D3hot. At the time of this writing, runtime power management is disabled by default for USB devices, due to problems with some devices not functioning properly. Figure 11.5 illustrates an example Tunables window.

11.4 **LatencyTOP**

Similar to PowerTOP, LatencyTOP is a monitor, also written by Arjan van de Ven, for measuring the duration that user space applications spend in a blocked state, along with the underlying reason.

In order to instrument the kernel scheduler to obtain this data, the kernel must be built with LatencyTOP support. This is controlled via two Kconfig options, CONFIG_HAVE_LATENCYTOP_SUPPORT and CONFIG_LATENCYTOP. Most Linux distributions only enable these options for their debug kernels.

```
$ grep LATENCYTOP /boot/config-'uname -r'
CONFIG_HAVE_LATENCYTOP_SUPPORT=y
CONFIG_LATENCYTOP=y
```

LatencyTOP communicates to user space through the procfs filesystem. Controlling and accessing this information requires root privileges. Data collection is enabled or disabled by writing either a "1" or "0" into /proc/sys/kernel/latencytop. Once data collection is enabled, latency statistics for the entire system are accessed through the /proc/latency_stats file. Additionally, the latency statistics for each specific process can be accessed via the latency file within that processes' procfs directory, for example, /proc/2145/latency.

The first line of each of these files is a header, which identifies the LatencyTOP version. This header is then followed by zero or more data entries. Each of these entries take the form of three integers followed by a string. This string contains the function call stack, starting from the far right, with each function call separated by a space. This call stack only traces kernel functions, so the function on the far right is always a system call invocation. The first integer represents the number of times this function call stack has occurred. The second integer represents the total microseconds of latency caused by this call stack. The third integer represents the largest latency in microseconds of one invocation of this call stack (van de Ven, 2008).

For example:

```
# cat /proc/630/latency
Latency Top version : v0.1
1 881 881 poll_schedule_timeout do_sys_poll SyS_poll system_call_
fastpath
1 9 9 futex_wait_queue_me futex_wait do_futex SyS_futex system_call_
fastpath
```

In this example, the process has made two system calls, poll(2) and futex(2). Each of these calls occurred once, with the invocation of poll(2) blocking for 881 μs, and the invocation of futex(2) blocking for 9 μs.

Aside from manually reading these files or enabling or disabling data collection, there is a GTK+ graphical interface and a ncurses-based command-line interface. The data displayed within these interfaces is the same, although they do provide a few conveniences, such as automatically starting and stopping data collection, and printing the process name next to the pid.

11.5 SYSPROF

Sysprof is a monitor that measures how much time is spent in each function call. Time per function is reported with two different metrics, cumulative time and self time. Cumulative time measures the time spent within a function, including all function calls invoked from within that function. Self time measures the time spent within a function, excluding all function calls invoked from within that function, i.e., just the cost of the function itself. This level of detail makes Sysprof very useful for algorithmic analysis.

11.5.1 COLLECTION

Originally, Sysprof had its own kernel module, which is called sysprof-module, for collecting data. Starting around 2009, Sysprof began leveraging the kernel's perf counter infrastructure, thus obviating the need for a separate module. At the time of this writing, Sysprof unconditionally uses the software clock counter, `PERF_COUNT_SW_CPU_CLOCK`, although support for the hardware cycle counter, `PERF_COUNT_HW_CPU_CYCLES`, is also implemented. Reading through the commit log, it appears that the hardware counters were disabled due to issues with some hardware platforms not working properly. If desired, reenabling the hardware counters appears trivial.

There are two methods for collecting data in Sysprof, the GTK GUI and the command-line interface. Both methods require the associated permissions for opening a perf event file descriptor, as configured via the `perf_event_paranoid`, as described in Chapter 8.

The GTK GUI is invoked via the `sysprof` command. Figure 11.6 is a screenshot of the interface. To begin collecting system-wide results, click the Start button in the menubar. As samples are collected, the sample count will increment. Once the operation being profiled is complete, stop the collection by selecting the Profile button in the menubar. At this point, the three views, labeled Functions, Callers, and Descendants, will populate. These results can be saved for later inspection via the Save As option under the Profiler menu.

The Descendants view organizes the results as a hierarchical tree of modules, with each module representing a different process. The root of this tree, which will always have a total time of 100%, is labeled "Everything." The root's children each correspond to a process running on the system. The cumulative time represents what percentage of time sampled was spent in the given process during data collection. Each process's children represents a function call, and each function call's children

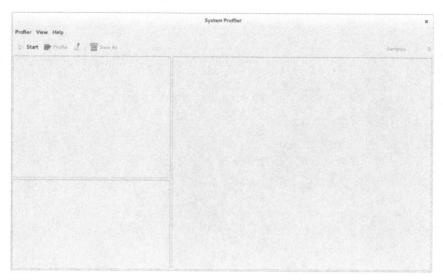

FIGURE 11.6

Sysprof's GTK interface.

represent function calls from that function. Double-clicking on a node will update the related Functions and Callers views, based on the selected node.

The Functions view displays a sorted list of the functions that consumed the most time. By default, the Functions view sorts based on the total time, which highlights the hottest call chains. Sorting this view by self time highlights the most expensive functions in the profile. Single-clicking on an element of the Functions view will update the Descendants view and Callers view, with the call stack information for that element.

Finally, the Callers view displays the call sites for the highlighted function, i.e., where the current function was called from, and the percentage distribution of those calls.

More information, along with the source code, can be found at http://sysprof.com/.

REFERENCES

Free Software Foundation, 2014, 09a. GCC(1) Manual Page.
Free Software Foundation, 2014, 09b. GCOV(1) Manual Page.
Osier, J., Fenlason, J., 1992. GNU gprof.
Sandmann, S., 2013. Sysprof Source Repository. https://git.gnome.org/browse/sysprof/.
van de Ven, A., 2008,01. latencytop.c. ${LINUX_SRC}/kernel/latencytop.c. Linux Kernel Source File.
van de Ven, A., 2009, 10. latencytop.c. Latencytop user space tool source.
van de Ven, A. 2014. Powertop Source Repository. https://github.com/fenrus75/powertop.

PART

Optimization
Techniques

3

Toolchain Primer

CHAPTER

12

CHAPTER CONTENTS

A *toolchain* is a set of tools for building, inspecting, and modifying software. All of the optimization techniques explained in this book, in one way or another, rely on support from the toolchain. As such, despite the fact that the majority of developers are intimately familiar with the toolchains they frequently use, the author feels compelled to review them to ensure all readers are on the same page. The major components of a toolchain include, but aren't limited to, a compiler, an assembler, and a linker.

The *compiler* is responsible for parsing source files written in a high-level programming language, such as C. The files are first translated into an intermediate language, used internally to the compiler. This intermediate language allows for the compiler to analyze program flow and optimize accordingly. After the optimization phase is complete, the compiler outputs assembly code, which is passed directly to the assembler.

The *assembler* is responsible for translating the instruction mnemonics, used in human-readable assembly, into the binary opcodes expected by the processor. Unlike the compiler, the assembler's output typically has a one-to-one relationship with the assembly source, except in the case of pseudo-instructions, which may translate to multiple, or even zero, instructions. The output produced by the assembler is a binary object file.

Finally, the *linker* is responsible for combining the sections from each binary object file, resolving symbol references, and producing the final output, whether an executable or library. The exact layout of the linker output can be controlled through a linker script, which, for each section, defines the ordering, offsets, and virtual memory addresses.

While these tools are used every time source code is built into an executable or library, there are many other important pieces of the toolchain. Some tools allow for inspection of object files, such as `nm` and `objdump`, which display the information encoded in the object file in a human-readable form. Other tools allow for the modification of object files, such as `strip` and `objcopy`.

In Linux, there are three major toolchains: the GNU compiler toolchain (GCC), the Low Level Virtual Machine toolchain (LLVM), and the Intel® C and C++ Compilers (ICC).

GCC is the most common toolchain, without a doubt, consisting of multiple projects, including binutils, which provides the tools for creating and modifying binary object files, the GNU compiler collection, which provides the compiler and frontends for multiple programming languages, the GNU debugger , as well as other build tools, such as GNU autotools, and GNU Make. In fact, so many open source projects, such as the Linux kernel, rely on so many GCC-specific behaviors and extensions, that most of the other toolchains strive to maintain at least some level of compatibility with GCC.

Another common toolchain present on Linux is LLVM. While a much younger project than GCC, LLVM has been progressing rapidly and has attracted much attention for its modular design and static analysis capabilities.

The last of the major toolchains is the Intel® compiler, designed specifically for producing heavily optimized code for Intel® processors. The Intel compiler is available free for noncommercial use on Linux. More information is available at https://software.intel.com/en-us/c-compilers.

This chapter focuses mostly on the GNU toolchain, due to its ubiquitous nature and the fact that many of its extensions are supported by other toolchains for compatibility. The author will do his best to point out areas where the different idiosyncrasies of the toolchains can be problematic.

12.1 COMPILER FLAGS

The first step in leveraging the compiler to produce better code is to learn how to control the compiler's optimization stages and instruction generation. These are selected through the use of command arguments to the compiler, often called compiler flags or CFLAGS.

Looking at the list of individual optimizers available in GCC can be daunting, partially due to the large number of options available. To remedy this problem, GCC exposes predefined optimization levels that automatically toggle the appropriate optimizers. These levels are selected by the -O compiler flag, a capital letter O.

The levels, and this is fairly standard between different compilers, are described in Table 12.1. The exact optimizers enabled at each level can be manually queried with

Table 12.1 GCC Optimization Levels

Level	CFLAG	Description
0	-O0	No optimizations enabled.
1	-O1	Optimizations are enabled that reduce code and execution time, but don't significantly increase compilation time.
2	-O2	All optimizations are enabled that reduce code and execution time, excluding those that involve a tradeoff between code size and speed.
3	-O3	Enables all optimizations at Level 2, plus those that can drastically increase code size and those that may not always improve performance.
s	-Os	Optimizes for size. Similar to Level 2, except without optimizations that could increase code size, plus additional optimizations to reduce code size.
fast	-Ofast	Optimization Level 3, plus additional optimizations that may violate the language standards.
g	-Og	Enables any optimizations that do not interfere with the debugger or significantly increase the compilation time.

the -Q option. An explanation of each of these optimizations is typically available in the GCC man page. For instance, to determine the optimizers enabled at -O2:

```
$ gcc -Q -O2 --help=optimizers
```

Aside from what optimizations the compiler can perform on the program flow, there are two other important considerations, the first being which instructions the compiler can generate and the second being which platform those instructions are tuned for.

Like the optimizers, the compiler's use of each instruction set extension is controlled through compiler flags. These take the form of -m<feature> and -mno-<feature>. For example, GCC accepts -msse3 and -mno-sse3 to enable and disable SSE3 instructions, respectively. Multiple instruction set extensions can be enabled simultaneously.

Rather than specifying the individual instruction sets, a specific processor profile can be specified in the -march=<arch> compiler flag. This will enable all of the instruction sets that are listed within GCC's profile for that architecture. If compiling for the local system, a special architecture profile exists entitled native, which automatically detects and enables all of the instruction sets supported by the underlying processor. Table 12.2 highlights some of the more recent architecture profiles, along with the feature sets they enable.

In order to select a specific processor type for the compiler to optimize for, set the -mtune=<type> compiler flags. The architectural profiles used for -march are valid values for -mtune.

While selecting which instruction set extensions the compiler can generate is a fairly straightforward process, determining whether the compiler should generate them is slightly more involved. When making this decision, it's important to realize that the compiler can generate these instructions throughout the entire program without any runtime checks as to whether the underlying processor supports those instructions. If the executable or library attempts to execute one of these instructions on a processor that doesn't support that necessary instruction set extension, the processor will raise a #UD, an UnDefined opcode exception. This processor exception will be trapped by the Linux kernel, which will send a SIGILL, the POSIX illegal instruction signal, to the offending process. While this signal can be caught, the default signal handler will terminate the process and produce a core dump.

Table 12.2 Modern GCC -march Profiles and Their Supported Features

Profile	SSE	SSE2	SSE3	SSSE3	SSE4.1	SSE4.2	Intel® AVX	Intel® AVX2
core2	•	•	•	•				
corei7	•	•	•	•	•	•		
corei7-avx	•	•	•	•	•	•	•	
corei7-avx2	•	•	•	•	•	•	•	•

Thus, the instruction set enabled for the compiler to automatically generate at compile time must be the lowest common denominator of the hardware the software is designed to support. Section 12.3 will explain how to remedy this problem.

12.2 ELF AND THE x86/x86_64 ABIs

In Linux, the execve() system call is used to load and execute a stored program in the current process. To accommodate this, the stored program must convey information to the kernel regarding how the associated code should be organized in memory, among other bits of information. This information is communicated through the various pieces of the executable file format, which the kernel must thus parse and handle accordingly.

Linux supports parsing and executing multiple file formats. Internally, Linux abstracts the implementations for each of these file format handlers via the linux_binfmt struct. Each handler is responsible for parsing the associated file format, creating the necessary state, and then starting the execution. For example, the reason that it's possible to invoke execve() on shell scripts beginning with the line "#! <program> <program arguments>" is because there is an explicit handler, binfmt_script, dedicated to parsing files with that prefix, executing the program, and then passing the script to that program.

These linux_binfmt handler implementations, along with the common execve() code, can be found in ${LINUX_SRC}/fs/binfmt_*.c and ${LINUX_SRC}/fs/exec.c.

While Linux supports multiple executable file formats, the most commonly used format on Linux is the Executable and Linkable Format (ELF). The ELF standard was published by the UNIX Systems Laboratories, and was intended to provide a single executable format that would "extend across multiple operating environments" (UNIX System Laboratories, 2001).

ELF defines three different object types: relocatable files, executable files, and shared object files. Relocatable files are designed to be combined with other object files by the linker to produce executable or shared object files. Executable files are designed to be invoked via execve(). Shared object files are designed to be linked, either by the linker at build time, or at load time by the dynamic linker. Shared object files allow for code to be referenced via shared libraries.

The ELF format is comprised of two complementary views.

The first view, the linking view, is comprised of the program sections. Sections group various aspects such as code and data into contiguous regions within the ELF file. The linker is responsible for concatenating duplicate sections when linking multiple object files. For example, if object file foo.o defines a function foo() and a variable x, and object file bar.o defines a function bar() and a variable y, the linker would produce an object file whose code section contained the functions foo() and bar() and whose data section contained variables x and y.

The ELF specification defines special sections that are allocated for specific tasks, such as holding code or read-only data. These special sections can be identified by the leading dot in their name. Developers are also free to define their own custom sections.

A sampling of some common special sections and their usage is described below:

.text Holds executable instructions.
.bss Holds uninitialized, i.e., initialized to zero, data. Since all of the variables in the .bss section have a value of zero, the actual zeros aren't physically stored in the file. When the file is loaded, the corresponding memory region is zeroed.
.data Holds initialized data.
.rodata Holds read-only data.
.strtab A string table containing a NULL-terminated string of each symbol or section name. The first and last entries are NULL bytes.
.symtab A symbol table containing entries for locating symbols. Includes the symbol name, as an index into the .strtab section, the symbol type, the symbol size, etc.

In GAS, the GNU assembler, the current section is selected via the `.section` pseudo-op. Some popular special sections can also be selected through their corresponding pseudo-ops, e.g., `.data`, or `.text`, which switches to the `.data` or `.text` sections, respectively.

The second view, the execution view, is comprised of segments. Unlike sections, which represent the file layout, segments represent the virtual memory segments during execution. These segments are described in the Program Header table, which contains the information needed by the kernel to structure the code in memory. This table consists of the Load Memory Address (LMA) and Virtual Memory Address (VMA) for each memory segment, along with other information, such as the alignment requirements and size in memory. To accommodate on-demand loading of virtual memory segments, the ELF format stipulates that a segment's virtual address and file offset must be congruent modulo the page size.

12.2.1 RELOCATIONS AND PIC

One important aspect of building and loading an executable object is the handling of external symbols, i.e., symbols exposed in other ELF objects. There are two different techniques for dealing with external symbols. The first technique, static linking, occurs completely at link time while the second technique, dynamic linking, occurs partially at link time and partially at load time.

Statically linking an executable fully resolves all external symbols at link time. To accomplish this, the external dependencies are explicitly copied from their ELF objects into the executable. In other words, the executable includes all of the user space code needed for it to run. While this alleviates the need for resolving symbols at load time, it comes at the cost of increased executable size, memory usage, and update effort.

The increased executable size is caused by the inclusion of the program's dependencies. For instance, if an executable relies on functions from the C runtime, such as printf, the full printf implementation from libc must be copied into the executable. The exact size increase depends, since modern linkers only copy the needed bits, ensuring that the code size only pays for what the software uses.

The increased memory usage is caused by the redundant copies of functions between executables. For instance in the previous example, each statically linked executable that uses printf must have its own copy of the printf implementation, whereas otherwise all of the executables can share one implementation. The author imagines that some readers might argue that static linking actually reduces memory usage, since unused objects from libraries aren't loaded into the process image. While it is true that with dynamic linking the full library, including unused objects, will be mapped into the virtual address space of the process, that doesn't necessarily translate to that full library being loaded into physical memory. Each page of the library will only be loaded from disk into memory once it has been accessed, and once these pages have been loaded they can be shared between multiple executables.

The increased update effort is caused by the fact that the only way to update the external dependencies used by an executable is to recompile that executable. This also makes it more difficult to determine what version of a library a specific executable is using. This can obviously be a serious issue when determining whether an executable is susceptible to a published security vulnerability in one of its dependencies. With dynamic linking, only the shared library needs to be recompiled.

Unlike with static linking, dynamic linking doesn't fully resolve the location of external dependencies until run time. At link time, the linker creates special sections, describing the external dependencies that need to be resolved at run time. When the object is loaded, this information is used by the dynamic linker to finish resolving the external symbols enumerated within the object. This process is referred to as symbol *binding*. One this is complete, control is transferred to the executable.

The linker creates an PT_INTERP entry into the object's Program Header. This entry contains a NULL-terminated filesystem path to the dynamic linker, normally ld.so or ld-linux.so. This is the dynamic linker that will be invoked to load the necessary symbols.

The linker also creates a .dynamic section that includes a sentinel-entry-terminated array of dynamic properties. Each of these entries is composed of a type and value. A full list of the supported types and their subsequent meanings can be found within the ELF specification. A few of the important types are described below.

DT_NEEDED Array elements marked with this type represent the names of shared libraries required for external symbol resolution. The names can either be the SONAME or the filesystem path, relative or absolute. The value associated with this type is an offset into the file's string table. A list of values of this type can be obtained either by reading the section, with a command like readelf -d, or at execution time via setting the LD_TRACE_LOADED_OBJECTS environment variable. For convenience, ldd is a utility that will set the environment variable and execute the program.

DT_SONAME The shared object name of the file. The value associated with this type is an offset into the file's string table. This value is set via the linker with the -soname= LDFLAG.

DT_RPATH The search library search path. The value associated with this type is an offset into the file's string table. This value is set via the linker with the -rpath= LDFLAG.

DT_HASH The location of the symbol hash table. The value associated with this type is the table address.

DT_TEXTREL Whether the relocations will update read-only code.

Each of the entries in the .dynamic section marked DT_NEEDED are loaded by the dynamic linker and then searched for the necessary symbols. At link time, the linker creates a .hash section, which consists of a hash table of the symbol names exported within the current file. This hash table is used to accelerate the search process at run time.

Unlike executables, which are always loaded at a fixed address known as build time, shared objects can be loaded at any address. Otherwise, it would be possible for conflicts to arise where two objects expect to be loaded at the same address.

In order to handle this, the symbols in shared objects must be *relocatable*. The ELF format supports many different types of relocations; a full description of each kind can be found within the ELF specification. While the programmer isn't required to manually handle these relocations, it is necessary to understand what happens behind the scenes, because it impacts both performance and security.

When building relocatable code, the linker uses a dummy base address, typically zero, with each symbol value set to the appropriate offset from the base address of the symbol's section. Each time one of these addresses is used in the code, the linker creates an entry in that section's corresponding relocation section. This entry contains the relocation type, that determines how the real address should be calculated, and the location of the code that needs to be updated with the real address. The relocation section takes the form of .rel.section_name or .rela.section_name, where section_name is the section containing that relocation.

At runtime, the dynamic linker iterates the relocation section. For each entry, the real address is calculated and then corresponding code is patched with the resulting address. This has three important ramifications. First, a significant number of relocations can hurt application load performance. Second, the code pages in memory must be writable, since the dynamic linker needs to update them with the relocations, and thus security is reduced. Third, since the code pages are modified by the relocations, they can't be shared between processes, since each process will have different addresses, and thus this leads to increased memory usage.

Obviously binding a large number of symbols before execution begins can be devastating to the application's load time. Even worse, there is no guarantee that all of these resolved symbols will actually be needed during execution. In order to alleviate this issue, ELF supports lazy binding, that is, where symbols are resolved the first time they are actually used. To accommodate this, function calls occur indirectly through the Procedure Linkage Table (PLT) and Global Offset Table (GOT). The GOT contains the calculated addresses of the relocated symbols, while the PLT is used as a trampoline to that address for function calls.

Each entry in the PLT, except the first, corresponds to a specific function. Rather than directly calling the relocated symbol, the code jumps to the function's PLT entry. The first instruction in a function's PLT entry jumps to the address stored in the function's corresponding GOT entry. Initially, before the symbol address has been bound, the GOT address points back to the next instruction in the PLT entry, that is, the next instruction after the PLT's first jump instruction. This next instruction pushes the symbol's relocation offset onto the stack. Then the next instruction jumps to the first PLT entry, which invokes the dynamic linker to resolve the relocation offset pushed onto the stack. Once the dynamic linker has calculated the relocated address, it updates the relevant entry in the GOT and then jumps to the relocated function.

For future invocations of that function, the code will still jump to the function's PLT entry. The first instruction in the PLT will jump to the address stored in the GOT, which will now point to the relocated address. In other words, the cost of binding the symbols occurs the first time the function is used. After that, the only additional cost is the indirect jump into the PLT.

Another problem with the dynamic linker patching code at runtime is that the code pages must be writable and are dirtied, that is, modified. Writable code pages are a security risk, since those pages are also marked as executable. Additionally, dirty pages can't be shared between multiple processes and must be committed back to disk when swapped out. To solve this problem, the relocations need to be shifted from the code pages to the data pages, since each process will require its own copy of those anyway. This is the key insight of Position Independent Code (PIC).

The PLT is never modified by relocations, so it is marked read-only and shared between processes. On the other hand, each process will require its own GOT, containing the specific relocations for that process. In PIC, the PLT can only indirectly access the GOT.

The method for addressing the GOT in the PLT works slightly differently between the 32- and 64-bit ELF formats. In both specifications, the address of the GOT is encoded relative to the instruction pointer. For 64-bit PIC, access to the GOT is encoded as an offset relative to the current instruction pointer. This straightforward approach is possible because of *RIP*-relative addressing, which is only available in 64-bit mode. For 32-bit PIC, the ELF ABI reserves the *EBX* register for holding the base address of the GOT.

Since the instruction pointer isn't directly accessible in 32-bit mode, a special trick must be employed. The CALL instruction pushes the address of the next instruction, the first instruction after the function returns, onto the stack so that the RET instruction can resume execution there after the function call is complete. Leveraging this, a simple function can read that saved address from the stack, and then return. In the GNU libc implementation, this type of function is typically called __i686.get_pc_thunk.bx, which loads the program counter, i.e., the instruction pointer, into the *EBX* register. Once the instruction pointer is loaded into *EBX*, the offset of the GOT is added.

While PIC improves security, by keeping the code pages read-only, and can improve memory usage, by preventing the code pages from being dirtied by relocations, it has a negative impact on performance. This impact is caused by all of the indirect function calls and data references. The impact is much more significant on 32-bit, where the loss of the *EBX* register also leads to increased register pressure.

Because dynamic linking allows for an application to be built once, but utilize different versions of the same shared library, it can be useful when benchmarking. By default, the dynamic linker searches for shared libraries in the paths configured via /etc/ld.so.conf, or, in modern distros, /etc/ld.so.conf.d. The configured paths can be overridden by setting the LD_LIBRARY_PATH environmental variable. As such, a user conducting performance benchmarking can modify this environmental variable to run the benchmark with multiple revisions of the same library, in order to measure the differences. For instance:

```
$ ls
project0 project1 bench
$ export LD_LIBRARY_PATH=project0/
$ ldd bench
        linux-vdso.so.1 =>  (0x00007fffeaffe000)
        libc.so.6 => /lib64/libc.so.6 (0x000000371a000000)
        /lib64/ld-linux-x86-64.so.2 (0x0000003719c00000)
        libproject.so => /home/jtk/lpa/project0/libproject.so
                       (0x000000392ea00000)
$ ./bench > result_version0
$ export LD_LIBRARY_PATH=project1/
$ ldd bench
        linux-vdso.so.1 =>  (0x00007fffeaffe000)
        libc.so.6 => /lib64/libc.so.6 (0x000000371a000000)
        /lib64/ld-linux-x86-64.so.2 (0x0000003719c00000)
        libproject.so => /home/jtk/lpa/project1/libproject.so
                       (0x000000392ea00000)
$ ./bench > result_version1
```

The LD_PRELOAD environment variable can be defined as a colon-separated list of libraries the dynamic linker should load first. To see how this can be used to intercept and instrument functions in a shared library, refer to the buGLe and Apitrace tools described in Sections 10.2 and 10.3 of Chapter 10.

12.2.2 ABI

The Application Binary Interface (ABI) standardizes the architectural interactions between various system components. The ABI defines items, such as the calling conventions, structure layout and padding, type alignments, and other aspects that must remain consistent between various software components to ensure compatibility and interoperability. This section focuses on considerations when dealing specifically with the C ABI.

Natural alignment

Alignment refers to the largest power of two that an address is a multiple of. In binary, this has the interesting property of being the first bit after zero or more consecutive zeros starting from the least significant bit. So for instance, the binary numbers 00001000, 11111000, 11011000, and 00111000 all have an alignment of 8. Using this knowledge, whether a specified address, x, meets the alignment criteria, a, given that a is a power of two, can be determined by:

```
1   #include <inttypes.h>
2   #include <assert.h>
3
4   static inline int is_aligned(uintptr_t x, int a)
5   {
6           assert(a && !(a & (a -1)));
7           return !(x & (a - 1));
8   }
```

Unlike some architectures, Intel® Architecture does not enforce strict data alignment, except for some special cases. The C standard specifies that, by default, types should be created with regards to their natural alignment, i.e., their size. So for instance, an integer on both x86 and x86_64 architectures has a natural alignment of 4 bytes, whereas a long integer would have a natural alignment of 4 bytes on x86, and 8 bytes on x86_64.

Calling conventions

Calling conventions describe the transfer of data between a function callee and caller. Additionally, the conventions describe which function, callee or caller, is responsible for cleaning up the stack after the function call. Without standardized calling conventions, it would be very difficult to combine multiple object files or libraries, as functions might lack the ability to properly invoke other functions.

The calling convention for x86 is known as cdecl. Functions written to this specification expect their arguments on the stack, pushed right to left. Since the CALL instruction pushes the return address, that is, the address of the next instruction after the function call returns, onto the stack, the stack elements can be accessed starting at offset 4 of the stack pointer.

The calling convention for x86_64 is similar, but is designed to take advantage of the extra registers available when the processor is in 64-bit mode. Rather than passing all arguments on the stack, arguments are passed in registers, with the stack being used to handle any extras. The first integer argument is passed in the *RDI* register, the second in the *RSI* register, the third in the *RDX* register, the fourth in the *RCX* register, the fifth in the *R8* register, and the sixth in the *R9* register. Floating point arguments are passed in the *XMM* registers, starting at *XMM*0 and ending at *XMM*7.

Typically, immediately on being invoked, a function sets up a frame pointer, that is, a special reserved register that contains the base address for the current stack frame. Saving the base of the stack frame for each function is useful for unwinding the stack for debugging purposes, such as recording the stack trace. On both x86 and x86_64, the *EBP* register is used. Note that for compiler-generated code, the frame pointer can be omitted or emitted with the `-fomit-frame-pointer` and `-fno-omit-frame-pointer` CFLAGS.

If the return value of the function is an integer, it is passed between the two functions in the *EAX* register. The register used for returning a floating point value depends on the architecture. Because `cdecl` on x86 was established before SIMD was ubiquitously available, floating point values are returned in *st*(0), that is, the top of the x87 floating point stack. On x86_64, floating point values are returned in the *XMM*0 register, as x86_64 requires the presence of SSE2.

Note that since the 32-bit ABI requires floating point values to be returned at the top of the x87 stack, for some small functions, consisting of only one or two scalar SIMD instructions, the cost of translating from x87 to SSE and back may outweigh any performance gains obtained by utilizing SSE. When in doubt, measure.

For both x86 and x86_64, the caller of the function is responsible for cleaning up the stack after the function call has returned. This is accomplished by incrementing the stack pointer to offset any elements that were pushed onto the stack. The x86 ABI requires that the stack be word-aligned before a function call; however, GCC actually performs, and expects, a 16-byte stack alignment (Whaley, 2008). The x86_64 ABI requires that the stack be aligned to 16-bytes prior to a function call, that is, excluding the instruction pointer pushed onto the stack by the `CALL` instruction.

Finally, the calling conventions also specify which registers must be preserved across function calls, and which registers are available as scratch registers. Understanding this, and the purpose of the general purpose registers, will help plan data movement in order to avoid a lot of unnecessary register copies. For the x86 ABI, a function invocation must preserve the *EBP*, *EBX*, *EDI*, *ESI*, and *ESP* registers. For the x86_64 ABI, a function invocation must preserve the *RBP*, *RBX*, *R*12, *R*13, *R*14, and *R*15. In other words, before these registers can be used, their inherited values must be pushed into the stack, and then popped back before returning to the calling function. In order to save stack space and the extra instructions, favor putting data in scratch registers, which aren't required to be saved, over preserved registers, if possible.

12.3 CPU DISPATCH

As mentioned in Section 12.1, only the instructions present in the software's minimum hardware requirement can be enabled for the compiler to freely generate.

Sometimes, this is a non-issue, as the software being compiled isn't intended to be distributed to other computers. A source-based Linux distribution, such as Gentoo, is a prime example. One reason why Gentoo users are able to achieve better performance than binary-based distributions is that their CFLAGS can be set to optimize for their exact hardware configuration.

This comes as a stark contrast to software that is distributed in an already-compiled binary format. Whereas the Gentoo user's applications and libraries are compiled to target their individual system, a binary-based distribution, such as Fedora, has to compile its applications to run on the minimum hardware requirement.

One startling ramification of this is that, depending on how often the minimum hardware configurations are increased, many hardware resources, and subsequent performance opportunities, remain unexploited. This is especially concerning when considering the trend of introducing specialized instruction set extensions in order to improve performance.

To summarize the problem succinctly, the majority of users own modern microarchitectures, such as the Second, Third, or Fourth Generation Intel® Core™ processors, and yet are running software that is essentially optimized for the fifteen year old Intel® Pentium® Pro processor.

Obviously, this situation is less than optimal, but luckily there is a solution. The solution, however, is a bit more complicated than just enabling a compiler flag. Instead, it involves targeting specific areas that can benefit from the use of newer instructions, providing multiple implementations for those areas, and then ensuring that the proper implementations run on the proper architectures.

The tools and techniques introduced in Part 2 aid with the first aspect, finding the areas that can benefit, and the rest of the chapters in Part 3 aid with the second aspect, creating the optimized implementations. The rest of this section will focus on the final aspect, ensuring that the proper implementations run on the proper architecture.

12.3.1 QUERYING CPU FEATURES

The first step in selecting the proper implementation of a function at runtime is to enumerate the processor's functionality. For the x86 architecture, this is accomplished with the CPUID instruction. Since the kernel also uses this information, a cached version is also available through procfs.

CPUID

CPUID, the CPU Identification instruction, allows the processor to query, at runtime, the processor's supported features. Due to the large amount of information available, information is cataloged into topical "leaves." A leaf is selected by loading the corresponding leaf number into the *EAX* register prior to invoking CPUID. The basic information leaf numbers start at 0, whereas the extended function leaf numbers start at 0x80000000.

Since CPUID has been updated with new features since its introduction, when using a potentially unsupported leaf, it's necessary to first verify that the leaf is supported. This is achieved by querying the first leaf, either 0 for the basic information leaf or 0x80000000, and checking the value of the *EAX* register, which is set to the maximum supported leaf.

Some leaves have sub-leaves, which can be selected using the *ECX* register. The resulting data is returned in the *EAX*, *EBX*, *ECX*, and *EDX* registers. A comprehensive list of these leaves and their subsequent meanings can be found in Volume 2 of the *Intel Software Developer's Manual*, under the Instruction Set Reference for CPUID.

Consider Listing 12.1, which uses CPUID to check whether the processor supports the Intel® AVX instruction extensions. Line 10 selects the Basic Information Leaf which, as described in the Intel SDM, contains, among other data, a bit to indicate whether Intel AVX is supported by the processor. Line 11 executes CPUID, and thus loads the relevant information described in the leaf into the *EAX*, *EBX*, *ECX*, and *EDX* registers. Line 12 masks out all of the bits except the single bit of interest in the appropriate register. Finally, Line 13 moves the masked value into the return value, *EAX* due to x86 calling conventions. Technically, if we were concerned about returning the exact bit value, we would right-shift the bit into the least significant bit position; however this is unnecessary since C interprets zero as false, and all other values as true, and thus it is simply enough to return a nonzero value for the truth case.

```
1    .text
2
3    # ECX Bit 28 : AVX extensions
4    #define AVX_MASK (1 << 28)
5
6    /* int cpu_has_avx(void); */
7            .globl  cpu_has_avx
8    cpu_has_avx:
9            pushl   %ebx              # Preserve EBX on stack
10           movl    $0x01, %eax       # 01H = Basic Information Leaf
11           cpuid                     # Clobbers EAX, EBX, ECX, and EDX
12           andl    $AVX_MASK, %ecx   # Clears all bits except bit 28
13           movl    %ecx, %eax        # return AVX_MASK if supported, or 0
14           popl    %ebx              # Restore EBX to original value
15           ret
```

LISTING 12.1

A function to check for Intel® AVX support with CPUID.

Another important consideration for utilizing CPUID is its associated cost. CPUID is a serializing instruction that flushes the processor's execution pipeline, hence its usage in conjunction with the RDTSC and RDTSCP instructions to accurately measure clock cycle counts while accounting for instruction pipelining, as described in Section 5.3.1 of Chapter 5. As such, executing CPUID frequently degrades performance, and thus should be avoided in performance-sensitive contexts.

In cpu_has_avx() from Listing 12.1, we were only interested in checking for Intel AVX support; however, if we were interested in checking for multiple pieces of information, it would be best to perform CPUID as few times as necessary, as dictated by the information leaves.

Each toolchain provides a separate method for invoking CPUID without writing assembly. Section 12.5.3 contains more information on using compiler intrinsics. GCC provides the cpuid.h header file that defines __get_cpuid()

and __get_cpuid_max(). The __get_cpuid() function takes the leaf number, along
with pointers to four unsigned integers, to store the values returned in each register.
Listing 12.2 demonstrates how to use __get_cpuid() to check for SSE4.2, Intel
AVX, and Intel® AVX2 support.

Notice that the feature checks at lines 17, 20, and 27 are wrapped with preprocessor checks for whether the bit masks are defined. This is because older toolchain
versions that lack support for these features won't have these masks defined, leading
to compilation errors. The downside of this approach is that the feature checks will
only be performed if the compiler supports the feature. This could be resolved by
checking for what the bit mask preprocessor defines, and manually defining them in
the case they aren't already defined.

GCC checks the leaf number against the maximum supported leaf and returns
false in the case where the request leaf is unavailable. At the time of this writing,
Clang provides the same functions as GCC, but doesn't perform the maximum leaf
check.

```
1   #include <cpuid.h>
2
3   static int has_sse42;
4   static int has_avx;
5   static int has_avx2;
6
7   #define BASIC_LEAF      0x1
8   #define EXTENDED_LEAF   0x7
9   void x86_feature_check(void)
10  {
11          int ret;
12          unsigned eax, ebx, ecx, edx;
13
14          ret = __get_cpuid(BASIC_LEAF, &eax, &ebx, &ecx, &edx);
15          if (ret) {
16  #ifdef bit_SSE4_2
17                  has_sse42 = ecx & bit_SSE4_2;
18  #endif
19  #ifdef bit_AVX
20                  has_avx = ecx & bit_AVX;
21  #endif
22          }
23
24  #ifdef bit_AVX2
25          ret = __get_cpuid(EXTENDED_LEAF, &eax, &ebx, &ecx, &edx);
26          if (ret) {
27                  has_avx2 = ebx & bit_AVX2;
28          }
29  #endif
30  }
31
```

```
32   int cpu_has_sse4_2(void)
33   {
34          return has_sse42;
35   }
36
37   int cpu_has_avx(void)
38   {
39          return has_avx;
40   }
41
42   int cpu_has_avx2(void)
43   {
44          return has_avx2;
45   }
```

LISTING 12.2

Using GCC's CPUID Intrinsics.

As of GCC 4.8, GCC adds a new builtin designed to simplify the above, __builtin_cpu_supports(). This builtin takes a string to the feature name, such as "sse4.1" or "avx2", and returns true or false, depending on what the processor supports. Listing 12.3 shows how this feature simplifies Listing 12.2, assuming support for GCC pre-4.8 isn't a requirement.

```
1    int cpu_has_sse42(void)
2    {
3           return __builtin_cpu_supports("sse4.2");
4    }
5
6    int cpu_has_avx(void)
7    {
8           return __builtin_cpu_supports("avx");
9    }
10
11   int cpu_has_avx2(void)
12   {
13          return __builtin_cpu_supports("avx2");
14   }
```

LISTING 12.3

Using GCC's builtins.

ICC provides the _may_i_use_cpu_feature() function for querying for specific feature support. This function takes as an argument a mask corresponding to the features in question. A list of supported features and examples can be found in the ICC documentation.

Procfs

Technically, all CPU feature queries on Intel Architecture are facilitated through the CPUID instruction; however the Linux kernel, since it needs to be aware of the supported features, executes CPUID at boot and caches the result. Within the kernel, these results can be queried by using the relevant macros such as boot_cpu_has() or cpu_has(). Outside of the kernel, in user space, the results are exposed through the cpuinfo file in the procfs filesystem.

Procfs is a special memory-backed filesystem that exposes kernel data structures through a hierarchical directory and file interface. Unlike a standard filesystem, the files within procfs and sysfs don't physically exist. Instead, the VFS file operations, such as opening the file, hook into special functions that gather and generate the desired content on demand. For procfs support, the kernel must be compiled with CONFIG_PROC_FS, which is enabled on practically every Linux kernel. The standard convention is that procfs is mounted at /proc, although this isn't a technical requirement.

The cpuinfo file is located at the top-level procfs directory and contains all of the relevant processor information, such as model, family, frequency, and a list of supported features. The file contains one entry for each logical processor.

The flags field contains a space-delimited list of CPU features for which the kernel has detected support.

One common issue with the flags field is knowing which strings map to which features. For some, the answer is obvious, such as the SSE2 extensions mapping to the string "sse2." For others, the answer is less than obvious, such as the SSE3 extensions mapping to the string "pni", an acronym for Prescott New Instructions.

Understanding which string to search for requires a remedial understanding of how the cpuinfo file is generated. All of the x86 processor features are listed in:

${LINUX_SRC}/arch/x86/include/asm/cpufeature.h.

Each feature is represented by a preprocessor define beginning with X86_FEATURE, e.g., X86_FEATURE_XMM3. The value of the define is the mask used to check for support with CPUID. Finally, each line ends with a C-style comment. Here, within the comment, the name exposed to user space is defined, enclosed within double quotes. If the double quotes are missing from the comment, the macro name is used instead. If the double quotes are empty, the feature is omitted from the cpuinfo file.

Some select excerpts from cpufeature.h are shown in Listing 12.4. The first two selections, X86_FEATURE_TSC and X86_FEATURE_MSR, are represented in the flags field as "tsc" and "msr", respectively, since they lack any string designator in the comments. The third, fourth, and fifth features would appear in the list as "dst", "sse", and "sse2", respectively. Finally, the last example won't appear in the cpu feature list at all.

```
1   #define X86_FEATURE_TSC         (0*32+ 4) /* Time Stamp Counter */
2   #define X86_FEATURE_MSR         (0*32+ 5) /* Model-Specific
                                                 Registers */
3   #define X86_FEATURE_DS          (0*32+21) /* "dts" Debug Store */
4   #define X86_FEATURE_XMM         (0*32+25) /* "sse" */
5   #define X86_FEATURE_XMM2        (0*32+26) /* "sse2" */
6   #define X86_FEATURE_SYSCALL32   (3*32+14) /* "" syscall in ia32
                                                 userspace */
```

LISTING 12.4

Examples from cpufeature.h.

During kernel compilation, this header is parsed by a script that generates an array of all processor capabilities supported by the kernel. It is this array that is iterated when a file descriptor to cpuinfo is opened. The code that generates the content of cpuinfo can be found at ${LINUX_SRC}/arch/x86/kernel/cpu/proc.c.

Since procfs is part of the kernel ABI, the feature names shouldn't change, and thus it is only necessary to look up the names in cpufeature.h once.

12.3.2 RUNTIME DISPATCHING

Once the processor information has been detected, it is possible to leverage this information to ensure that the best-performing implementation runs for the current system. The rest of this section iterates a number of techniques for accomplishing this.

Branching

The simplest method for runtime dispatching is to add a branch that chooses the proper implementation. Listing 12.5 builds on the cpu_has_avx() function from Listing 12.1 in order to select which version of function foo() will be executed, depending on whether the cpu supports Intel AVX.

```
1   extern int cpu_has_avx(void);
2   extern void foo(void);
3   extern void foo_avx(void);
4
5   void dispatch_foo(void)
6   {
7           if (cpu_has_avx())
8                   foo_avx();
9           else
10                  foo();
11  }
```

LISTING 12.5

Dispatching the proper implementation of foo().

The advantage to this technique is its simplicity, and the fact that it doesn't rely on any toolchain extensions.

The disadvantages to this technique are that it potentially adds a branch into a hotpath and adds an additional function call.

The first disadvantage, the added branch, tends to be negated by speculative execution. The processor's branch predictor is incredibly adept at discovering patterns in the history of branches taken. Since the processor features won't dynamically change at runtime, the branch taken on each function invocation will be constant, and thus after the first time evaluating the branch, all subsequent branches should be predicted correctly, thus removing the cost of the branch completely. When in doubt, measure. Chapter 13 goes into further detail on branch prediction.

Function pointers

Another common technique for runtime dispatching is through function pointers. Before any of the dispatched functions are invoked, the processor features are detected and function pointers are set to the appropriate implementation. Then all access to the dispatched functions occurs through these pointers.

This approach removes the branching and extra function call that were disadvantages of the simple branching technique. Instead, the dispatching decision occurs only once.

Listing 12.6 exemplifies this concept for two functions `foo()` and `bar()`. In this example, the implementation sets are predefined, although this isn't a requirement.

```
1   #include <stddef.h>
2   extern void foo(unsigned *data, size_t len);
3   extern void foo_sse42(unsigned *data, size_t len);
4   extern void foo_avx2(unsigned *data, size_t len);
5
6   extern void bar(int x, int y);
7   extern void bar_sse42(int x, int y);
8
9   struct impl {
10          void (*foo)(unsigned *data, size_t len);
11          void (*bar)(int x, int y);
12  };
13
14  const struct impl basic_impl = {.foo = foo,       .bar = bar};
15  const struct impl sse42_impl = {.foo = foo_sse42, .bar = bar_sse42};
16  const struct impl avx2_impl  = {.foo = foo_avx2,  .bar = bar_sse42};
17
18  extern int cpu_has_sse42(void);
19  extern int cpu_has_avx2(void);
20
21  const struct impl *x86_get_impl(void)
22  {
23          if (cpu_has_avx2())
24                  return &avx2_impl;
25          if (cpu_has_sse42())
26                  return &sse42_impl;
27          else
28                  return &basic_impl;
29  }
```

LISTING 12.6

Dispatching via function pointers.

ELF IFUNC

As described in Section 12.2, ELF symbols have an associated type. Functions are normally of type STT_FUNC. On modern Linux systems, with a binutils version newer than 2.20.1 and a glibc version newer than 2.11.1, there is GNU extension to the ELF format that adds a new function type, STT_GNU_IFUNC. The "I" in "IFUNC" stands for indirect, as the extension allows for the creation of indirect functions resolved at runtime.

Each "IFUNC" symbol has an associated resolver function. This function is responsible for returning the correct version of the function to utilize. Similar to lazy symbol binding, the resolver is called at the first function invocation in order to determine what symbol should be loaded. Once the resolver has been run, all future function calls will invoke the given function.

Listing 12.7 demonstrates how an "IFUNC" symbol can be used.

```
1   #include <stddef.h>
2
3   extern void foo(unsigned *data, size_t len);
4
5   void foo_c(unsigned *data, size_t len)
6   {
7           /* ... */
8   }
9
10  void foo_sse42(unsigned *data, size_t len)
11  {
12          /* ... */
13  }
14
15  void foo_avx2(unsigned *data, size_t len)
16  {
17          /* ... */
18  }
19
20  extern int cpu_has_sse42(void);
21  extern int cpu_has_avx2(void);
22
23  void foo(unsigned *data, size_t len)
24          __attribute__((ifunc ("resolve_foo")));
25
26  static void *resolve_foo(void)
27  {
28          if (cpu_has_avx2())
29                  return foo_avx2;
30          else if (cpu_has_sse42())
31                  return foo_sse42();
32          else
33                  return foo_c();
34  }
```

LISTING 12.7

Dispatching via IFUNC ELF Extension.

The downside to this method is that it is an extension to the ELF standard and therefore will not be portable to other toolchains or systems. Also, support for older Linux distributions can be problematic, since support has only been available for five years and has not made it into some older enterprise distributions.

Dynamic linking

For 32-bit x86, the dynamic linker, `ld.so`, supports the concept of hardware capabilities. Each predefined capability, listed in the manual page, corresponds to a search directory, which will only be utilized if the underlying processor architecture supports that feature. For example, if the SSE2 feature is available, the linker will include the contents of the `/usr/lib/sse2/` directory in the library search path.

As a result, it's possible to leverage this functionality by building multiple versions of a shared library, each with different processor functionality enabled, and installing them into the appropriate directories. The benefit of this approach is that no runtime functionality checks need to occur, since the library compiled with certain processor features will only be used when run on a processor that supports those features. The drawbacks to this approach are that there will be multiple versions of the library, corresponding to each possible combination of supported features, and that this feature is only available on 32-bit systems.

The author includes this technique for completeness, since in general, the other approaches are much better. Providing multiple versions of a shared library means a significant extra testing burden, and the runtime checking for processor features can easily be performed outside of any hotspot, during code initialization, making it irrelevant.

12.4 CODING STYLE

If the tools discussed in Part 2 have led to a hotspot, where the problems are mostly missed optimization opportunities or simply bad code generation, the next step is not to jump directly into rewriting the code in assembly. Instead, it is much more preferable to coax the compiler into generating better code. This typically occurs by providing the compiler with as much information as possible about the context of the code, in order to enable better optimizations.

This section provides some useful techniques for writing code in such a way that actively helps the compiler to improve performance.

12.4.1 POINTER ALIASING

Two pointers are said to alias when they both point to the same region of data, what the C specification would refer to as an object. For the compiler, determining pointer aliasing is important for both correctness and performance.

Before diving into the specifics, consider the simple example presented in Listing 12.8, where every element of an array of doubles is set based on the value of a double referenced via the second pointer.

```
1    #include <stddef.h>
2    void foo(double *x, double *y, size_t len)
3    {
4            size_t i;
5
6            for (i = 0; i < len; i++)
7                    x[i] = *y * 2.0;
8    }
```

LISTING 12.8

A victim of pointer aliasing.

The output produced for Listing 12.8 by GCC, at the normal optimization level 2, is shown in Listing 12.9. Since this was compiled as x86_64, the function arguments x, y, and len, are passed into the function in the RDI, RSI, and RDX registers, respectively. The compiler chose RAX to store the i loop offset, and thus avoids using any registers that are required to be preserved on the between function calls.

Notice that the inner loop, starting at offset 0x10 thanks to the nop that aligns the loop entry address to 16 bytes, loads the value of $*y$ as a scalar double into the SSE XMM register $XMM0$. At offset 0x14, $*y * 2.0$ is calculated, using the fact that $*y + *y == *y * 2.0$ to avoid the potentially more expensive multiplication instruction. Then the value of xmm0 is copied into the appropriate displacement in x, i.e., $(uintptr\_t)x + sizeof(double[i])$.

```
1    0000000000000000 <foo>:
2       0:   48 85 d2               test    %rdx,%rdx
3       3:   74 21                  je      26 <foo+0x26>
4       5:   31 c0                  xor     %eax,%eax
5       7:   66 0f 1f 84 00 00 00   nopw    0x0(%rax,%rax,1)
6       e:   00 00
7      10:   f2 0f 10 06            movsd   (%rsi),%xmm0
8      14:   f2 0f 58 c0            addsd   %xmm0,%xmm0
9      18:   f2 0f 11 04 c7         movsd   %xmm0,(%rdi,%rax,8)
10     1d:   48 83 c0 01            add     $0x1,%rax
11     21:   48 39 c2               cmp     %rax,%rdx
12     24:   77 ea                  ja      10 <foo+0x10>
13     26:   f3 c3                  repz retq
```

LISTING 12.9

GCC -O2 output from Listing 12.8.

This raises the question, "Since the value of *y isn't explicitly changed in the function, why doesn't the compiler hoist the load out of the loop?"

The answer is that the compiler doesn't know whether the value of *y changes due to pointer aliasing. Consider for example the situation where $x[0] = 1.0$ and $y = \&x[0]$. In this case, the first loop iteration would set $x[0] = 1.0 * 2.0$. Then the next loop iteration would set $x[1] = 2.0 * 2.0$. If the compiler were to hoist the load of $*y$ out of the loop, the code would incorrectly produce $x[0] = x[1] = 2.0$.

The C specification provides compiler writers with rules, called strict aliasing rules, with regards to when the language allows pointers to alias, allowing compiler writers to optimize the cases where pointers are *not* allowed to alias. These rules are incredibly important for programmers to understand, because violating the rules can lead to the compiler generating incorrect code.

Section 6.5 paragraph 7 of the C specification states:

"An object shall have its stored value accessed only by an lvalue expression that has one of the following types:

- *a type compatible with the effective type of the object,*
- *a qualified version of a type compatible with the effective type of the object,*
- *a type that is the signed or unsigned type corresponding to the effective type of the object,*
- *a type that is the signed or unsigned type corresponding to the qualified version of the effective type of the object,*
- *an aggregate or union type that includes one of the aforementioned types among its members (including, recursively, a member of a subaggregate or contained union, or*
- *a character type"*

The first four rules essentially state that a pointer may alias another pointer of the same type, regardless of whether the types differ in signedness, signed and unsigned, or qualification, const and volatile. So for instance, a pointer of type unsigned int *, and a pointer of type signed int *const, in the same scope could alias. The fifth rule extends this concept to include structures and unions. For convenience, the sixth rule allows any pointer to be aliased by a char pointer.

So going back to the code in Listing 12.8, assume that the programmer knows that *y* will never alias *x*, and wants the compiler to optimize the code accordingly, by hoisting the load of *y* out of the loop.

The C99 specification introduced the restrict qualifier, that informs the compiler that the restricted pointer is the sole pointer that accesses the object it points to. Listing 12.10 adds the restrict qualifier to the pointers *x* and *y*.

```
1   #include <stddef.h>
2   void foo(double *restrict x, double *restrict y, size_t len)
3   {
4           size_t i;
5
6           for (i = 0; i < len; i++)
7                   x[i] = *y * 2.0;
8   }
```

LISTING 12.10

Pointer Aliasing With restrict.

Notice that the `restrict` qualifier modifies the pointer type, not the object type. Looking at the output from GCC, produced in an identical fashion to Listing 12.9, Listing 12.11 shows that GCC performed the loop hoisting optimization, reducing the numbers of instructions in the inner loop from four to two. Now when using the `restrict` keyword and *x* and *y* overlap, there will be trouble, so care must be taken by the programmer to ensure that this optimization is valid.

```
1    0000000000000000 <foo>:
2       0:    48 85 d2                test    %rdx,%rdx
3       3:    74 19                   je      1e <foo+0x1e>
4       5:    f2 0f 10 06             movsd   (%rsi),%xmm0
5       9:    31 c0                   xor     %eax,%eax
6       b:    f2 0f 58 c0             addsd   %xmm0,%xmm0
7       f:    90                      nop
8       10:   f2 0f 11 04 c7          movsd   %xmm0,(%rdi,%rax,8)
9       15:   48 83 c0 01             add     $0x1,%rax
10      19:   48 39 c2                cmp     %rax,%rdx
11      1c:   77 f2                   ja      10 <foo+0x10>
12      1e:   f3 c3                   repz retq
```

LISTING 12.11

GCC -O2 output from Listing 12.10.

One important caveat is that while the C language supports the restrict keyword, assuming the compiler supports at least the C99 specification, the C++ language does not. However G++, the C++ frontend for GCC, does expose the concept as an extension, via the __restrict or __restrict__ keywords.

C support does require that the compiler implement the C99 specification. Since the 99 in C99 stands for the year 1999, that is, over 15 years from the time of this book being written, the author considers that requirement reasonable.

12.4.2 USING THE APPROPRIATE TYPES AND QUALIFIERS

As shown in Section 12.4.1, providing the proper hints to the compiler can aid in optimization. In many cases, these hints are provided to the compiler through types and their qualifiers.

Signed versus unsigned

Types come in two different flavors, signed and unsigned, as specified by the corresponding `signed` and `unsigned` qualifiers. If no qualifier is given, a signed type is assumed. As the reader is probably aware, signed types reserve a bit, the most significant bit, to store whether the value is negative or positive. Negative integers on Intel Architecture are stored in the two's complement format. On the other hand, unsigned types do not reserve a sign bit, but instead are always treated as positive, increasing the potential range of values that can be stored and also providing standard defined behavior in the case of overflow and underflow. Adding these stronger constraints allows the compiler to optimize these types more aggressively in some situations.

Const

The const qualifier informs the compiler that the type modified by the qualifier will not change. This actually serves two purposes, as it can enable additional optimizations as well as causing compiler errors if an attempt is made to modify a constant variable.

An important aspect of the const qualifier is that it can modify either a value or pointer. For instance, the const int type represents a signed integer whose value cannot be changed. On the other hand, a const char *const type represents a constant pointer, that is, a pointer that never changes, that points to a character whose value never changes.

Marking strings as const can cause strings to move from the ELF .data section to the .rodata section. This can also enable string merging, where two constant strings that overlap can be merged into one string. For instance, consider the strings const char *const str0 = "testing 123" and const char *const str1 = "123". The second string, str1, only requires four characters: "1", "2", "3", and "\0", the NULL sentinel. These four characters can be found as the last four characters in the first string, str0, and therefore only the first string needs to be stored, with the second string simply pointing at the last 4 bytes of the first string. This size optimization can only occur when both strings are marked as constant.

Volatile

The volatile qualifier informs the compiler that the modified variable may be updated in ways the compiler doesn't have visibility into. The canonical example of this is a pointer to a memory mapped device, where the value written may not be the same value later read from that address. Without this qualifier, the compiler would incorrectly optimize away the memory accesses due to its limited understanding of the situation.

The problem with the volatile qualifier is that it forces the compiler to disable every memory optimization. Fetched memory accesses can't be reused or cached, resulting in a significant degradation in performance. Only use this qualifier if it is absolutely necessary.

12.4.3 ALIGNMENT

On modern Intel Architectures, unaligned memory accesses are less significant than they used to be. Since memory accesses are satisfied by fetching entire cache lines, the only big penalty paid for an unaligned access is if it splits a cache line, resulting in two cache lines needing to be loaded, and then the relevant values spliced. For the most part, the majority of important alignments will be taken care of automatically by the compiler.

Some instruction set extensions, especially SIMD, are sensitive to memory alignment, with special instructions for accessing unaligned and aligned data. Also, data structure layouts can benefit from strategic alignment. For example, false sharing issues can be avoided by ensuring that two variables accessed by two different processors are sufficiently aligned to ensure they reside in separate cache lines.

As mentioned in "Natural alignment" section, by default elements on the stack are allocated with their natural alignment. Memory regions returned by malloc(3) are aligned to 8 bytes. There are four methods for obtaining memory with a larger alignment.

The first method uses the alignment macros introduced with the C11 language specification and defined in stdalign.h. The alignof() macro, and the corresponding _Alignof keyword, return the alignment requirement of the specified variable or type. The alignas() macro, and the corresponding _Alignas keyword, specify the alignment for a variable. If the parameter is numeric, it specifies the alignment. If the parameter is a type, it specifies the alignment to be equivalent to that type's alignment requirement. For instance, the following are equivalent:

```
alignas(32) unsigned foo[8];
alignas(alignof(__m256i)) unsigned foo[8];
alignas(__m256i) unsigned foo[8];
```

The second method uses the compiler's variable attributes with the aligned property. This attribute is supported by GCC, LLVM, and ICC; although, the author does have experience with some compiler versions treating this attribute as a hint that can be ignored. For example, to achieve 16-byte alignment for a variable, foo.

```
unsigned __attribute__((aligned(16))) foo;
```

The third method uses the posix_memalign(3) function, which provides similar functionality to malloc(3), in that it allocates heap memory, but with the requested alignment instead. Memory regions allocated with posix_memalign(3) are freed with free(3). The function signature is self-explanatory:

```
int posix_memalign(void **memptr, size_t alignment, size_t size);
```

The final technique is to perform the alignment manually. For an alignment requirement a, any address is between 0 and $a - 1$ bytes from an aligned address. Therefore, allocate an extra $a - 1$ bytes, increment the pointer by $a - 1$ bytes, and then round down to the aligned address. For example:

```
1  void *alloc_align(void **out, const size_t align, const size_t size)
2  {
3          void *ret;
4
5          assert(align && !(align & (align - 1)));
6          *out = malloc(size + align - 1);
7          ret = (uintptr_t)*out + align - 1;
8          ret = (uintptr_t)ret & ~(align - 1);
9          return ret;
10 }
```

Notice that in this example, two pointers are returned. The first pointer, returned in out, contains the unaligned pointer returned by malloc(3). The second pointer, returned in *EAX* by the function, contains the aligned pointer. In this case, since the memory was allocated with `malloc(3)`, it is necessary to use the original unaligned pointer to `free(3)` the memory. Calling `free(3)` on an address that wasn't returned by `malloc(3)` results in undefined behavior.

12.4.4 LOOP UNROLLING

Loop unrolling is a technique for attempting to minimize the cost of loop overhead, such as branching on the termination condition and updating counter variables. This occurs by manually adding the necessary code for the loop to occur multiple times within the loop body and then updating the conditions and counters accordingly. The potential for performance improvement comes from the reduced loop overhead, since less iterations are required to perform the same work, and also, depending on the code, the possibility for better instruction pipelining.

While loop unrolling can be beneficial, excessive unrolling degrades performance. Because modern processors execute instruction out-of-order so aggressively, in many cases loop unrolling effectively occurs in hardware, with a better scheduling of resources than can be performed at compile time. Additionally, the compiler may automatically perform loop unrolling.

Since loop unrolling is a tradeoff between code size and speed, the effectiveness of loop unrolling is highly dependent on the loop unrolling *factor*, that is, the number of times the loop is unrolled. As the factor increases, code size increases, leading to potential issues with the front end, such as icache misses. The only way to determine the best unrolling factor is through measurement.

12.5 x86 UNLEASHED

After having attempted the techniques described above for goading the compiler into generating better instruction sequences with suboptimal results, the next possibility is to manually generate the desired instructions by writing assembly. This section explores the three dissimilar techniques for integrating assembly with C, with each technique involving the compiler to a varying degree.

The first technique, standalone assembly, completely bypasses the compiler, providing the most freedom to write optimized code. With this freedom comes the responsibility of properly following the ABI requirements, such as the function calling conventions.

The second technique, inline assembly, seamlessly integrates assembly into C code, allowing the developer to write small snippets of optimized code that can interact with local C variables and labels. While the compiler doesn't modify the instructions written with inline assembly, it still handles, or can handle, some aspects like register allocation or calling conventions.

Finally, the third technique, compiler intrinsics, relies completely on the compiler to produce the desired instruction sequence, but in doing so frees the developer from worrying about any aspects of the ABI. Compiler intrinsics are C functions that have a one-to-one or many-to-one relationship with specific instructions.

It's important to note that while some of these techniques are more powerful than others, it's generally possible to do the same things with any of them. As an analogy, consider compiler intrinsics to be like a watch hammer, inline assembly to be like a claw hammer, and standalone assembly to be like a sledgehammer. Any of these hammers are capable of driving a nail, but using the right tool for the job tends to make that job seem much easier.

12.5.1 STANDALONE ASSEMBLY

As the name implies, standalone assembly involves writing full routines and data structures in assembly that are separate from the C source files. Instead of being compiled by the C compiler, these source files are assembled, using the assembler, into an object file, which can then be used like any other ELF object file. Compliance with the ABI ensures interoperability between C and assembly. Following the GNU Makefile implicit rules, assembly files typically end with a .s or .S suffix. By default, files ending with .s are passed to the assembler, whereas files ending with .S are first run through the C preprocessor to produce a .s file, and then are assembled. Use of the C preprocessor allows for the sharing of C header files between C and assembly code. Another common suffix is .asm.

Many different assemblers exist for Linux, but the most common are the GNU assembler, as, the Netwide Assembler, nasm, and YASM. The GNU assembler and YASM support both the AT&T and Intel instruction syntaxes. Due to its ubiquitous nature, the author tends to use AT&T syntax and target the GNU assembler, as this tends to be the most commonly available; however, the decision on what assembler or format to use really depends on personal preference.

Symbols, which can mark data or text regions, are exported, for linking, via the .globl pseudo-op. Local symbols, that is, symbols whose names are not saved in the object file, begin with the prefix ".L". Unique local labels, for situations where only a temporary symbol is desired, can be created by using a positive integer for the symbol name. The numbered label can then be referred to via the number, suffixed by either "f" or "b." The "f" suffix indicates that the numbered label occurs after the current instruction, while the "b" suffix indicates that the numbered label occurs before the current instruction.

In order to reserve space for uninitialized variables or declare initialized ones, a series of pseudo-ops exist. A memory region is reserved for a symbol in the .bss section, by using the .lcomm pseudo-op. This takes the format .lcomm SYMBOL, SIZE. For instance, to define an uninitialized buffer of 256 bytes named bar:

```
.bss
.lcomm bar, 256
```

The pseudo-op for reserving a memory region with a given value in one of the various data sections depends on the size of the region. For instance, the following are all equivalent:

```
.data
var0:    .byte    0xFF, 0xFF, 0xFF, 0xFF, 0xFF, 0xFF, 0xFF, 0xFF
var1:    .word    0xFFFF, 0xFFFF, 0xFFFF, 0xFFFF
var2:    .int     0xFFFFFFFF, 0xFFFFFFFF
var3:    .quad    0xFFFFFFFFFFFFFFFF
```

There are also an `.ascii` and an `.asciz` pseudo-op, which create string data. The difference between `.ascii` and `.asciz` is that the second creates a NULL-sentinel terminated string, while the first does not.

Listing 12.12 demonstrates how to write a function, `foo()`, in assembly that properly follows the x86_64 ABI in order to allow invocation from C. The function declaration begins at line 9, whereas line 8 exports the function symbol to the linker. Lines 10 through 13 set up the stack frame, and lines 30 through 32 clean up the stack frame, in the reverse order of setup.

As mentioned in "Calling conventions" section, the stack must be 16-byte aligned at the time of a function call, such as the call to the `printf(3)` function on line 23. Because of this, it is safe to assume that the current stack on entering this function was 16-byte aligned before the 8-byte return address was pushed onto the stack by the CALL instruction. Then two 8-byte registers are pushed onto the stack on lines 10 and 11. The first PUSH instruction returns the stack pointer to 16-byte alignment, but the second PUSH instruction reduces the stack to only 8-byte alignment. In order to remedy this, there are a couple of options, including subtracting another 8 bytes from the stack pointer. In order to make this point clear, the example explicitly rounds the stack pointer down to the next 16-byte multiple, line 13. The original stack offsets before the alignment can be accessed through *RBP*.

Once the stack frame is initialized, the function loops over the function parameter, invoking `printf(3)` each iteration. The *R12* register is used for the loop counter, since *R12* is a preserved register, and therefore the call to `printf(3)` won't clobber it. Notice how the function arguments are loaded into the *RDI*, *RSI*, and *RDX* registers prior to the function call.

Also, note the different types of labels and their usages. Lines 16 and 34 are both temporary local labels, referenced using the "f" and "b" suffixes, at lines 25 and 28. Line 29 contains a named local label, with the ".L" prefix, and is referenced at line 18.

```
1    .section .rodata
2
3    msg:    .asciz   "Loop Iteration %d\n"
4    err:    .asciz   "printf output error\n"
5
6    .text
7
8            .globl foo
9    foo:
10           pushq    %rbp
11           pushq    %r12
12           movq     %rsp, %rbp
```

```
13          andq    $-16, %rsp
14
15          movq    %rdi, %r12
16   1:
17          test    %r12, %r12
18          jz      .Ldone
19
20          movq    $msg, %rdi
21          movq    %r12, %rsi
22          movq    $0, %rdx
23          call    printf
24          cmp     $0, %rax
25          jle     2f
26
27          decq    %r12
28          jmp 1b
29   .Ldone:
30          movq    %rbp, %rsp
31          popq    %r12
32          popq    %rbp
33          ret
34   2:
35          movq    $err, %rdi
36          movq    $0, %rsi
37          call    printf
38          jmp     .Ldone
```

LISTING 12.12

Example Assembly Function Following the x86_64 ABI.

12.5.2 INLINE ASSEMBLY

While standalone assembly provides the most control, sometimes it is more desirable to write the majority of a function in C, with only a small subset of the code in assembly. To accomplish this, most compilers support some level of inline assembly, that is, the embedding of assembly instructions directly into C source files.

GCC, along with LLVM and ICC, support an extended inline assembly syntax, that allows for C variables to be utilized in the assembly, while the compiler handles moving the variables into the proper format. This syntax takes the following form:

```
__asm__ __volatile__ {
        "INSTRUCTIONS\n\t"
        "INSTRUCTIONS\n\t"
        ...
: Input Variables
: Output Variables
: List of Clobbered Resources
};
```

Table 12.3 GCC Inline Assembly Constraints

Constraint	Variable Referenced As
r	Any general purpose register
m	Memory operand
o	Offsetable operand (e.g., -4(%esp))
i	Immediate integer operand
E	Immediate floating point operand
a	RAX or EAX
b	RBX or EBX
c	RCX or ECX
d	RDX or EDX
S	RSI or ESI
D	RDI or EDI
x	Any SSE register

The optional __volatile__ attribute informs the compiler that the instructions have side-effects not visible to the compiler. This prevents the compiler from optimizing these instructions out of the executable and from significantly moving the instructions.

The input and output variables are a comma delimited list of variables of the form [name] "constraint" (variable). A list of popular constraints on x86 can be found in Table 12.3. Constraints can be modified with prefixes. Input operands must be marked as writable, with either "=", which specifies that the operand is write-only, or "+", which specifies that the operand is read and written. Be careful with constraints, as incorrect constraints can lead to miscompiled programs.

The clobbered list is a comma delimited list of strings, each containing the names of the registers the instructions modify. There are also two special resources that can be specified in the clobbered list, "memory", which informs the compiler that memory was changed, and "cc", which informs the compiler that the *EFLAGS* condition register was changed. Resources clobbered in the input and output lists do not need to be listed in the clobbered list.

When writing inline assembly, the author recommends testing the constraints on multiple compilers, as some compilers, such as LLVM, are significantly more restrictive in what they accept. At the time of this writing, ICC will complain if there are empty lists at the end of the declaration.

12.5.3 COMPILER INTRINSICS

Compiler intrinsics are built-in functions provided by the compiler that share a one-to-one, or many-to-one, relationship with specific instructions. This allows the specific instructions to be written using high-level programming constructs and frees the developer from worrying about calling conventions, register allocation, and instruction scheduling. Another advantage to utilizing compiler intrinsics is that, unlike standalone or inline assembly, the compiler has visibility into what is occurring and perform further optimizations.

Unfortunately, compiling intrinsics with GCC can be somewhat annoying. This stems from the fact that certain instruction sets can only be generated by the compiler when they are explicitly enabled in the CFLAGS. However, when the instruction sets are enabled in the CFLAGS, they are enabled to be generated *everywhere*, that is, there is no guarantee that all of the instructions will be protected by a `CPUID` check. For example, attempting to compile Intel AVX2 compiler intrinsics without the `-mavx2` compiler flag will result in compilation failure.

In order to bypass this problem, intrinsic functions should be isolated to separate files. These files must only contain functions that are dispatched based on the results of `CPUID`. This is the only way to guarantee that all instruction set extensions are properly dispatched at runtime.

Each instruction set extension typically has its own header file. However, since the instruction sets build upon one another, only the main top level header files should be directly included. This main header file for all x86 intrinsics functions is `x86intrin.h`, which is typically located in the `include` directory under `/usr/lib/gcc`.

The intrinsics function that corresponds to a specific instruction can be determined by looking at the related instruction documentation in the Intel *Software Developer's Manual*, under the instruction reference. Each instruction that supports a corresponding intrinsics function has a section entitled `Intel C/C++ Compiler Intrinsic Equivalents`, which lists the intrinsic signature.

Intrinsics that support larger SIMD registers add new variable types for representing the larger width registers. For instance, `__m128` represents a general 128-bit SSE register, while `__m128i` represents a 128-bit SSE register storing packed integers.

REFERENCES

Drepper, U., n.d. Static Linking Considered Harmful. http://www.akkadia.org/drepper/no_static_linking.html.

Free Software Foundation, 2013, 08a. AS(1) Manual Page.

Free Software Foundation, 2013, 11b. GCC(1) info page.

Free Software Foundation, 2014, 09. GCC(1) Manual Page.

Intel Corporation, 2013, 10. Intel 64 and IA-32 Architectures Software Developer's Manual. Computer Hardware Manual.

ISO Joint Technical Committee JTC1, Subcommittee SC 22, Working Group 14, 2007, 10. ISO/IEC 9899:TC3 Draft. C language Specification.

ISO Joint Technical Committee JTC1, Subcommittee SC 22, Working Group 14, 2011, 10. ISO/IEC 9899:2011 Draft. C language Specification.

Matz, M., Hubicka, J., Jaeger, A., Mitchell, M., 2005, 01. AMD64 ABI Draft.

Torvalds, L., Anvin, H.P., Shimamoto, H., et al., 2014, 06. Source for /proc/cpuinfo. ${LINUX_SRC}/arch/x86/kernel/cpu/proc.c. Linux Kernel Source.

The Santa Cruz Operation, Inc., 1996. System V Application Binary Interface: Intel386 Architecture Processor Supplement.

UNIX System Laboratories, 2001. Executable and Linkable Format (ELF).

Whaley, R.C., 2008, 12. Bug 38496—Gcc misaligns arrays when stack is forced follow the x8632 ABI. https://gcc.gnu.org/bugzilla/show_bug.cgi?id=38496. Bugzilla Entry.

Youngdale, E., 1994. binfmt_elf.c. ${LINUX_SRC}/fs/binfmt_elf.c. Linux Kernel Source.

Branching

13

CHAPTER CONTENTS

As discussed in Chapter 1, the instruction pointer contains the address of the next instruction to be executed. After the current instruction is executed, the instruction pointer increments to the next instruction, and so on. A *branch* introduces a deviation from this incremental behavior. Instead of incrementing to the next instruction, the branching instruction loads the instruction pointer with the address of an instruction at a different code region.

Every branch can be classified as either conditional or unconditional. As the names imply, a *conditional branch* may or may not change the instruction flow, while an *unconditional branch* will always alter the flow. Most programmers tend to associate the concept of branching with the first category, conditional branches, since these are the most visible forms. This kind of branch corresponds to the conditional and looping constructs exposed by programming languages, such as `if` or `for` statements. The other kind of branch, an unconditional branch, corresponds to control flow changes, such as calling into or returning from a function.

Due to the superscalar nature of the execution pipeline found in Intel® processors, comprised of many different parallel execution units, it is more efficient to keep the pipeline full, executing multiple instructions simultaneously, than to let instructions trickle in, executing the instructions serially. In an attempt to keep the execution pipeline fully utilized, the processor, in hardware, performs an optimization referred to as speculative execution. With *speculative execution*, upon approaching a branch, the processor predicts which branch will be taken. It will then use this guess to begin, possibly prematurely, executing the instructions from the predicted branch path. In the case of a correct guess, referred to as a *branch hit*, the instructions from both code paths can be interleaved, utilizing any idle execution units. This not only leads to more efficient pipeline usage, but also the branch is effectively free.

In the case where the guess was incorrect, referred to as a *branch miss*, the prematurely executed instructions from the incorrect branch path amount to wasted work. The execution pipeline is flushed to remove the partially executed instructions, and the typical branch overhead is experienced. It's important to note that speculative execution doesn't hurt performance in a branch miss, since it merely tries to fill idle execution resources with potentially beneficial work. Without it, every branch would suffer from overhead.

Despite some popular beliefs, branch misses are not restricted to conditional branching. Each processor contains a ring-buffer cache, which is responsible for storing the return address of each function call. While a CALL instruction pushes the return address onto the processes' stack, it also places the return address into this buffer. When a RET instruction is found, the last pointer inserted into this ring buffer is used as the guess for speculative execution. In the case where either the cache overflows, that is, the function call stack exceeds the number of entries in the buffer, or where a CALL instruction doesn't have a corresponding RET instruction, this pointer is incorrect, leading to a branch miss on the function return. In order to avoid this, *ensure that each CALL instruction has a corresponding RET instruction, and vis-versa.* The toolchain should handle this automatically, but it is something to be cognizant of when writing assembly. This mistake is especially common when writing a thunk to get the program counter for 32-bit PIC!

Also, and perhaps more importantly, *avoid writing code that results in deep stack traces.* This is especially problematic for recursive code. The typical number of entries in the processor's ring-buffer cache is sixteen return addresses, so be wary of going much deeper. If possible, inline small functions to reduce the stack depth. To determine the balance between the cost of increased code size due to excessive function inlining and the cost of unconditional branch misses, *measure*.

While speculative execution never hurts performance, it can be poorly utilized by software, leading to a high performance opportunity cost, that is, the performance that could have been achieved had the code been tuned better. In general, the optimizations discussed in this chapter focus on avoiding the overhead associated with a branch. Granted, on modern Intel® Architectures, this overhead is minute, but bad speculation can still cause performance to suffer. The fastest branch is the branch that never occurs, either by not being present within the code, or by being correctly predicted.

13.1 AVOIDING BRANCHES

This section focuses on optimizing branching by reducing the number of overall branches. Obviously, the overhead of a branch miss can't be felt if the branch is missing from the code. Additionally, the branch prediction logic within each processor core maintains a cache of the recent branches encountered and their resulting targets. As the number of branches in an application increases, the pressure on this cache also increases, potentially reducing branch prediction accuracy. Conversely, as the number of branches in an application decreases, the pressure on this cache also decreases, potentially leading to more accurate predictions.

13.1.1 EXTRA WORK AND MASKING

By definition, a conditional branch optionally executes a segment of code. In some cases, this optional code must only execute in certain circumstances, that is, it has side effects that would affect correctness. In other cases, this optional code has no consequences to correctness, but just simply doesn't need to be executed in every circumstance. Obviously in the former case the branch is unavoidable; however, in the latter case, the branch itself *may* be more expensive than performing the actual work contained within that branch. This is a result of the highly parallel nature of the execution pipeline, as described in Section 2.2.3 of Chapter 2.

Remember though, a correctly predicted branch is essentially free, so *doing more work to avoid a well-predicted branch will hinder, not help, performance*. The only way to determine whether its worth branching or just to do the work is to profile and measure.

For computations, branches can sometimes be avoided by utilizing masks. A *mask* is simply a value that gates which bits are used from another value. While this section will mostly focus on integer operations, masks are also very important when writing SIMD code, where branching functionality is severely limited and can drastically hurt parallelism.

The easiest way to explain this concept is probably with an example. Consider the following function, foo(), where the variable x is only added to the variable y if x is positive.

```
1   int foo(int x, int y)
2   {
3           if (x > 0)
4                   y += x;
5           return y;
6   }
```

Assume that foo() is showing up on the CPU cycles profile as a hotspot, and that Top-Down Hierarchical analysis has identified branch prediction for this branch as the primary culprit. Is it possible to remove the branch from foo()?

To begin, consider what is known about this branch. First, it checks the sign of the integer x, so any mask will need to be crafted out of this information. Second, the x variable is a signed integer, and signed integers on x86 encode positive and negative numbers with a sign bit. This sign bit is located in the high order bit, which is also referred to as the most significant or leftmost bit. Therefore, isolating this bit will provide the information needed to generate the mask. The next step is to determine how this bit can be transformed in order to affect the value of x so that it can be added to y unconditionally.

Ideally, for negative values of x, where the sign bit is set, the mask should be zero. This is because a mask of zero, when combined with the value of x with a bitwise and operation, will result in $x = 0$, allowing for the addition to occur without any effect. For positive values of x, where the sign bit is not set, the mask should be all ones. This is because a mask of all ones, when combined with the value of x with a bitwise and operation, will result in the value of x being unchanged, allowing for the addition to occur as expected.

The key observation needed for converting the sign bit into the mask is that negative integers are encoded using their two's complement. Therefore, the encoding for negative one, where all bits are set, corresponds to the requirements for the mask when the sign bit is positive. By shifting the sign bit, located in the high order bit, right to the low order bit, also known as the least significant or rightmost bit, the result is a value of either one, in the negative case, and zero, in the positive case. Thus, subtracting one from this result will generate the desired masks. For example, the previous function foo() without the branch:

```
1   int foo(int x, int y)
2   {
3           unsigned hob = (unsigned)x >> (sizeof(int[CHAR_BIT])-1);
4           return y + (x & (hob - 1));
5   }
```

Notice that on line 3, the variable x is first cast from a signed integer type to an unsigned integer type. This is because the behavior when performing a bitwise shift to the right on a negative integer is implementation-defined by the C standard. On x86, there are two types of shift instructions, arithmetic and logical, used on signed and unsigned integers respectively. Logical shifts to the right, the SHR instruction, always fill the leftmost bits with zeros. Arithmetic shifts to the right, the SAR instruction, always fill the leftmost bits with the sign bit of the shifted value. For example, a 32-bit negative integer arithmetically shifted to the right 31 times would produce a result of $0xFFFFFFFF$, since the sign bit would propagate to every other bit position. At the same time, a 32-bit positive integer arithmetically shifted to the right 31 times would produce a result of zero. Therefore, using an arithmetic right shift would create the proper mask, once the mask's bits had been inverted with a logical not operation, instead of subtracting one from the mask value, as is done on line 4. The cast to the unsigned type, which according to C precedence rules occurs before the bitshifting operator, on line 3 ensures that the code only performs an unsigned bitwise shift to the right, the behavior of which is defined in the C standard as filling the leftmost bits with zeros. Additionally, operating on an unsigned integer instead of a signed integer does not affect creation of the mask, since unsigned underflow is well-defined in the C specification and produces the same result.

The sizeof(int[CHAR_BIT])-1 calculation on line 3 is simply a portable way of determining the number of bits in an integer. The syntax of the size calculation exploits the fact that the sizeof operator multiplies an array type by the number of indices, thereby multiplying CHAR_BIT, which the C standard defines to be the number of bits in a byte, with the number of bytes in an integer. Therefore, the hob variable contains the contents of the high order bit shifted into the low order bit.

Another way to avoid branching in this example is to leverage the conditional move, CMOV, instruction. This instruction only performs the data movement if the condition code is met. Since the instruction pointer is only incremented, this instruction doesn't classify as a branch. With any decent C compiler, this instruction is typically generated automatically for any ternary operator. For example, another way to remove the branch from the previous example:

```
1   int foo(int x, int y)
2   {
3          int tmp = x > 0 ?
4                  x : 0;
5          return y + tmp;
6   }
```

LISTING 13.1

C-Style.

```
1   foo:
2          mov     $0, tmp
3          cmp     $0, x
4          cmovg   x, tmp
5          add     tmp, y
6          mov     y, %eax
7          ret
```

LISTING 13.2

Pseudo x86.

13.1.2 COMBINING AND REARRANGING BRANCHES

As described in "Flow control" section of Chapter 1, every instruction either sets or clears zero or more arithmetic status flags in the EFLAGS register. While these status flags can be used to control the execution flow, they are not branches. Branches only correspond to instructions that actually modify the instruction pointer. For conditional branches, that means instructions such as JCC, where CC represents a condition code.

Consider the following simple branching example, implemented in a high-level programming language on the left, and the equivalent, although unoptimized, x86 on the right:

```
1   if ( x == 0 && y == 0 ) {
2          // fallthrough case
3   }
4   // continue path
```

LISTING 13.3

C-Style.

```
1          cmp     $0, x
2          jne     .Lcontinue_path
3          cmp     $0, y
4          jne     .Lcontinue_path
5          # fallthrough case
6   .Lcontinue_path:
7          # continue path
```

LISTING 13.4

Pseudo x86.

First, notice that although there is only one if statement in the high-level programming language, there are still two x86 branching instructions, on lines 2 and 4. Each of these branching instructions correlates to one of the two checks performed within the if condition. At the same time, it would be fallacious to assume that the number of branch instructions is always the same as the number of checks performed in the high-level language. For example, in this situation the compiler might determine during one of its optimization passes that the variable x is always 0, and therefore completely omit that check, resulting in only a single branch instruction actually occurring. Additionally, the compiler might determine that x can never be 0, and therefore completely omit the entire branch code path. The only way to know for certain is to check the assembly generated by the compiler.

Second, notice that the left-most branch, $x == 0$, is evaluated before the right-most branch, $y == 0$. This behavior is guaranteed by the C specification, which specifies that the logical and, &&, and logical or, ||, operators are sequence points between their two operands. A sequence point ensures that all values and side effects produced before the sequence point will be evaluated before code after the sequence point.

As a result of this behavior, if the left-most branch condition evaluates to false, then the right-most branch is completely skipped. This observation can be exploited to reduce the total number of branches executed by arranging branches such that the most influential branches, that is, the branches that are most likely to determine whether the entire code path is taken or not, are executed before less influential branches.

For example, consider the situation where three conditions must be met as a prerequisite for a code path. Assume that using a tool like gcov has revealed the probabilities of these three branches evaluating to true are 80%, 75%, and 10%. According to these measurements, the best order for the branches would start with the condition that is only true 10% of the time, followed by the branch that is true 75% of the time, and then finally the branch that is true 80% of the time.

This concept extends beyond the logical C operators to any sequence point within the C language. For example, considering the following optimal arrangements:

```
1   void foo(void)
2   {
3           if (very_likely_condition)
4                   return;
5           if (somewhat_likely_condition)
6                   return;
7           if (not_likely_condition)
8                   return;
9           /* do something */
10  }
11
12  void bar(void)
13  {
14          if (not_likely_condition) {
15                  if (somewhat_likely_condition) {
16                          if (very_likely_condition) {
17                                  /* nested fallthrough */
18                          }
19                  }
20          }
21          /* do something */
22  }
```

Notice that in the previous listing, the function foo()'s branches were listed in the reverse order to those in function bar(), that is, moving from most likely to least likely as opposed to least likely to most likely. This is because foo()'s branches result in the control flow leaving foo(), and therefore skipping its other branches. The point here is not to always follow a specific ordering, but instead to think about how to reduce the actual number of branches executed.

Third, going back to the examples in Listings 13.3 and 13.4, notice that two non-branching instructions, on lines 1 and 3, are used to perform the actual comparisons. The CMP instruction performs integer subtraction on the two operands. Unlike the normal integer subtraction instruction, the CMP instruction discards the result and only modifies the relevant arithmetic flags for later use by a conditional instruction. The TEST instruction is similar to the CMP instruction, but performs a bitwise and operation instead of integer subtraction. Therefore, the TEST and CMP instructions each modify a different set of arithmetic flags.

In this case, the CMP instruction subtracts the immediate operand, the integer zero, and the other operand, the variable x or y. When comparing for equality with a conditional instruction, either with the equal, e, or not-equal, ne, condition codes, the arithmetic flag representing a zero result, ZF, is checked. Obviously, this is because the difference of two equivalent numbers is zero. At the same time, the ZF is also set by arithmetic and logical instructions that produce a zero result. This flag can also be checked with the zero, z, or not-zero, nz, condition codes.

This observation can be leveraged to reduce the number of branches performed in this example. For example, if both the x and y variables are zero, then the sum of those variables will also be zero. Therefore, instead of branching on the condition of each variable, it is possible to branch on the sum of these variables, that is, checking whether $x + y == 0$. Of course, this is only possible if it is guaranteed that x and y won't offset to 0, e.g., $x = -1$ and $y = 1$. Since in this example the result of the summation isn't saved, this would require either using a temporary variable to avoid modifying the actual contents of x and y. Assuming that both x and y are unsigned, and therefore can't offset to zero, the previous example could therefore be reduced from two branches to only one branch. For example:

```
1  if ( x + y == 0 ) {
2          // fallthrough case
3  }
4  // continue path
```

LISTING 13.5

C-Style.

```
1          mov     x, tmp
2          add     y, tmp
3          jnz     .Lcontinue_path
4          # fallthrough case
5  .Lcontinue_path:
6          # continue path
```

LISTING 13.6

Pseudo x86.

13.2 IMPROVING PREDICTION

The branch prediction logic in the more modern x86 architectures is *very* good at detecting patterns in the branch paths taken. As a result, a lot of the traditional advice about optimizing branch prediction is no longer valid. Typically, this advice would focus on improving prediction by providing hints to the processor that would help the branch predictor choose the correct path, or on organizing branch targets to follow static prediction rules. While these techniques will improve branch prediction for older platforms, and they won't hurt branch prediction for newer platforms, they won't be producing performance gains on modern platforms.

Instead, since the branch predictor excels at finding patterns, branch optimizations should focus on reorganizing branches, such that they follow some predictable pattern.

Branch hint prefixes have already been mentioned as an ineffective optimization technique for modern x86 architectures. The two prefixes, $0x2E$, which hinted that the branch wouldn't be taken, and $0x3E$, which hinted that the branch would be taken, modified the static prediction rules used by the branch predictor. The static prediction rules are no longer used, so neither are the prefixes.

13.2.1 PROFILE GUIDED OPTIMIZATION

Unlike the other techniques in this chapter, profile guided optimization is a technique for optimizing branch prediction that doesn't involve any changes to the source code. Instead, it comprises of a series of steps that are designed to provide the compiler with feedback about the application's behavior. This feedback is then used by the compiler to provide further optimizations. While all of the compiler's optimizations benefit from this additional information, in the author's personal experience, profile guided optimization is capable of providing impressive performance gains when branch prediction is the limiting bottleneck.

In order to accomplish this, the software must be built not once, but twice. The first build is not designed to be used regularly. Instead, it instruments the code with special functions that monitor and record the software's behavior at runtime. This instrumented binary will then be run on a workload designed to replicate the typical workloads expected by the software. As the execution of this representative workload finishes, the trace of the application's behavior is saved to the filesystem, and will be used later by the compiler. It's worth noting that profile guided optimization can be performed on any binary, that is, both on executable applications and libraries. In the case of a shared library, the binary executable, that links against the shared library in order to exercise it, will also need to be compiled with the instrumenting compiler flags, as will the library itself.

At this point, the software is ready to be built again. At compile time, the compiler parses the traces generated by the first build during execution, and then uses those results to make informed decisions about the optimizations and layout of the code. The resulting binary, with its tailored optimizations, will hopefully result in a performance increase. The key to successful profile guided optimization is the availability of an accurate representative workload.

At the time of this writing, all three of the major compiler toolchains, GCC, LLVM, and the Intel® C and C++ compilers (ICC), all support profile guided optimization, although LLVM requires a newer release, as support wasn't available until early 2014.

Interestingly, LLVM supports two different methods for profile collection. The first type, which is the same as GCC and ICC, instruments the binary during build to collect results. The second type, which deviates from the typical profile guided optimization flow, eschews instrumentation and instead allows feedback to be submitted to the compiler from the `perf(1)` infrastructure. For this to work, the binary needs to be built with debugging information, and a special tool must be used to convert the output from `perf(1)` into something the compiler can parse. In the author's opinion, this is an excellent feature, designed to obviate the two-build requirement that has prevented profile guided optimization from obtaining wide usage. As such, the author patiently awaits to see how this functionality will evolve and affect the other compilers.

In order to generate the first, instrumented, build, each compiler uses a similar, but unfortunately different, compiler flag. For GCC, the flag is `-fprofile-generate`, for LLVM, it is `-fprofile-instr-generate`, and for ICC, it is `-prof-gen`.

After using this flag, for both building and linking, the resulting binary will generate additional tracing files upon execution. The number, name, and formatting of those tracing files is compiler specific. GCC generates one trace file, ending with a `.gcda` suffix, per object file. For instance, `foo.o` would have a corresponding `foo.gcda`. On the other hand, ICC and LLVM only generate one trace file, representing the entire trace. ICC trace files end with a `.dyn` suffix, while LLVM traces end with a `.profraw` suffix.

Once the trace file, or files, has been collected, a different compiler flag is used to inform the compiler to locate, parse, and utilize them. For GCC, this flag is `-fprofile-use`, for LLVM, the flag is `-fprofile-instr-use=filename`, and for ICC, the flag is `-prof-use`. The result from this build is ready for benchmarking.

REFERENCES

Free Software Foundation, 2014, 09. GCC(1) Manual Page.

Gerber, R., Bik, A.J.C., Smith, K.B., Tian, X., 2006, 03. The Software Optimization Cookbook: High-Performance Recipes for IA-32 Platforms. Intel Press, Hillsboro, OR.

Intel Corporation, 2013, 10. Intel 64 and IA-32 Architectures Software Developer's Manual. Computer Hardware Manual.

Intel Corporation, 2014, 10. Intel 64 and IA-32 Architectures Optimization Reference Manual. Order Number: 248966-030.

Intel Corporation, 2014. Intel® C++ Compiler XE User and Reference Guide.

LLVM Project, 2014, 10. `llvm-profdata`—Profile Data Tool.

Patterson, D.A., Hennessy, J.L., 2007. Computer Organization and Design: The Hardware/ Software Interface, third ed. Morgan Kaufmann, Burlington, MA.

The Clang Team, 2014. Clang: Profile Guided Optimization.

Optimizing Cache Usage

14

CHAPTER CONTENTS

In an ideal world, all data could be stored in the fastest memory available to the system, providing uniform performance to all segments of data. Unfortunately, this currently isn't feasible, forcing the developer to make tradeoffs with regards to which data elements are prioritized for faster access. Giving preference to one chunk of data comes with the opportunity cost of potentially having given preference to a different data block.

Section 1.1.1 in Chapter 1 introduced the fundamentals of a tiered storage hierarchy. This hierarchy is organized such that each level is faster, but more expensive and less dense, than the level below it. This concept is illustrated in Figure 14.1.

If data accesses were uniformly distributed, that is, the probability of a data access to every address or every block was equal, then performance would suffer immensely. Luckily, the principle of *temporal data locality* observes that previously accessed data is likely to be accessed again soon after. Leveraging this observation, which is not a law, it is possible to improve performance by caching recently used data elements from a slower medium in a faster medium.

The effectiveness of such a cache is typically measured with the percentage of cache hits. A *cache hit* is a data access that was satisfied from the cache. A *cache miss* is a data access that was not satisfied from the cache, and therefore had to access one or more slower tiers of storage.

While this chapter primarily focuses on a particular caching layer, the CPU cache implemented in hardware, caching occurs throughout the storage hierarchy, in both hardware and software. For example, the Linux kernel will prefetch the contents of a

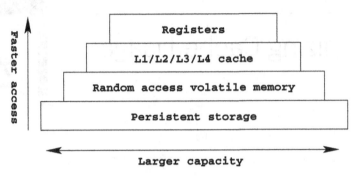

FIGURE 14.1

Storage hierarchy.

file from a disk drive, placing the data into memory pages. These memory pages are then put into the kernel's page cache, so when an application requests them, they are immediately available. For more information on this feature, read the related documentation for the readahead(2) system call, which allows the developer to request this behavior.

When optimizing an application that is suffering from high latency resource accesses, consider adding a cache in a higher tier of storage. Analyzing the data access patterns should provide insight into whether a cache can improve performance. If so, the next step involves selecting algorithms for determining what data is stored in the cache, how long entries are kept, and the search algorithm for finding entries.

14.1 PROCESSOR CACHE ORGANIZATION

Whereas the rapid advancements in processor technology have yielded significant performance increases between processor generations, the advancements in memory technology haven't been keeping the same aggressive pace. As a result, memory is a fairly common bottleneck. As mentioned in Chapter 2, the Intel® 80486 introduced an on-chip data and instruction cache for reducing the effect of memory latency on performance. Prior to the 80486, memory caches did exist, but they were not physically located on the processor die and therefore were not as effective. Continuing through Chapters 2 and 3, the processor's caches have grown to meet the needs of increasing memory sizes. Consider that the cache on the 80486 was 8-KB, whereas the cache on a modern high-end Intel® Xeon® processor can be almost 40-MB.

The overarching storage hierarchy can also be seen within the organization of the processor cache. The cache is divided into multiple levels, with the highest tier providing the fastest access and the smallest density and the lowest tier providing the slowest access and the largest density. The lowest cache tier the processor supports is referred to as the *Last Level Cache* (LLC). A LLC miss results in an access to physical memory. The number of cache levels and their capacities depends not only on the microarchitecture, but also on the specific processor model.

The highest tier is the Level 1 (L1) cache. Originally, this cache was introduced in the 80486 as a *unified cache*, meaning that it stored both instructions and data. Starting with the P6 microarchitecture, there are two separate L1 caches, one dedicated to storing instructions and one dedicated to storing data. A cache that only stores instructions is referred to as an *icache*. Conversely, a cache that only stores data is referred to as a *dcache*. The P6 microarchitecture also added a unified Level 2 (L2) cache. Both L1 caches and the L2 cache are duplicated per-core, and are shared between the core's Hyper-Threads. On the other hand, the unified Level 3 (L3) cache is an uncore resource, i.e., it is shared by all of the processor's cores.

When the execution unit needs to load a byte of memory, the L1 cache is searched. In the case where the needed memory is found, a L1 cache hit, the memory is simply copied from the cache. On the other hand, in the case of a L1 cache miss, the L2 is searched next, and so on. This process repeats until either the data is found in one of the caches, or a cache miss in the LLC forces the memory request to access physical memory. In the case where the data request missed the L1 cache but was satisfied from a different level cache, the data is loaded into the L1 first, and then is provided to the processor.

At this point, the reader may be wondering how such large caches are searched so quickly. An exhaustive iterative search wouldn't be capable of meeting the performance requirements needed from the cache. In order to answer this question, the internal organization of the cache must be explained.

Intel® Architecture uses a *n*-way set associative cache. A *set* is a block of memory, comprised of a fixed number of fixed size memory chunks. These fixed size memory chunks, each referred to as a *cache line*, form the basic building block of the cache. The number of *ways* indicates how many cache lines are in each set (Gerber et al., 2006).

To reduce the number of cache entries that must be searched for a given address, each set is designated to hold entries from a range of addresses. Therefore, when searching for a specific entry, only the appropriate set needs to be checked, reducing the number of possible entries that require searching to the number of ways. Each set is encoded to a range of physical addresses.

14.1.1 CACHE LINES

Fundamentally, the concept of a cache line represents a paradigm shift in memory organization. Previously, memory could be considered as just an array of bytes, with each memory access occurring on demand, and in the size requested. For example, if the processor loaded a word, the corresponding address would be translated into a physical address, which would then be fetched as a word. As a result, if the address of the word was unaligned, it would require the processor to perform two aligned loads and then splice the results together, making the memory access more expensive. With the introduction of cache lines, the execution unit no longer fetches data from memory directly, instead all data memory requests, except for two exceptions, are satisfied from the L1 cache. As a result, all requests to physical memory occur in the granularity of the cache line size. Consider how this affects the previous example of loading an unaligned word. Rather than just loading the needed 16 bits, the full cache line containing the word is loaded. Therefore, the unaligned property of the address only significantly impacts performance if the unaligned word also crosses two cache lines.

As mentioned above, there are two exceptions to all data passing through the L1 cache. The first exception is data loads from regions of memory which are marked as not cacheable. The ability to disable caching for certain memory regions is required for memory mapped I/O, as the values at those addresses are actually the contents of device registers, which may be updated by the respective peripheral. These regions are configured either by the Page Attribute Table (PAT) entry in the page tables or via the Memory Type Range Registers (MTRR) MSRs. For almost all situations, the Linux kernel should handle these regions properly, so this shouldn't be an issue for user space.

The second exception is the nontemporal instructions, such as MOVNTDQA. These instructions are used to stream chunks of data in and out of memory, bypassing the cache. This is useful for loading or storing data that the programmer doesn't want to be cached because it is unlikely to be accessed again soon and adding it to the cache may evict other temporal data.

All data that is accessed with nontemporal instructions is evicted from every level of the cache. As a result, nontemporal hints can *reduce* performance if used incorrectly. When measuring the performance of algorithms containing nontemporal instructions, it is important to account for the cost of future accesses to that data.

For example, consider the memcpy(3) function. For functions like these, that operate on large chunks of memory, it is typically best to access each element in the largest width possible. As a result, the memcpy(3) implementation in glibc is optimized with SIMD instructions, in order to take advantage of the larger vector registers. Substituting these temporal load and store instructions with their nontemporal versions might appear to make the memcpy(3) operation faster; however, unlike the current implementations, which keeps the data cache warm, the nontemporal implementation would evict all of that data from the cache. In other words, the memcpy(3) operation may complete faster, but overall performance will decrease.

14.2 QUERYING CACHE TOPOLOGY

The configuration of the cache, including the number of cache levels, size of each level, number of sets, number of ways, and cache line size, can change. Some of these aspects, like the cache line, lack fluidity, while other aspects, such as the size of each cache level, change per processor model. Because of this, when writing software that optimizes based on these factors, it makes sense to automatically detect these values at runtime rather than hard-coding them.

This section demonstrates a few different methods for retrieving this data, leaving the reader to determine which approach best suits his needs.

CPUID

As with essentially any relevant processor information, the cache details on Intel Architecture are exposed via the CPUID instruction. In fact, multiple CPUID leaves report information about the cache.

The Basic CPUID Information leaf, *EAX* = 2, reports the type and size of each cache, TLB, and hardware prefetcher. Each of the result registers are loaded with a descriptor corresponding to an exact description of one of the resources. Multiple CPUID invocations may be necessary in order to retrieve all of the information. In order to encode so much information in so few bytes, each descriptor is merely a number, referencing a table entry in the Intel® *Software Developer Manual* (SDM) that describes the full configuration. Because of this, in order to properly interpret these entries dynamically, a copy of the data in that table from the SDM must be included in the code.

The Deterministic Cache Parameters Leaf, *EAX* = 4, reports the properties of a specific cache. Each cache is identified by an index number, which is selected by the value of the *ECX* register upon invocation of CPUID. This index can be continually incremented until a special NULL cache type is returned, indicating that all cache levels have been iterated. Unlike the Basic CPUID Information leaf, this leaf encodes the information, such as the cache line size, number of ways, and number of sets, in bitfields returned in the registers. Because it doesn't require a pre-populated table, this approach yields itself to programmability better than the other leaf. Listing 14.1 provides an example of how to iterate the caches using this leaf, and how the reported information should be interpreted.

```
1   #include <stdio.h>
2   #include <assert.h>
3
4   #ifdef __PIC__
5   static inline void cpuid(unsigned *restrict const a,
6                            unsigned *restrict const b,
7                            unsigned *restrict const c,
8                            unsigned *restrict const d)
9   {
10          __asm__ __volatile__ (
11                  "xchg %%ebx, %1\n\t"
12                  "cpuid\n\t"
13                  "xchg %1, %%ebx\n\t"
14          : "+a" (*a),
15            "+r" (*b),
16            "+c" (*c),
17            "+d" (*d)
18          );
19  }
20  #else    /* Non PIC */
21  static inline void cpuid(unsigned *restrict const a,
22                           unsigned *restrict const b,
```

```
23                              unsigned *restrict const c,
24                              unsigned *restrict const d)
25   {
26          __asm__ __volatile__ (
27                  "cpuid\n\t"
28          : "+a" (*a),
29            "+b" (*b),
30            "+c" (*c),
31            "+d" (*d)
32          );
33   }
34   #endif
35
36   enum cache_type {          /* From Table 3-17 of Volume 2 SDM */
37          TYPE_NULL = 0,
38          TYPE_DATA = 1,
39          TYPE_INST = 2,
40          TYPE_UNIF = 3,
41          TYPE_MAX  = 4,
42   };
43
44   static const char *const type_str[TYPE_MAX] = {
45          [TYPE_NULL] = "NULL",
46          [TYPE_DATA] = "Data Cache        ",
47          [TYPE_INST] = "Instruction Cache",
48          [TYPE_UNIF] = "Unified Cache      "
49   };
50
51   union ax {
52          unsigned e;
53          struct cache {  /* From Table 3-17 */
54                  unsigned type : 5;
55                  unsigned lvl  : 3;
56                  /* Skip Rest */
57          } b;
58   };
59
60   union bx {
61          unsigned e;
62          struct cache_sz { /* From Table 3-17 */
63                  unsigned linesz_m1 : 12;
64                  unsigned parts_m1  : 10;
65                  unsigned ways_m1   : 10;
66          } b;
67   };
68
69   void iterate_caches(void)
```

```
70   {
71           unsigned cache_idx = 0;
72
73           static_assert(sizeof(union ax) == sizeof(unsigned),
74                   "bitfield A wrong");
75           static_assert(sizeof(union bx) == sizeof(unsigned),
76                   "bitfield B wrong");
77
78           while (1) {
79                   const char *const units[] = {" B", "KB", "MB", "GB",
80                                                 NULL };
81
82                   union ax ax;
83                   union bx bx;
84                   unsigned cx, dx, cache_sz;
85                   const char *const *unit_str;
86
87                   ax.e = 0x4;
88                   cx = cache_idx;
89                   cpuid(&ax.e, &bx.e, &cx, &dx);
90
91                   if (ax.b.type == TYPE_NULL)
92                           break;
93
94                   cache_sz = (bx.b.ways_m1 + 1) * (bx.b.parts_m1 + 1) *
95                           (bx.b.linesz_m1 + 1) * (cx + 1);
96
97                   unit_str = &units[0];
98                   while (cache_sz >= 1024) {
99                           if (*(unit_str + 1) == NULL)
100                                  break;
101
102                          cache_sz /= 1024;
103                          unit_str++;
104                  }
105
106                  printf("(Index %d) %3d%s L%d %s [Line Size: %dB]\n",
107                          cache_idx, cache_sz, *unit_str, ax.b.lvl,
108                          type_str[ax.b.type], bx.b.linesz_m1 + 1);
109
110                  cache_idx++;
111          }
112  }
```

LISTING 14.1

Using CPUID to determine cache sizes.

For example, running this function on a Second Generation Intel® Core™ processor produces:

```
1  $ ./get-cache
2  (Index 0)  32KB L1 Data Cache         [Line Size: 64B]
3  (Index 1)  32KB L1 Instruction Cache [Line Size: 64B]
4  (Index 2) 256KB L2 Unified Cache      [Line Size: 64B]
5  (Index 3)   6MB L3 Unified Cache      [Line Size: 64B]
```

Sysfs

The CPUID leaves described in the previous section can also be accessed via the sysfs interface. In this case, the CPUID leaves are iterated, with the results cached, when sysfs is initialized. Performing a read(2) on these files looks up the relevant data in the cache. The code that iterates the cache information, along with the code that executes when these files are accessed can be seen at ${LINUX_SRC}/arch/x86/kernel/cpu/intel_cacheinfo.c.

The cache information cache is stored per logical processor, so the cache sysfs directory can be found under the cpu sysfs directory, located at /sys/devices/system/cpu/.

For example, looking at the cache available to cpu0 on the same processor as the CPUID example from the previous section:

```
1  $ ls /sys/devices/system/cpu/cpu0/cache/
2  index0  index1  index2  index3
3  $ cat /sys/devices/system/cpu/cpu0/cache/index0/type
4  Data
5  $ cat /sys/devices/system/cpu/cpu0/cache/index0/size
6  32K
7  $ cat /sys/devices/system/cpu/cpu0/cache/index0/coherency_line_size
8  64
```

14.3 PREFETCH

Earlier in this chapter, the principle of data locality was introduced as one of the prime motivations for utilizing caching. Whereas that motivation revolved around *temporal* data locality, another observation of data locality can also benefit performance. The principle of *spatial data locality* observes that if one address is accessed, other addresses located near that address are also likely to be accessed.

In order to benefit from this observation, Intel processors support the *prefetching* of cache lines. When a cache line is prefetched, it is loaded from memory and placed into one, or more, levels of the processor cache, not because the executing code immediately needs it, but because it *may* need it. If successful, when the cache line is requested, it is already close to the processor, thus completely masking the memory latency for the load operation. Additionally, since the prefetch request occurs without an immediate need for the data, the load can be more flexible with regards to memory bandwidth. This allows for prefetches to be completed during lulls in memory accesses, when there is more available bandwidth, and translates to more available bandwidth later, since the prefetched memory loads are already in the cache, and don't require a memory access.

Prefetching occurs in one of two ways, either through the hardware prefetcher or through the software prefetching instructions. For the most part, the hardware prefetcher operates transparently to the programmer. It leverages the principle of spatial data locality to prefetch cache lines spatially colocated with the cache lines currently being accessed. On modern Intel platforms, the hardware prefetcher is very effective at determining which cache lines should be loaded, and loading them before they are needed. Despite this, tailoring data organization and access patterns to improve data locality can make the hardware prefetcher even more effective.

On the other hand, software prefetching instructions give the programmer the ability to hint at what cache lines should be loaded and into which cache level. The PREFETCH instruction encodes this information as a memory pointer operand, pointing to the address whose cache line should be loaded, as well as an instruction suffix, determining which cache level the cache line should be loaded into. Unlike most instructions that operate on memory, the PREFETCH instruction doesn't generate a fault on an invalid memory address, so it is safe to use without regard for the end of buffers or other edge conditions. This yields itself well to heuristics, such as prefetch *n* bytes ahead in this array each loop iteration. When deciding how far ahead to prefetch, the general rule of thumb is to prefetch data that won't be needed for about one hundred clock cycles and then use measurements to refine the lookahead value (Gerber et al., 2006).

It's important to note that software prefetching instructions only provide a hint, not a guarantee. This hint may be disregarded or handled differently depending on the processor generation. In the author's personal experience, the hardware prefetcher is often effective enough to make software prefetching unnecessary. Instead, focus on improving data locality and reducing the working set. That being said, there are some unusual memory access patterns where software prefetching can benefit.

14.4 IMPROVING LOCALITY

Since the concept of caching relies heavily on the principles of temporal and spatial data locality, it follows that efficient cache usage requires optimizing for data locality. Therefore, when organizing a data structure's memory layout, it is typically beneficial to *group variables used together into the same cache line*. The exception to this rule is if the variables are going to be modified concurrently by two threads. This situation is discussed in more detail in Chapter 15.

The `pahole` tool is capable of displaying the layout of data structures, partitioned by cache line. This is accomplished by providing an ELF file, including executable and object files, as an argument to `pahole`. For instance, the command `pahole foo.o` will display all of the structures present within the ELF object file foo.o. In order for this to work correctly, the ELF file must contain its debugging information.

Using this information, it is possible to rearrange a data structure's memory layout to improve locality. As always, any changes should be measured and verified with benchmarking to ensure that they actually improve performance. For example, consider the following structure:

```
1   struct bad_locality {
2           int x;
3           char strdata[252];
4           int y;
5   };
```

In this example, assume that profiling has identified that code utilizing this structure is suffering from performance penalties due to cache line replacements, that is, cache lines are loaded and then prematurely evicted. Also assume that the accesses to this structure frequently use bad_locality.x and bad_locality.y together, and don't often use bad_locality.strdata. Now, consider the output from pahole, which has been adjusted to fit the page width of this book, for this structure:

```
1   struct bad_locality {
2           int      x;                      /*      0     4 */
3           char     strdata[252];           /*      4   252 */
4           /* --- cacheline 4 boundary (256 bytes) --- */
5           int      y;                      /*    256     4 */
6
7           /* size: 260, cachelines: 5, members: 3 */
8           /* last cacheline: 4 bytes */
9   };
```

Notice that bad_locality.x and bad_locality.y are separated by four cache lines. Because of this, two separate cache lines, one for each member, will need to be loaded to complete any operation involving both integers. Also, as the gap between the two cache lines grows, the probability of both cache lines being present in the L1 dcache simultaneously decreases, potentially increasing the time required to fetch these elements from memory. On the other hand, by rearranging this structure, so that bad_locality.x and bad_locality.y share a single cache line, the number of cache lines that need to be loaded is halved. In other words, the struct would be rearranged into:

```
1   struct better_locality {
2           int x;
3           int y;
4           char strdata[252];
5   };
```

Another situation to consider is the behavior of a memory layout when grouped together as an array. Continuing with the previous example, consider how the `better_locality` struct will behave when stored in an array of a few thousand elements, back-to-back.

Assume that the first element starts aligned to the cache line size, and therefore starts on the first byte of a new cache line. This first element will consume four whole cache lines and 4 bytes of the fifth cache line, that is 260 mod 64 = 4. As a result, the second element will start at the fifth byte of the cache line which was partially used by the first element. Since this second element starts at an offset of 4 bytes in its first cache line, it will require an extra 4 bytes in its last cache line, that is (4 + 260) mod 64 = 8, and so on. This trend will continue, with each element shifting the next element over to the right until a multiple of the cache line size is reached, at which point the trend will start over again. As a result, every sixteenth element of the array, 64/(260 mod 64) = 16, will result in `better_locality.x` and `better_locality.y` being split between two cache lines. While in this example, this phenomenon may seem to be very innocuous, the pattern illustrated here, where elements in an array have their position shifted due to the previous elements, can play havoc with variables that have strict alignment requirements.

There are three obvious approaches to resolving this issue. The first trades size for speed by adding extra padding to each struct entry. Since this example is concerned with keeping `better_locality.x` and `better_locality.y` together, an extra 4 bytes would be sufficient to ensure they never were separated. This could also be achieved by padding the structure with an extra 60 bytes, so it wouldn't use any partial cache lines, that is, `sizeof(struct better_locality)` mod 64 = 0.

The second possibility, rather than adding padding to increase the size of each array element, would be to instead decrease the size. Naturally, the feasibility of this approach would depend on whether the reduction in range affected correctness. In the example, this could be accomplished either by reducing both integer fields to shorts, removing 4 bytes from the character array, or a combination of both.

The third possibility would be to split the structure into two distinct structures, one containing the integer fields, and one containing the character array. This option relies on the assumption that `better_locality.x` and `better_locality.y` are used together, and that these are not often used with `best_locality.strdata`. In the case where this assumption holds, this option most likely will provide the best results.

REFERENCES

Carvalho de Meo, A., n.d. pahole(1) Manual Page.
Gerber, R., Bik, A.J.C., Smith, K.B., Tian, X., 2006, 03. The Software Optimization Cookbook: High-Performance Recipes for IA-32 Platforms, Intel Press, Hillsboro, OR.
Intel Corporation, 2013, 10. Intel 64 and IA-32 Architectures Software Developer's Manual. Computer Hardware Manual.
Intel Corporation, 2014, 10. Intel 64 and IA-32 Architectures Optimization Reference Manual. Order Number: 248966-030.

Exploiting Parallelism

CHAPTER CONTENTS

Parallelism, the act of performing two or more operations simultaneously, is a topic that has generated lots of interest and headlines within the last decade. Part of this fascination stems from the shift of the consumer market away from uniprocessor (UP) systems to widely available symmetric multiprocessing systems (SMP). Another part of this interest stems from the simplification of GPGPU, that is writing general purpose code for the GPU, which is a dedicated parallel processor. This simplification has transformed highly parallel vector processing from a niche aspect of the high performance computing (HPC) segment into something very accessible to everyone. Regardless of the modern attention, research into parallelism, and its associated challenges, traces back to the 1950s, predating the x86 architecture by more than twenty years.

Unfortunately, one hazard of the modern hype is the misconception that parallel means fast, or that every task yields itself well to parallelization. On the contrary, *many tasks can't be parallelized in a manner that improves performance*, and often parallel code will run slower than serial code. It is important to keep in mind that parallelism isn't a silver bullet for performance. On the contrary, just like all of the other aspects introduced within this book, properly wielding parallelism requires measurement and careful analysis in order to determine whether it is an appropriate solution for a given problem.

The most commonly discussed levels of parallelism utilize multiple threads and multiple processes. The decision between these two techniques typically revolves around whether the address space should be shared or isolated between the two components. In Linux, both threads and processes are created with the `clone(2)` system call, and processes can also be created with the `fork(2)` system call.

The concept of pipes and filters, that is, filters being the applications and pipes being the glue that connects multiple filters in order to build complicated commands out of simplistic ones, is a fundamental aspect of the UNIX philosophy. Every filter, whether executed interactively in a terminal emulator or noninteractively in a shell script, is executed by first creating a new process. This is achieved via the fork(2) system call, which duplicates the calling process into a new process. To change this new duplicate process into a different command, the execve(2) system call is invoked by the new child process. This system call replaces the current process image with the image described by the executable specified.

Since the workflow of creating a new process and then immediately loading a new process image to begin executing a different command is incredibly common, the fork(2)/execve(2) code path within the Linux kernel is heavily optimized. That being said, process and thread creation is still very expensive. In this situation, because execve(2) immediately replaces the current process image with a new image, the copying of the parent process into the child process, performed by the fork(2) system call, is unnecessary. In order to avoid these unnecessary data copies, Linux processes are created with Copy on Write (COW). With COW, rather than performing a deep copy of the parent's resources into the new process, the child's process resources point to the parent's, but are marked as read-only. If the child process calls execve(2), or doesn't perform any modifications to the address space, no copies are performed. On the other hand, if the child process does perform a write operation, then the write operation on the read-only pages will fault, giving the kernel time to perform the actual copies required for the new process.

As an aside, COW illustrates an important point about performance measurements. Hopefully the reader can see that without understanding COW, attempting to benchmark the overhead of process creation would probably be misleading. The system call API provides a nice abstraction of hardware functionality for user space; however, in order to measure the abstraction, at least a basic understanding of the lower layer and implementation is required. A wise teacher once told the author that operating systems are nothing but "lies, tricks, and deceptions."

There are already many excellent resources covering the use of parallel threads and processes. Some of the author's favorites include:

1. *Is Parallel Programming Hard, And, If so, What Can You Do About It* by Paul McKenney
2. *Modern Operating Systems* by Andrew Tanenbaum

Additionally, Intel develops an open source library, Intel® Threading Building Blocks (Intel® TBB), that is designed to aid in writing high performance parallel code. Intel TBB is a cross-platform C++ library which adds parallel algorithms and containers, while also providing primitives for defining parallel tasks. These parallel tasks are then automatically scheduled by the Intel TBB library, in order to provide better performance. The Intel TBB library is dual-licensed under the GPLv2 with the (libstdc++) runtime exception and a commercial license, and is typically available in most Linux distribution's package managers. More information on Intel TBB can be found at https://www.threadingbuildingblocks.org/.

15.1 SIMD

Single Instruction Multiple Data (SIMD) instructions were introduced into the x86 architecture with the MMX™ technology, and continue to be incredibly significant to performance on modern x86 with the SSE and Intel® Advanced Vector Set Extensions (Intel® AVX) instruction set extensions. As the name implies, a single SIMD instruction performs the same operation, not on one data element, but on *many* simultaneously. Their purpose is to provide the general purpose processor with some of the benefits and capabilities of a vector processor.

Whereas vector processors are typically more parallel, that is, they can operate on larger data sets, providing SIMD functionality directly in the processor architecture provides some unique advantages. For example, when writing GPGPU kernels, special care must be taken to reduce the number of data copies, since PCIe bandwidth is usually a significant bottleneck. As a result, GPGPU can be impractical for use cases that require data to bounce back and forth between the CPU and GPU. On the other hand, SSE and Intel AVX resources are located close to the processor's other execution resources, and can fully benefit from the processor caches. As a result, parallelization with SIMD has much lower setup costs, which make it more practical for situations where other forms of parallelism, such as threading, are too expensive.

The SIMD functionality of the processor depends on which instruction set extensions are supported. While it is always a good practice to check for support for all features used, since these extensions compound upon each other, Intel® processors typically don't support one extension without supporting all prior extensions. For instance, if a processor supports SSE3, it will typically also support SSE2, SSE, and so on.

Originally, the MMX extensions added instructions designed to perform integer operations; however, unlike the later extensions, the MMX registers aliased to the x87 stack. This simplified operating system support, since no new state needed to be saved on a context switch, but complicated the simultaneous use of MMX and x87 operations. In general, MMX isn't frequently used anymore.

The Intel® Pentium® III introduced the Streaming SIMD Extensions (SSE). This extension added new larger registers, which aren't part of the x87 stack, and instructions for operating on both integer and floating point values. Over time, the functionality of SSE has been steadily augmented through a number of extensions, which each add new instructions. These extensions include SSE2, SSE3, SSSE3, SSE4.1, and SSE4.2. The extra S in SSSE3 stands for Supplemental, that is, Supplemental Streaming SIMD Extensions 3.

The Intel® Advanced Vector Extensions (Intel® AVX) were introduced with the Second Generation Intel® Core™ processor family. Once again this increased the register width, with a new set of registers and instructions. The Intel AVX instructions only focused on floating point operations, while the second extension, Intel® AVX2, introduced with the Fourth Generation Intel® Core™ processor family, added integer operations. Intel AVX also introduced the VEX instruction encoding, which is capable of supporting non-destructive versions of instructions. With a destructive form of an instruction, one operand serves as both the source and destination for the operation, that is, one of the source operands is clobbered. On the other hand, with VEX encoded non-destructive instruction forms, neither source operand is modified and a third operand is added for the destination.

Intel has already released the documentation for the next Intel AVX extension, Intel® Advanced Vector Extensions 512 (Intel® AVX-512). This extension is not called AVX3 because that would imply an extension that simply adds new instructions to Intel AVX. Instead, Intel AVX-512 increases the register width from Intel AVX, and uses a different encoding, known as EVEX.

When attempting to determine whether a code segment is a prime candidate for vectorization, there are a few characteristics to look for. First, the code should be a self-contained loop. In other words, the loop shouldn't call any external functions on each data element within the loop, unless that function can be recreated in SIMD instructions. Second, there should be no data dependence between each loop iteration. If this doesn't hold true, it can be difficult to achieve a high level of parallelism. Third, the loop computation shouldn't require any branching, although masks can often be used to avoid branching. Review Section 13.1 in Chapter 13 for more information on techniques to avoid branches.

15.1.1 SIMD REGISTERS

In order for the instructions to operate on multiple data elements, each data element is *packed* into special extra-wide registers. There are sixteen SSE registers, *XMM*0 through *XMM*15, that are each 128 bits wide, although only eight of these registers are available in 32-bit mode with the other eight requiring 64-bit mode. There are sixteen Intel AVX registers, *YMM*0 through *YMM*15, that are each 256 bits wide. Finally, there are thirty-two Intel AVX-512 registers, *ZMM*0 through *ZMM*31, which are each 512 bits wide. So for instance, a 256-bit Intel AVX register can hold thirty-two packed bytes, sixteen packed words, eight packed dwords, eight packed IEEE 754 floats, four packed qwords, four packed IEEE 754 doubles, two packed 128-bit SSE values, or one 256-bit value.

The most straightforward and most efficient method to load these packed values into a SIMD register is by loading contiguous elements from an array. This is accomplished mainly by different forms of two instructions, MOVDQA and MOVDQU, that load the appropriate number of bytes beginning at the memory operand provided. The MOVDQA and MOVDQU instructions load 16-B and store them in a SSE register. The VMOVDQA and VMOVDQU instructions load 32-B and store them in an Intel AVX register. As time has passed, the expectations and abilities of SIMD have evolved, resulting in the presence of multiple other instructions that perform data loads, such as MOVAPS,

MOVAPD and LDDQU. At the times of their various introductions, these instructions all had slightly different internal behaviors, allowing for performance tuning for different situations; however on modern x86, they are all essentially identical.

Data alignment

The data load instructions typically come in two distinct versions, one with the suffix containing the letter "A", and one with the suffix containing the letter "U." Sometimes this letter is the last letter in the suffix, such as in the case of MOVDQU and MOVDQA, and sometimes it is not, such as in the case of MOVAPS and MOVUPS. This letter designates instructions that only operate on aligned data, corresponding to the letter "A" for aligned, and instructions that operate on both unaligned and aligned data, corresponding to the letter "U."

Each register size has a corresponding alignment requirement, the natural alignment. In other words, the 128-bit SSE registers have an alignment requirement of 16 bytes, that is, 128 bits, the 256-bit Intel AVX registers have an alignment requirement of 32 bytes, that is, 256 bits, and the 512-bit Intel AVX-512 registers have an alignment requirement of 64 bytes, that is, 512 bits. Attempting to perform an aligned load, or store, on a memory operand that doesn't meet this alignment requirement will result in a fault occurring, causing the process to receive a SIGBUS, or sometimes a SIGSEGV, signal. The default signal handler in both cases is to generate a core dump and then terminate the process.

The reason for providing instructions that only operate on aligned memory operands is that aligned loads and stores are significantly faster than their unaligned counterparts.

Originally, utilizing an unaligned load or store instruction would result in the more expensive unaligned load or store occurring, regardless of whether the memory operand was aligned or not. Starting with the Second Generation Intel® Core™ processor family, there is extra logic in the unaligned load and store instructions that checks for an aligned memory operand and, if found, performs the aligned operation instead. This optimization in hardware improves performance in the situations where the alignment isn't explicitly known and where software is written to always perform the unaligned load or store, to avoid the possibility of generating a fault. Unfortunately, this optimization has also resulted in some confusion about the performance impact of data alignment.

The reason for this confusion stems from the fact that using an unaligned load instruction no longer guarantees an actual unaligned data load, making it very easy to create misrepresentative microbenchmarks supposedly disproving the performance impact of alignment. On the contrary, data alignment does make a significant impact on performance. This is especially true for Intel® Atom™ processors.

This confusion is further compounded by the fact that, excluding the streaming instructions, loads and stores are satisfied by the cache, as opposed to directly accessing RAM. Therefore, an unaligned load that is contained within one cache line causes no extra penalty; however, by definition, there is no guarantee that an unaligned address doesn't straddle two cache lines. In this situation, where two cache lines are needed to satisfy the load or store, the processor needs to internally perform two aligned loads and then splice the result together, resulting in the extra penalty. This too can lead to misleading microbenchmarks.

As a result, any time data is being loaded into or stored from a SIMD register, the resulting memory operand should be explicitly aligned, either through the C11 `alignas()` macro, the POSIX `posix_memalign(3)` function, the compiler variable attribute, or manually. When aligning both the source and destination are not possible, favor alignment of the destination. For more information about specifying data alignment, see Section 12.4.3 in Chapter 12.

On newer microarchitectures, once the data is aligned, the selection of an aligned or unaligned instruction doesn't matter. As a result, the author tends to prefer using the unaligned instructions, since they provide identical performance as the aligned instructions, but also provide safety in the case of an unaligned operand, i.e., the program won't crash. The reader may be wondering how an unaligned operand could occur if the data was explicitly aligned; however, this does occasionally happen, typically with compiler variable attributes. The author has experience with compilers completely ignoring a variable's alignment attribute, resulting in a fault (Cryil, 2012).

Handling unknown alignment

In many situations, the programmer will be unable to guarantee the alignment of an address at compile time. Since the additional overhead of performing unaligned loads can be significant enough to negate any performance benefits from vectorization, it may be beneficial to use a hybrid approach consisting of both vectorized and nonvectorized implementations. In this approach, the nonvectorized implementation of the algorithm is used to "single-step" until an aligned address is found. For an alignment requirement of n, any address is either a multiple of n, and therefore meets the requirement, or is anywhere from 1 to $n - 1$ bytes away from the next aligned address. This technique relies on the nonvectorized code incrementing the address in a manner that alignment is possible. Once the aligned address is reached, the vectorized code can be utilized.

Assuming that the desired alignment is a power of two, which is a safe assumption for Intel processors, checking for alignment can be performed quickly with a logical and instruction. This takes advantage of the property of an integer's binary representation, where a power of two is represented by a single set bit, and a power of two minus one is represented as every bit prior to the power of two's bit being set. For example, 16 is represented as 10000_2 and 15 is represented as 01111_2. Using this knowledge, checking whether a number is a multiple of a power of two is as simple as checking whether any of the bits below that power of two's corresponding bit are set.

Consider the following example, where this hybrid approach is used to combine a byte-by-byte nonvectorized and SSE vectorized implementation.

```
1   #include <inttypes.h>
2
3   void foo(char *x, size_t x_sz)
4   {
5           /* Single-Step until aligned address */
6           while ((uintptr_t)x & (16 - 1) && x_sz) {
7                   /* Nonvectorized byte-by-byte algorithm */
8                   x_sz--;
9                   x++;
10          }
11
12          /* Bulk of operations w/ aligned data */
13          while (x_sz >= 16) {
14                  /* Vectorized SSE algorithm */
15                  x_sz -= 16;
16                  x += 16;
17          }
18
19          /* Finish up leftovers */
20          while (x_sz) {
21                  /* Nonvectorized byte-by-byte algorithm */
22                  x_sz--;
23                  x++;
24          }
25  }
```

15.1.2 SIMD OPERATIONS

All SIMD operations, besides those responsible for moving data, can be classified as either operating horizontally or vertically. Operations that are performed *vertically* occur between the corresponding positions of two separate registers. On the other hand, operations that are performed *horizontally* occur between all of the positions of one register. These two concepts are illustrated in Figures 15.1 and 15.2. The majority of SIMD operations are performed vertically, as vertical operations provide more parallelism and better performance. When possible, avoid horizontal operations by organizing data in a manner that yields itself to vertical operations.

In order to design data structures, programmers typically organize memory by grouping all of the fields needed for describing a single logical unit. In other words, a struct is organized to contain all of the attributes needed to describe a single instance of the data structure. If multiple instances are required, an *array of structures* is created.

For example, consider the situation where an array of structures exists for a series of data points, each represented by struct aos. The function foo() in this example iterates over this array and for each element performs floating point addition between the two elements, aos.x and aos.y, storing the result into a different array.

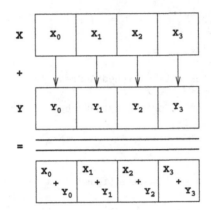

FIGURE 15.1

Vertical SIMD addition.

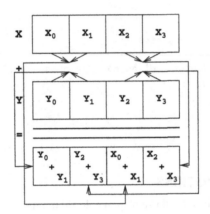

FIGURE 15.2

Horizontal SIMD addition.

```
1   struct aos {
2          double x;
3          double y;
4          /* other fields */
5   };
6
7   void foo(struct aos *in, size_t insz, double *out)
8   {
9          size_t i;
10
11         for (i = 0; i < insz; i++, in++) {
12                 out[i] = in->x + in->y;
13         }
14  }
```

Assuming that foo() shows up on a performance profile as consuming a large percentage of cycles, this function is a good candidate for vectorization. Unfortunately the current memory organization, an array of structures, is less than optimal for vertical vectorization. This organization leads to poor utilization of the caches and memory bandwidth, since more data is fetched than is required, and the extra fields increase the chance for the data to be evicted from the cache before it is needed again. Additionally, there will be overhead for swizzling the data into the correct format, which potentially could negate any benefit from parallelizing the calculation.

The most efficient method for loading this data into the SIMD registers is sequentially. By reorganizing the layout of memory, it is possible to better accommodate this data flow. Ideally, the structure would be organized as groups of multiple units, rather than each struct representing a single unit. In other words, rather than organizing memory as an array of structures it would be better to organize them as a *structure of arrays*. This isn't a strict requirement, but it will benefit performance. Continuing the previous example, the function foo() is easy to vectorize once the data is arranged accordingly:

```
1   #include <inttypes.h>
2   #include <immintrin.h>
3
4   struct soa {
5           double *x;
6           double *y;
7           size_t len;
8           /* other fields */
9   }
10
11  void foo_avx(struct soa *in, double *out)
12  {
13          size_t sz = in->len;
14          double *x = in->x;
15          double *y = in->y;
16
17          while ((uintptr_t)out & (32 - 1) && sz) {
18                  *out = *x + *y;
19
20                  x++;
21                  y++;
22                  out++;
23                  sz--;
24          }
25
26          while (sz >= 4) {
27                  __m256d x_ymm, y_ymm, r_ymm;
28
29                  x_ymm = _mm256_loadu_pd(x);
```

```
30                  y_ymm = _mm256_loadu_pd(y);
31                  r_ymm = _mm256_add_pd(x_ymm, y_ymm);
32                  _mm256_store_pd(out, r_ymm);
33
34                  x += 4;
35                  y += 4;
36                  out += 4;
37                  sz -= 4;
38          }
39
40      if (sz >= 2) {
41                  __m128d x_xmm, y_xmm, r_xmm;
42
43                  x_xmm = _mm_loadu_pd(x);
44                  y_xmm = _mm_loadu_pd(y);
45                  r_xmm = _mm_add_pd(x_xmm, y_xmm);
46                  _mm_store_pd(out, r_xmm);
47
48                  x += 2;
49                  y += 2;
50                  out += 2;
51                  sz -= 2;
52          }
53
54      if (sz)
55                  *out = *x + *y;
56  }
```

First, notice on lines 4 through 9, how the layout of memory differs from the definition of struct aos. This structure is designed for describing multiple elements, as opposed to just one. Second, notice that the first while loop, starting on line 17, single-steps until the *destination* array is aligned. Throughout the function, unaligned loads are used for the source arrays. Ideally, both of these arrays will be aligned correctly during allocation, but the code will work correctly either way. Third, notice that both SSE and Intel AVX are used in a complementary fashion. Of course, it will also be necessary to ensure that this function is only called on processors that support Intel AVX and SSE.

Although each SIMD register can be logically decomposed into a set of packed values, this concept is not enforced. For example, it is completely valid to load an array of unsigned integers into a SIMD register, then perform an operation on that register designed for unsigned words, then an operation designed for signed bytes, and then an operation designed for strings, assuming that this sequence produces the results the programmer desires.

To control how the contents of a SIMD register are interpreted, each instruction typically provides different forms for operating on different types. For example, to perform an addition operation on packed values, there are the ADDPS, ADDPD,

`PADDB`, `PADDW`, `PADDD`, `PADDQ` instructions, which operate on packed single-precision floats, double-precision doubles, bytes, words, double-words, and quad-words types, respectively.

There are far too many instructions to cover them all here. Some of the special purpose SIMD instructions are covered in Chapter 16. Instead, the rest of this section provides a key for determining what an instruction does, based on its name. The following abbreviations should provide insight into the instruction's meaning:

H (if first or second letter of instruction) Horizontal Operation, e.g., `HSUBPS` (Horizontal Subtraction on Packed IEEE 32-bit floats) and `PHADDW` (Horizontal Addition on Packed 16-bit words)

H (if not at beginning) High Lane, e.g., `PSHUFHW` (Shuffle Packed High Words)

L Low Lane, e.g., `PSHUFLW` (Shuffle Packed Low Words)

PS Packed Single (multiple IEEE 32-bit floats), e.g., CMPPS (Compare Floats)

PD Packed Double (multiple IEEE 64-bit doubles), e.g., CMPPD (Compare Doubles)

SS Scalar Single (1 IEEE 32-bit float), e.g., CMPSS (Compare Scalar Single)

SD Scalar Double (1 IEEE 64-bit float), e.g., CMPSD (Compare Scalar Double)

REFERENCES

Cryil, B., 2012, 07. Bug 45351—general protection fault in raid5, load_balance. https://bugzilla.kernel.org/show_bug.cgi?id=45351. Kernel Bugzilla Entry.

Intel Corporation, 2013, 10. Intel 64 and IA-32 Architectures Software Developer's Manual. Computer Hardware Manual.

Intel Corporation, 2014, 10. Intel 64 and IA-32 Architectures Optimization Reference Manual. Order Number: 248966-030.

Special Instructions

16

CHAPTER CONTENTS

The x87 floating point instructions were added to the x86 instruction set in order to alleviate some common software problems. Over the years, the Intel® Architecture has collected quite a few specialized instructions that are designed to simplify the lives of developers and improve performance. One of the associated challenges is that as the number of instructions increases, it can be hard for someone not familiar with the architecture to find these helpful instructions. The author thought it fitting to close the book by highlighting some of these lesser known instructions. Additional information can be found in the whitepapers listed at the end of each section and within the Intel® *Software Developer Manual* and *Optimization Reference*.

16.1 INTEL® ADVANCED ENCRYPTION STANDARD NEW INSTRUCTIONS (AES-NI)

The Intel® AES New Instructions (AES-NI) extension adds seven new instructions designed to accelerate AES encryption and decryption.

Typically, one of the largest challenges to the wide adoption of various security measures is performance. Despite the value users place on security, their behavior is strongly influenced by what they perceive to improve their performance, and what they perceive to impede their performance. As a result, providing high performance encryption and decryption is a prerequisite for enabling ubiquitous encryption.

Before the introduction of these dedicated AES instructions, the standard technique for improving AES performance was via a lookup table. This approach has been shown to be susceptible in practice, not just in theory, to side-channel attacks. Rather than exploiting a weakness in the cryptographic algorithm, side-channel attacks instead focus on accidental data leakage as a result of the implementation. In the case of AES lookup table implementation, the side-channel attack performs cache-timing to sample what cache lines are accessed by the AES implementation. Eventually enough samples are collected to reveal the key used in the encryption or decryption process. As a result, not only do the AES-NI instructions improve performance, but they also provide additional security against these types of attacks.

16.1.1 FURTHER READING

1. http://www.intel.com/content/www/us/en/architecture-and-technology/advanced-encryption-standard--aes-/data-protection-aes-general-technology.html
2. http://www.intel.com/content/dam/doc/white-paper/enterprise-security-aes-ni-white-paper.pdf

16.2 PCLMUL-PACKED CARRY-LESS MULTIPLICATION

Introduced in the AES-NI extensions first available in the Intel® Westmere processor generation, the PCLMUL instruction performs carry-less multiplication of two 64-bit integers stored in SIMD registers, storing their product as a 128-bit integer. As the name implies, carry-less multiplication performs integer multiplication but ignores any carry digits that would normally propagate to the next place. Because carry-less multiplication is one of the steps for performing multiplication in the Galois Field, this instruction is capable of accelerating many different operations. This PCLMUL instruction was added with the AES-NI extension in order to accelerate the Galois Counter Mode (GCM) of AES. Another common usage of PCLMUL is to accelerate the CRC calculation for arbitrary polynomials.

Since each 128-bit SSE register is capable of holding two packed 64-bit values, the first operand, in AT&T syntax, is an 8-bit immediate that encodes which of the two packed quad words should be used in the second and third operands. The first bit of the lower nibble of this immediate represents the location in the third operand, which will be used as both a multiplier source and as the final destination for the product. The first bit of the higher nibble, that is, the fifth bit of the byte, represents the second operand. A value of zero in either of these bits encodes the low packed quad word, while a value of one encodes the high packed quad word. Aside from the SSE version, Intel® AVX added a VEX encoded nondestructive version.

16.2.1 **FURTHER READING**

- http://www.intel.com/content/dam/www/public/us/en/documents/white-papers/fast-crc-computation-generic-polynomials-pclmulqdq-paper.pdf
- http://www.intel.com/content/dam/www/public/us/en/documents/white-papers/fast-crc-computation-paper.pdf
- https://software.intel.com/en-us/articles/intel-carry-less-multiplication-instruction-and-its-usage-for-computing-the-gcm-mode/

16.3 **CRC32**

The SSE4.2 instruction extensions add a CRC32 instruction for calculating the 32-bit CRC for the $0x11EDC6F41$ polynomial. For computing a CRC with a different polynomial, use the PCLMUL instruction. Aside from data integrity checks, the CRC32 instruction can also be used as a fast hash function.

16.3.1 **FURTHER READING**

- http://www.intel.com/content/dam/www/public/us/en/documents/white-papers/hash-method-performance-paper.pdf

16.4 **SSE4.2 STRING FUNCTIONS**

Aside from the CRC32 and POPCNT instructions, the SSE4.2 instruction set extension adds functionality for performing common string operations with SIMD instructions. This new functionality revolves around comparing, searching, and validating strings with five new instructions.

Four of the five new instructions vary slightly in behavior and follow the general format of PCMPxSTRy, where x and y are variable characters that control the string length interpretation and result format, respectively. These are two possible values for x, the character "E," for explicit length strings, and the character "I," for implicit length strings. Implicit length strings are terminated with a sentinel character, that is, standard C strings terminated with a NULL character. On the other hand, explicit length strings require the length of the strings to be loaded into general purpose registers. As a result, the implicit length forms, PCMPISTRy, are designed for working on text strings and will automatically stop processing when a NULL character is encountered. On the other hand, the explicit length forms, PCMPESTRy, are designed for working on binary strings, where a NULL character isn't used as a sentinel.

For the explicit length forms, the string length of the second operand, in AT&T syntax, is stored in the *RDX* or *EDX* register, depending on the processor mode, while the length of the third operand is stored in the *RAX* or *EAX* register. Since the length

	7	6		4		2		0
0	Output	Polarity		Aggregation		Source size		

FIGURE 16.1

PCMPxSTRy immediate operand.

of the strings are only relevant to the instruction with regard to the values loaded into the SIMD registers, both lengths loaded into these general purpose registers are internally saturated, although the values stored in the actual registers aren't affected, to the maximum width of the SIMD register. This fact can be exploited in order to reduce the number of registers required for some string operations by also using the explicit length registers as counters.

The second form variable, the y variable, in the PCMPxSTRy form, controls the output format. This variable can either be the character "I" for index or "M" for mask. In index mode, the result is stored into the *ECX* register. In mask mode, the result of each comparison is stored in the destination operand as a mask.

Therefore, the four new PMPxSTRy instructions can be defined as follows:

PCMPESTRI Compares two explicit length strings, whose lengths are in *RDX/RAX* or *EDX/EAX* and stores the result in *ECX*.
PCMPESTRM Compares two explicit length strings and stores the comparison result in the destination SIMD register.
PCMPISTRI Compares two implicit length strings, stopping at the first NULL byte, and stores the result in the *ECX*.
PCMPISTRM Compares two implicit length strings, and stores the comparison result in the destination SIMD register.

The PCMPxSTRy instructions are designed to handle a lot of different scenarios. As a result, the first operand is an 8 bit immediate that controls the exact behavior of the comparison. This includes whether the comparisons occur between signed or unsigned characters or words, what should be reported, and so on. Figure 16.1 illustrates the format of this byte.

In order to communicate additional information about the result, the arithmetic flags in the EFLAGS register are overloaded with special meanings.

16.4.1 **FURTHER READING**

- https://software.intel.com/en-us/articles/schema-validation-with-intel-streaming-simd-extensions-4-intel-sse4

Index

Note: Page numbers followed by *f* indicate figures and *t* indicate tables.

Printed in the United States
By Bookmasters